ERASMUS,
the
ANABAPTISTS,
and the
GREAT COMMISSION

ERASMUS,
the
ANABAPTISTS,
and the
GREAT COMMISSION

Abraham Friesen

WILLIAM B. EERDMANS PUBLISHING COMPANY
GRAND RAPIDS, MICHIGAN / CAMBRIDGE, U.K.

© 1998 Wm. B. Eerdmans Publishing Co.

255 Jefferson Ave. S.E., Grand Rapids, Michigan 49503 /

P.O. Box 163, Cambridge CB3 9PU U.K.

Printed in the United States of America

03 02 01 00 99 98   7 6 5 4 3 2 1

Library of Congress Cataloging-in-Publication Data

Friesen, Abraham

Erasmus, the Anabaptists, and the Great Commission / Abraham Friesen

p.   cm.

Includes bibliographical references.

ISBN 0-8028-4448-0 (pbk.: alk. paper)

1. Anabaptists — Doctrines — History — 16th century.

2. Erasmus, Desiderius, d. 1536 — Influence.

3. Great Commission (Bible).   I. Title.

BX4931.2.F76   1998

284′.3 — dc21   97-45849

CIP

To
Lewis W. Spitz

Contents

Preface

After having completed the following study, I happened upon the commentaries on the Gospel of Matthew and the Acts of the Apostles just recently published in the "Believer's Church" series. Intrigued to learn whether the one or the other of the authors — or both — had recognized the unique Erasmian/Anabaptist interpretation of Christ's Great Commission I had made the center of my study, I read both with considerable anticipation. But neither the commentary on Matthew [Richard B. Gardner, *The Believer's Church Bible Commentary: Matthew* (Scottdale, PA. and Waterloo, Ont.: Herald Press,1991)], nor the one on Acts [Chalmer E. Faw, *The Believer's Church Bible Commentary: Acts* (Scottdale, PA. and Waterloo, Ont.: Herald Press, 1993)], so much as hinted at the way in which the Anabaptists had interpreted the Great Commission through the baptismal passages in Acts, never mind linking that interpretation to Erasmus's paraphrases of those two books of the Bible. If these two authors neither saw the interpretation nor traced it to Erasmus, it is probably safe to surmise that no one else has done so either. This should not be as surprising as it might at first appear to be since no one — aside from the sixteenth-century Anabaptists — picked it up from Erasmus. It was unknown before Erasmus and has remained so after him to the present day. Even Mennonites and the adherents of other believer's churches have forgotten about it. The above two commentaries attest to the latter fact.

   This study began — like the Renaissance concept of human nature — as an essay of indeterminate length. But as I pursued the various aspects of the topic, it began to expand — I hope in the right directions — a little here, more there, until it burst the bounds assigned it. As it grew, it was read by a number of persons; some at an earlier, others at a later stage of its development. Peter Klassen of Fresno State University and Victor G. Doerksen of the University of Manitoba read early versions; Victor Doerksen read it again in page proofs, as did Harry Loewen, Chair in Mennonite Studies emeritus of the University of Winnipeg, under whose auspices the first formulation of the subject matter took place. Robert Gundry of neighboring Westmont College, a leading scholar of Matthew's Gospel, was gracious enough to read the manuscript when it had neared completion. Jeffrey Burton Russell, a colleague here at the University of California, Santa Barbara, with whom I have shared many years of teaching a four-quarter sequence on the History of Christianity, read it just before it was sent to the publisher. And just in the last days, John D. Roth, editor of *The Mennonite Quarterly Review,* has also read it. To them all, I express my profound thanks. Their comments and criticisms have made this a better study. The interpretation, as the viewpoints expressed, however, remain very much my own, and I accept full responsibility for them, as I do for the errors and omissions that yet remain.

I am also grateful to the Historical Commission of the Mennonite Brethren Churches of North America for their grant in aid of publication. Their support was offered without having read the manuscript, so they bear even less responsibility for its content. Such support became necessary because I decided to go with a religious, commercial publisher — and Eerdmans was my publisher of choice — rather than an academic publisher because of the nature of the content, especially of the epilogue.

This study — had I indeed undertaken it — would have been very different were it not for the time spent at Stanford University as a doctoral student under the direction of Lewis W. Spitz. He it was who first initiated me into the intricacies of Christian humanism — "from Plato to Hegel," as one of his reading seminars would have it — and introduced me to the great minds that sought to reconcile "Athens with Jerusalem." Combining the irenic spirit of the Christian humanists with the religious convictions of Martin Luther, this preeminent scholar of the relationship of Christian humanism to the Reformation himself sought to repair the breach created during the

"Zeitalter der Glaubensspaltung" in many different ways. In my case, aware that I was a Mennonite who harbored some animosity to Luther and the other magisterial reformers for their treatment of the Anabaptists, he — one day — presented me with a Luther coat of arms in token of our personal reconciliation. (I no longer recall whether it was before or after my first seminar paper — on Thomas Muentzer, one of his "favorite" sixteenth-century characters — had been accepted for publication!) It is that same irenic spirit — which seeks to find ways to resolve the differences in the Christian community rather than add to them — I hope, that also animates this study, especially the epilogue. (Though the contest for the proper interpretation of the movement must be fought — as Joseph Lortz used to tell us with respect to ecumenism — without compromise.) For there can be little doubt that Erasmus's interpretation of Christ's Great Commission presented in his paraphrases of Matthew and Acts, which forms the centerpiece of this study — coming as it did just prior to his 1524 *Inquisitio de Fide* in which he proffered his solution to the growing rift between Catholic and Lutheran — was intended to serve an irenic purpose. But the Anabaptists, who absorbed this interpretation in a slightly modified form from Erasmus, have never been seen in such a light. Their position is nevertheless presented in the epilogue as the solution to the rift between evangelical and liberal Christians today. Erasmus's solution was rejected in his day; hopefully the present one will find a more favorable reception. But attempts at reconciliation such as the one embodied in the epilogue are always personal; they should nonetheless also be — as the Germans say — *sachlich*. I know it is the first; I hope it is also the latter.

Given the content of the study, then, and the spirit that animates it — as well as the immense debt I owe him — it is only right and fitting that I dedicate this book to Lewis W. Spitz — Christian, scholar, friend, and mentor extraordinaire.

Abraham Friesen
Santa Barbara, California
December 10, 1997

Introduction

The so-called Great Commission,[1] Christ's last words to his disciples just prior to his ascension into heaven, are contained in the last chapters of only two of the Gospels: Matthew and Mark. They are not identical, however. Whereas both relate the command to go forth into every part of the world to proclaim the gospel, only Matthew carries Christ's ostensible command to "baptize men everywhere in the name of the Father and the Son and the Holy Spirit." Mark has a much greater apparent emphasis on the primacy of faith, saying: "those who believe it [the gospel] and receive baptism will find salvation; those who do not believe will be condemned." This emphasis on faith continues in the immediately following sentence: "Faith will bring with it these miracles. . . ." The relationship between faith and baptism appears less clear in the Matthean account. But Matthew adds another statement not contained in the Mark account: "and teach them to observe all that I have commanded you."

Matthew's account of Christ's last will and testament is the only place where the command to baptize in the names of the Trinity is given. Yet in the Acts of the Apostles, every recorded instance of an apostolic baptism is performed only in the name of Jesus. This apparent discrepancy did not create problems until the time of the Arian controversy in the third and fourth centuries. Then suddenly, however, the trinitarian formula became important, as the decisions reached at the Council of Nicea clearly demonstrate. At the same time, the christological formula used by the apostles became problematical. How could one explain this apparent con-

1

tradiction? The debate begun by the Church Fathers over this issue has not yet ended.

New interpretations of events or literary documents do not necessarily, or even normally, appear full-blown, like Athena, from the head of Zeus. However, in the present case, a set of biblical passages, a new interpretation did appear full-blown from the mind of Erasmus. And yet, aside from the sixteenth-century Anabaptists, it has been passed over in virtual silence. Erasmus might later have wished that the Anabaptists had done so as well, for nowhere is it more true than in the relationship of Erasmus and the Anabaptists in the above context that once an idea has been formulated and set upon its course in the world, it may well take on a life of its own. What follows is the story of such an idea, formulated in Erasmus's paraphrases of the Gospel of Matthew and the Acts of the Apostles, but taking on a life of its own in the early Anabaptist movement.

When I arrived at Stanford University in the fall of 1963, it was my hope — in the due course of academic affairs — to write a doctoral dissertation on Erasmus and the Anabaptists. Instead, I wrote on the Marxist interpretation of the Reformation. A timely topic at the time, it is now — due to the vagaries of history — only of some mildly antiquarian interest. Erasmus and the Anabaptists, in contrast, remains a topic of more timeless interest. Indeed, as I hope to demonstrate in the present study, it is a topic that should be of interest not only to all students of the Reformation but to all students of Christianity.

An ardent admirer of Erasmus in my youth, today my feelings toward the great scholar are somewhat more ambivalent. Just last year I had the distinct honor of inaugurating the "Erasmus Society Lectures" at Westmont College. At the outset of my address, entitled "Erasmus: The Scholar as Christian," I suggested — half in jest — that the organizers might wish to rename the series after I had done. For there came a time when I believed Erasmus's Neoplatonism to have shaped his Christianity not only in significant but also in transformational ways. But studying his *Annotations* and *Paraphrases,* together with Craig R. Thompson's work on the Erasmian colloquy, *Inquisitio de Fide,* has significantly modified those views. As a result, I have become convinced that any attempt to understand Erasmus the Christian without taking all of his biblical scholarship into account can all too easily lead to the portrayal of a "liberal" Erasmus, the kind Preserved Smith spoke of in his 1923 biography when he wrote: "I discovered in Erasmus the champion, in his own day, of that 'undogmatic Christianity' now first coming into its own four hundred years after he proclaimed it."[2] Had I therefore written on the topic in 1965-1967 I would undoubtedly have written a very different book.

Though I had earlier wanted to write on Erasmus and the Anabaptists, the present study arose out of the conviction, slowly maturing during the late 1970s and early 1980s, that Anabaptism had been studied from far too narrow a perspective by its partisans. Part of this was intentional — to isolate Anabaptists from the mystics, the revolutionaries, and the humanists of the age; part of it was unintentional — done simply out of ignorance of the other movements and their history. Invited by Professor Harry Loewen, then of the University of Winnipeg, to deliver the *Mennonite Chair Lectures* in 1987, I therefore began exploring such topics as Anabaptism and Monasticism; Anabaptism and Humanism; and Reformation and Radicalism. The first appeared in the 1988 issue of the *Journal of Mennonite Studies;* the second some years later in the 1992 *Festschrift* for Lewis W. Spitz. The third has, thus far, resisted several not so valiant attempts at revision and is therefore still in gestation.

Though published, the essay on Anabaptism and Humanism remained, as Gerald Strauss quite correctly observed in a review in the *Catholic Historical Review,* more "suggestive" than definitive.[3] He also called for a response from someone without my "predilections," though he was careful not to say what these were! In any case, I hope to forestall any such person from putting pen to paper — to use an outmode[m]d metaphor — with the present study.

One of the more fundamental suggestions of the earlier essay had been that Erasmus was at least partially responsible for the rise of Anabaptism. Increasingly, therefore, the study turned into an inquiry into the intellectual origins of Anabaptism — perhaps a foolish enterprise given the relatively widespread, though largely uncritical, acceptance of the "polygenesis" argument.[4] But I must confess, I did not find that thesis compelling when it was first propounded, nor have I had occasion to alter my opinion since.[5] And I shall give my reasons *en passant.* Such a disagreement should come as no surprise since the question regarding the intellectual origins of Anabaptism has always been a controversial one, perhaps because virtually everyone who has turned to the topic has done so from a "Whig" perspective.[6] To demonstrate this it was therefore necessary, at the very outset, given the conflicting historiographical traditions, to deal, at least in summary fashion, not only with the main historiographical traditions touching on the problem but also with the more fundamental question of how one approaches the writing of religious history. I was the more inclined to do this since I have always had an interest in "the history of history" and, from time to time, have had occasion to study some of these interpretive traditions. Hence Chapter One. Furthermore, the controversial nature of the subject matter also required that I let the sources speak for themselves as much as possible. I have sought to keep them brief.

Chapter Two, then, begins with a general discussion of the state of the scholarship regarding Erasmus's relationship to the Anabaptists and suggests a different approach to the problem. Beginning with Paul Oskar Kristeller's definition of Renaissance humanism that emphasizes a set of disciplines with moral reform as their goal, the chapter proceeds to a discussion of the classical/Christian concept of *sapientia* (wisdom), which allowed humanists to bring human and divine matters into a relatively intimate relationship with one another. All of this was then placed into a Neoplatonic context that provided Christian humanists like Erasmus with the basic structure within which they thought. Christianity, too, came to be seen from within this Platonic framework, a framework that emphasized the movement "from things visible to things invisible," suggesting that "things visible" were shadows of their invisible ideals. As a consequence, Platonic Christianity came to deemphasize the external ritual of the religious service in favor of the moral and the "inner" spiritual — invisible — reality. When Erasmus therefore turned directly to the Bible, as he did in 1506 — resulting, eventually, in the publication in 1519 of the second edition of his Latin translation of the New Testament and his *Annotations* to it — he could speak of dealing as directly with the invisible — that is, with true reality — as any human might. Here the *shadows,* the physical reality, could be left behind and, as he said in his paraphrases, the *light of evangelical truth* could be emphasized. This approach led him to some — for many of his contemporaries — startling conclusions in his notes, conclusions about Christian pacifism, the oath, community of goods, and baptism that may well have influenced early Anabaptists.

The main argument, dealing with Erasmus's unique interpretation of Christ's Great Commission, is presented in Chapter Three. Balthasar Hubmaier and Peter Walpot, Anabaptists writing some fifty years apart, directly referred to this Erasmian interpretation, together with the biblical references cited. Not only did they cite Erasmus's notes and paraphrases directly, they also absorbed the structure of his argument. And it is the latter that became embedded in Anabaptist literature to such a degree that it shaped their theological thinking in determinative ways. This is not only demonstrated in their writings; it is also confirmed by the fact that virtually all of the leading Reformers and many Catholic polemicists felt compelled to address the Erasmian argument in their tracts against the Anabaptists. Had the argument not been present, and had it not been so compelling, they would most certainly not have had the occasion to do so. These Protestant and Catholic responses are presented in Chapter Four.

The impact that this interpretation had on the form and content of Anabaptist thought is investigated in Chapter Five. I argue that Erasmus's interpretation provided the Anabaptists not only with the structure within which the preaching of the gospel, conversion, baptism, and discipleship were brought into relationship with one another, but also with the content of each of these four categories.

Chapter Six, the conclusion to the main part of the study, then sets the problem of Reformer and radical into the wider context of the Reformation, arguing that the Nuremberg Imperial Edict of 6 March 1523 had much to do with the ultimate rupture between the two groups.

In the process of pursuing the various strands of this study, I was forced to address issues far outside the study's scope, issues that, for one reason or another, had either received little scholarly attention or at least not the attention they warranted. In the epilogue I therefore deal with the implications of the primary study for other areas of the history of Christianity, especially the role of the Great Commission in the missionary expansion of the early church; the argument that Matthew 28:18-20 was a later — after the Council of Nicea — interpolation into the Gospel; and the implication of the Erasmian interpretation for the rupture between Evangelical and liberal Mennonites in particular and Evangelical and liberal Christians in general. The epilogue was written on the assumption that once one has determined to address a controversial topic, one may as well be as comprehensive as possible.

1

Interpreting Anabaptism

Priests are not set apart to study Divinity, as Lawyers and Physicians are to study Law and Physick. The priests do not study Divinity so-called, but only how to maintain a certain System of Divinity. Thus the Popish, Mohametan, Lutheran, and Presbyterian Priests, study their several systems. Whereas Physicians are not ty'd down to Hippocrates, or Galen, or Paracelsus, but have all Nature and all Men's Observations before them, without any Obligation to subscribe implicitly to any one: nor have Lawyers any Rule, but the Law itself which lies before 'em, which they are at liberty to interpret according to its real Sense, being bound by no Articles or Subscriptions to interpret it otherwise.

Anthony Collins, *A Discourse on Free Thinking*, 1713[1]

These words of Anthony Collins, written at the close of the European wars of religion, contain a truth worthy of consideration. That truth, which even today hardly needs modification, is that theologians, or confessional historians, have sought to "maintain [or defend] a certain System of Divinity" rather than search dispassionately to establish the universal truths of Christianity. Not only have the "Popish, Mohametan, Lutheran, and Presbyterian Priests" studied only their own "several systems"; they have also declared these systems to be veritable embodiments of truth and attacked — indeed, declared to

6

be heretical — all those who would argue otherwise. Assuming that Collins is correct, why have they not followed the path of the physicians and lawyers? The answer would appear to lie in the very nature of the discipline. "Systems of Divinity" are deemed to embody ultimate truths upon which humans rest their salvation; law and science, relying on the inductive method and dealing with evolving temporal systems, make, or should make, no such claim. The former being the case, who would be so foolhardy as to hold theological tenets he or she did not believe to be true? And if these tenets are deemed to be theologically true, then surely history, if pursued correctly, must confirm them. Rather than return again and again to "search the Scriptures; for in them ye think ye have eternal life [John 5:39]," theologians and confessional historians have therefore repeatedly returned to the interpretation of the Scriptures given by their founders,[2] in the process tending only to confirm their various systems of divinity. In the West, until the beginning of the Renaissance, this interpretation was determined primarily by the Roman Catholic Church. And its argument that one had to abide by the interpretation — as Pope Leo put it in his bull threatening Luther with excommunication — of those teachers accepted by the Christian Church naturally led it away from a study of the Bible to the study of those teachers. Gradually, however, as that church grew more powerful, it also came increasingly under attack and other interpretations of its history began to appear; some, as we shall see, were based upon the argument that the primary source, not the secondary interpretations, ought to be the foundation of the edifice.

By the eve of the Reformation, two fundamentally antagonistic interpretations of the history of the Christian church began to confront one another increasingly. The one — that of the Catholic Church itself — taught that the church's ecclesiastical structure, its theology and liturgical practices, had been refined over the years. Combined with the theory of papal and conciliar infallibility that had been in the making at least since the twelfth century,[3] Catholic theologians and canon lawyers argued that the "modern" church, guided from its very inception by the Holy Spirit, had gradually made explicit, brought to fruition — indeed, perfected — what had only been implicit or even darkly veiled in the Scriptures and the primitive church.[4] Over time, therefore, the church had not only amplified but also improved upon the early apostolic church. Consequently, the latest teachers, those living in the age of ever

7

greater church perfection — in this case, the great Scholastics of the Middle Ages led by Thomas Aquinas — were deemed the best.[5] The term "accepted and approved," used with respect to these teachers even by Leo X in his bull of June 15, 1520, threatening Luther with excommunication, gave expression to the belief that the church was the final arbiter of correct scriptural interpretation and orthodox teaching. In that bull Leo enlisted the aid of St. Augustine to confirm this Catholic interpretation of church history, saying:

> We have found [after extensive examination], that these [Luther's] same errors, *as expected,* were not Catholic articles but *are opposed to the teachings or beliefs of the Catholic Church, and to the correct interpretation of the holy Scriptures, that has been accepted and approved by the Church;* a church that was held in such high esteem by St. Augustine that he said: he would not have believed the Gospel had the Church not been held in such [high] regard.[6]

Had not the church, after all, determined which books were to be considered canonical and held to be divinely inspired? And had she not, under attack from heretical groups in the third and fourth centuries, determined what was "orthodox"?[7]

Some, however, saw this as an essentially self-serving interpretation of church history that simply rationalized the existing ecclesiastical and theological status quo, making reform extremely difficult, if not impossible. Medieval heretics such as the Waldenses,[8] as well as critical intellectuals such as Dante Alighieri[9] and Marsiglio of Padua,[10] appear to have thought so, for they attacked the church's interpretation and reversed its judgment, insisting that the primitive church had been the purest and the apostles' interpretation of Christ's teachings the most reliable. It was to these one had to return. Rather than see a progression to ever greater perfection guided by the Holy Spirit, these critics saw in the church only decline from a primitive "golden age."

Christian humanists of the Renaissance, with their *ad fontes* emphasis, adopted this theory and built it into a formidable interpretation of church history consciously opposed to what they considered to be a morally bankrupt church. Proceeding from the historical premise that the oldest or earliest witnesses to any event or movement are invariably more reliable than later ones, Christian humanists asserted that the Bible, as the earliest and purest sourcebook of Christianity,

presented Christ's teachings in their purest form; and the most trust-
worthy interpreters of these teachings were the apostles. Next in
importance to the apostles as interpreters came the great Church
Fathers of the third to fifth centuries. The farther removed from the
original an interpreter stood, therefore, the more unreliable his interpretation, especially if he — like the Schoolmen of the Middle Ages
— relied more on the writings of Aristotle than on the Bible and was
more interested in "disputation than piety," as Erasmus charged in
the introduction to his *Enchiridion*.[11]

To undergird this argument, Christian humanists contrasted the
Renaissance popes of their day to Christ and his apostles — as did
Francesco Petrarca in his criticism of the Avignon papacy[12] — and the
corrupt Roman Catholic Church to the apostolic church — as did
Faber Stapulensis when he wrote in his 1522 *Introduction to the Gospels*:

> And pray God that the model of faith may be sought in the primitive
> church, which offered Christ so many martyrs, which knew no
> other rule than the Gospels, and no other end than Christ and
> which rendered its devotion to only one God in three Persons. . . .
>
> Why may we not aspire to see our age restored to the likeness
> of the primitive Church, when Christ received a purer veneration,
> and the splendor of His name shone forth more widely? . . . As the
> light of the Gospel returns, I say, which at this time begins to shine
> again. By this divine light many have been so greatly illuminated
> that, not to speak of other benefits, *from the time of Constantine, when
> the primitive Church, which had little by little declined, came to an end.*[13]

Was the history of the church to be judged by its latest — sixteenth-century — incarnation, or by Christ's teachings and the practices of the apostolic church? Advocates of church reform argued the
latter; defenders of the ecclesiastical status quo asserted the former.
When Luther, at the Leipzig Disputation, proclaimed the principle of
sola scriptura, he apparently went this Christian humanist position one
better, rejecting even the Church Fathers as necessarily authoritative
interpreters. To prove his contention, he cited the very same
Augustine Leo had enlisted in his defense of the church as sole arbiter
in matters Christian. Quoting from a letter of St. Augustine to Jerome
— a letter he had already cited at Leipzig and again at Worms —
Luther observed in 1523:

As is well known, these same teachers [the Church Fathers] did not always write or hold to the same, nor even to the correct, opinions. [Since this was the case, Luther] insist[ed] that they [the Church Fathers] did not, nor could they have, regarded the church more highly or ascribed [more] power to her than did St. Augustine, that special light of the Christian church, when he said: 'Only to those holy books called canonical do I ascribe the honor of believing that, no matter how holy or learned they may appear, I do not regard them as correct unless they convince me on the basis of Scripture and right reason.'[14]

Although Luther, in his attack on the Catholic Church, accepted the Scriptures as the Christian's sole authority, he would not, as John Headley has argued, accept the apostolic church as an absolute ecclesiastical norm.[15] Indeed, he repeatedly asserted that he and his Protestant contemporaries now possessed the gospel in an even clearer fashion than had the apostolic church.[16] The true church, he proclaimed, was not tied to any historical period but existed wherever the gospel was purely preached. Nevertheless, on at least one occasion during the years prior to 1523-1524, Luther conceded that the apostolic church might constitute a "tentative norm."[17] To a degree, therefore, the Reformer freed his interpretation of apostolic theology from its historical context in the apostolic church as portrayed in the Acts of the Apostles.

In his response to Leo's charge of heresy, however, Luther, now beginning to defend his own emerging theological position, may have contributed more to a Protestant interpretation of church history than he did with his theology. For in that papal bull, Leo placed Luther at the end of a long line of medieval heretics. In a classic reversal of Leo's particular judgment, and the church's judgment in general, Luther observed that "these heretics have done nothing against God; indeed, they committed a much more serious crime: they desired to possess the holy Scriptures and God's Word, and — poor sinners that they were — insisted that the pope live a moral life and preach the Word of God honestly and forthrightly, not threaten [innocent] people with papal bulls with the gay abandon of a drunken sailor."[18]

What Leo had intended as a damning association became, from a different theological perspective in Luther's hands, an honorable line of dissent to a church that had, for many years, hidden the Scriptures "under a bench."[19] From this perspective, Leo's "heretics" became Luther's legitimate precursors, eventually coming to be regarded in the writings of Protestant martyrologists such as John Foxe and Jean Crespin[20] as the "forerunners" of the Reformers. So widespread did this interpretation become that even John Henry Cardinal Newman, in the mid nineteenth century, could still refer to it in the following words: "The school of [Richard] Hurd, [Bishop of Worcester], and [Sir Isaac] Newton hold, as the only true view of history, that Christianity slept for centuries, except among whom historians called heretics."[21] In this view of church history, however, Christ's teachings — and their interpretation and implementation by the apostles — were no longer the criteria by which the church was to be judged; Luther's own teachings had taken their place. In a sense, the Reformer's position was not so different from the church's own approach to the problem: only the criteria by which the present church was to be judged had changed. The "heretics" of the Catholic past were therefore pressed into the service of the Lutheran (or Protestant) present. Like its Catholic counterpart, this Lutheran interpretation was also theologically self-serving. Both interpretations might therefore well be regarded as similar to, or religious versions of, what Herbert Butterfield once labeled the "Whig interpretation of history"[22] — seeking the origins of one's own present position and then judging the past from that vantage point.

This "Whig" approach to history is also reflected in the hermeneutical principles that Catholics and Reformers used to interpret the Scriptures; not so the humanists, however. This is nowhere more clearly illustrated than in the Reformation discussion of the biblical passages mentioned in the Introduction. These passages brought into sharp focus the contradiction between the trinitarian baptismal formula (in the Great Commission in Matt. 28:18-20) that Christ ostensibly commanded his followers to use and the christological formula used by the apostles as recorded in the Acts of the Apostles. As one might expect, this apparent discrepancy was exploited in the age of the Reformation for purely partisan purposes. Catholics, for example, confronted with Luther's attack on papal primacy and the church's claim to determine the correct interpretation of the Scriptures, argued that it was obvious from these passages that the apostles — as the "incipient" church — (to put it in Luther's terms) "not only had the power to be above, or even oppose, God's Word, but also to change it because this is what Paul did [Acts 19], even though he was only *one* member of the church."23 Such an assertion by sixteenth-century Catholic apologists would appear to contain the most extreme form of that argument for the superiority of the Catholic Church over the Bible that Priarias enunciated in his response to Luther's 95 Theses.24 Not only did these apologists argue that the church was *above* Scripture, they argued that the church could even *change* the teachings of Christ.25 To Luther this was tantamount to blasphemy.

In his attack on this Catholic position, however, Luther revealed his own exceptions to *sola scriptura,* a principle he had enunciated so forcefully at Leipzig in 1519. He did so in his own explanation of the above discrepancy between the trinitarian and christological baptismal formulas:

> Now if St. Paul had taught: No one shall baptize in accordance with Christ's teachings [to baptize] in the name of the Father and the Son and the Holy Spirit, and whoever shall do so shall be banned as a rebellious [son] of the church, then St. Paul would be doing what the pope-ass does, who teaches: No one is to take communion in both kinds according to the institution of Christ; whoever does so shall be excommunicated as a heretic, etc. St. Paul does not do this, however; rather, he allows Christ's baptismal order to stand. *For Christ did not forbid anyone to baptize in the name of Jesus Christ;* therefore it [St. Paul's baptism] remains the same baptism, whether it is performed in the name of Christ or that of the Trinity, since neither the one alone is commanded and the other forbidden. Thus, there is no changing of Christ's words or institution . . . but two ways of baptizing, neither of which is against the other, and both of which give the correct, complete and only [true] baptism.26

Just as Luther had taken pleasure in pointing out the flaws in the Catholic Church's interpretation of Scripture, even so Cochlaeus delighted to draw attention to the flaws in Luther's approach. In his 1529 *Defense of the Bishop of Meissen's Mandate against Luther's Attack,* he wrote:

> He [Luther] says, Christ did not forbid to baptize in the name of Jesus Christ, therefore it is right [to do so]. Therefore I should like

to say: it is not forbidden to baptize in the name of St. Peter. Thus, had they baptized in the name of St. Peter it would [also] be right. Oh, what sharp logic! On the other hand, he says that St. Paul did not forbid to baptize in the name of the Father, Son and Holy Spirit, the way that the pope-ass has forbidden to dispense communion in both kinds; therefore he did not have power to change things. But this cannot follow, for according to Luther one is not to change the Word of God.[27]

According to Cochlaeus and Eck, the Catholic Church had the power to supersede, indeed even to change, Christ's explicit commands; Luther argued that as long as something — like baptizing in the name of Jesus or, perhaps, even infant baptism — was not explicitly forbidden in the Bible, it was permissible.[28] In their own ways, therefore, both could justify moving beyond *sola scriptura* if the position they defended demanded it. John Henry Cardinal Newman was therefore right when he argued in his essay on the development of Christian doctrine:

> The common complaint of Protestants against the Church of Rome is, not simply that she has added to the primitive or the Scriptural doctrine, (for this they do themselves), but that she contradicts it, and moreover imposes her additions as fundamental truths under sanction of an anathema. For themselves they deduce by quite as subtle a method, and act upon doctrines as implicit and on reasons as little analyzed in time past as Catholic schoolmen.[29]

Erasmus — and in dependence upon him, the Anabaptists — approached the passages dealing with this apparent contradiction very differently, as we shall have occasion to note. Taking a historical approach derived from Renaissance humanism, Erasmus eschewed questions regarding a baptismal formula, or the question of the church's authority, or even the apparent conflict between the passage in Matthew and those in the Acts of the Apostles. Rather, he asked himself how Christ's disciples, his most intimate and knowledgeable followers, had interpreted the Great Commission. Not surprisingly, he found his answer in precisely the same passages in Acts that had formerly created the problem for the Church Fathers, and which the Catholics and Luther sought to exploit in their quarrel over the authority of the

13

church. Erasmus's quest led him back to Christ's own words and their interpretation by the apostles. This resulted — be it said here — in a much greater emphasis on *sola scriptura* than even that of Luther! The result, as we shall see, was a very different interpretation.

Just as the church's critics in the Middle Ages and the Renaissance were driven to adopt a different vantage point from which to justify their interpretation of church history, so the belief that a given theological position was the only logical and legitimate culmination of the church's development had of necessity to result in the overpowering desire to condemn all of one's theological opponents. It should not be surprising, therefore, to find that even the Reformers elected to adopt the same attitude toward their radical offspring that the Catholic Church had adopted toward them.[30] Even where Reformers were grudgingly forced to concede that at least some radicals lived exemplary Christian lives,[31] their opposition to the radicals, fueled by religious animosity and a nearly pathological fear of revolution, drove them to seek to discredit them. To accomplish this end, magisterial Protestants assigned the paternity of the entire movement to the arch-villain of the Reformation, Thomas Müntzer himself.[32] As their theme they adopted the refrain: from its inception under Müntzer to its culmination in Münster — a theme that employed the twin accusations of sedition and revolution to characterize the movement. This interpretation culminated in the not so immaculate historical conception of Heinrich Bullinger, Zwingli's successor in Zurich, who sought therewith to convince the world — as Zwingli had himself already attempted to do in his *Fidei Ratio* of 1530[33] — that Ulrich Zwingli had not been the father of Anabaptism, and that Zurich had not been the city of its origin.[34]

Anabaptist insiders, such as the authors of the sixteenth-century *Hutterite Chronicle* and Thieleman J. van Braght in his seventeenth-century *Martyrs' Mirror,* however, sought to clear the movement of these twin charges — in the south from any association with Thomas Müntzer,[35] and in the north from Jan of Leiden and the 1534-1535 uprising of the "saints" in Münster. Van Braght's was the more pressing concern, since Menno Simons, after whom virtually all Anabaptists eventually came to be called, had himself almost immediately after the Münster debacle been accused of being in league with the revolutionaries.[36] To disarm Menno's accusers and those of the later Dutch Anabaptists, van Braght appropriated the argument derived from Luther and the later Protestant martyrologists, and placed it into the service of Anabaptism. His "great chain of being," too, consisted of the Waldensian heretics, but he focused his attention on believers' baptism, which he traced all the way back to the apostolic church. Into this lineage he placed Menno Simons in order to free him from any contamination by the upstart, Jan of Leiden.[37] Whereas Protestants considered the "heretical" argument a legitimate device to use against their Catholic enemies, they objected when "their" heretics attempted to use the same weapon against them, saying, as did the eighteenth-century church historian Mosheim: "The modern Mennonites not only consider themselves as the descendants of the Waldenses, who were so grievously oppressed and persecuted by the despotic heads of the Roman church, but *pretend,* moreover, to be the purest offspring of these respectable sufferers, being equally averse to all the principles of rebellion, on the one hand, and all suggestions of fanaticism, on the other."[38]

Thus insiders and outsiders write the history of Anabaptism. The only early outsiders even remotely favorably disposed to that history were Spiritualists, such as Sebastian Franck,[39] and later German Pietists, like Gottfried Arnold[40] and Ludwig Keller,[41] themselves powerfully influenced by medieval mysticism.[42] The latter, however, were all drawn to the more mystical/spiritualist Anabaptists, notably to Hans Denck or, in the case of Arnold, even to David Joris. Pietists, in contrast to the *Confessio Augustana* that had anathematized Denck's mystical tendencies, including his universalism,[43] quite calmly and explicitly affirmed these very condemned tenets along with mysticism's concept of the "inner Word."[44] On occasion, Pietism also came to be tinged with rationalist proclivities, and in Keller's 1882 biography of Hans Denck, as Gustav Kawerau already noted in a personal letter to the author, rationalism and medieval mysticism came together.[45] Having selected Denck as his "ideal" Anabaptist,[46] Keller appropriated van Braght's "Waldensian origin" theory and built it into a "great chain of being" of his own in his 1885 *The Reformation and the Older Reform Parties,* a succession that began with Johanine Christianity and culminated in the Freemasons.[47] Carried through the ages by his "old evangelical brotherhoods," the theory seemed at first to favor the sixteenth-century Anabaptists and their Mennonite successors. In actual fact, however, Keller sought to legitimate his and Friedrich Fabri's[48] brand of Pietism and make it into a "third force" in the *Kulturkampf* of the day. But the entire edifice collapsed like a house of cards when the German Mennonites eventually refused to accept Denck as their sixteenth-century ideal type,[49] and Keller's historical reconstructions were destroyed by Paul Burckhardt, the Basel historian.[50]

Even Keller, therefore, apparently the most sympathetic of the Pietist outsiders, had pursued his own agenda in his interpretation of Anabaptism, an agenda that he never fully revealed to his nineteenth-century Mennonite admirers. Keller's reticence to divulge his motives eventually created considerable suspicion. Nonetheless, the young South German Mennonite John Horsch, beginning in 1885, came completely under his influence.[51] He remained so even after migrating to the United States in 1887 where he sought to realize Keller's own goal of publishing the entire corpus of what the latter called the "old evangelical" literature, with the writings of Hans Denck and the *German Theology* at its center. Between 1890 and 1900, however, Horsch underwent an intellectual — perhaps even spiritual — transformation under the auspices of American fundamentalism, for which he was later to become an eloquent spokesman.[52] Consequently, Horsch gradually rejected Hans Denck, his erstwhile "undogmatic" hero, eventually labeling him a "Liberalist." Menno Simons, on the other hand, rejected by Keller as too dogmatic, now became for Horsch — along with the Swiss Brethren — the "true"[53] Anabaptist. He described the latter as "Anabaptist Fundamentalists." Though he never openly voiced the sentiment, after his "conversion" Horsch must have come to believe that Keller, with his "undogmatic" hero in Hans Denck, had attempted to subvert Anabaptism, in the process misleading the more pietistic South German Mennonites while confirming the more rationalist Dutch and North German Mennonites in their liberal theology.[54]

Harald Bender, Horsch's son-in-law, teaching at a Goshen College apparently — at least in Horsch's opinion — caught in the tug-of-war between Mennonite fundamentalists and modernists, sought to forge an interpretation of Anabaptism as much as possible devoid of these polemical theological overtones in order to lead American Mennonites safely through the troubled theological waters bordered, on the one hand, by the Charybdis of American fundamentalism and, on the other, by the Scylla of liberalism/modernism. In order to do so, Bender appears to have followed the advice of an Erasmus — whom he sought to distance from the Anabaptist movement as much as possible — who had himself suggested during the theological confrontations of his age: "The sum of our religion is peace and unanimity, but these can scarcely stand unless we define as little as possible, and in many things leave each one free to follow his own judgment, because there is great obscurity in many matters, and man suffers from this almost congenital disease that he will not give in once a controversy has started." To avoid further theological wrangling, Bender may well have placed the central emphasis of his famous essay, as had Keller before him, on the *Nachfolge Christi.* In contrast to Keller, however, who asserted this on the basis of what he called Denck's "undogmatic Christianity," Bender argued simply that Anabaptism was the direct outgrowth of Protestant theology, though he did not characterize that theology any further. Such an assertion did little to negate Keller's argument of Anabaptism's "undogmatic" Christianity, or Horsch's predilection for a "fundamentalist" Menno, however. Yet when Bender consciously sought to divorce Anabaptism from Thomas Müntzer, on the one hand, and from the "liberal" humanist Erasmus, on the other, his unspoken reasons for doing so were those of his fundamentalist father-in-law. And when he labeled Menno Simons and the Swiss Brethren "normative" Anabaptists, he too was interpreting the sixteenth-century movement from his twentieth-century theological perspective. It is not surprising, therefore, that in the most recent past a Mennonite theologian has spoken of the "spiritual poverty" of Bender's Anabaptist vision.[55]

Whereas Horsch and Bender still sought to divorce Anabaptism from the twin accusations of sedition and revolution, the French Revolution had long since introduced a new perspective from which to read the apparently revolutionary events of the sixteenth century. For the French Revolution — preceded by what R. R. Palmer has called the age of democratic revolutions[56] — like no other event legitimated revolutions and drew attention to the social causes of political unrest. Historians such as Wilhelm Zimmermann, who was himself deeply enmeshed in the left-wing politics of the 1848 Revolution, therefore argued that such events became the means by which social and political progress could be achieved.[57] For Karl Marx and his followers, revolutions became the nodal turning points of world history in the long march toward the classless society.[58] The arbitrary goals — whether democratic or utopian — such interpreters set for history then became the criteria by which they in their turn judged the past. And so they too rewrote the history of the Reformation, making Luther into the villain of the piece;

while making a secularized Thomas Müntzer, the Anabaptists, and the peasants, however, into heroes.

Out of this last tradition has emerged the discipline of social history, the bourgeois cousin to the Marxist interpretation of history. Largely uninterested in theology,[59] sometimes even actively antagonistic to it,[60] these two approaches seek the root causes of revolution in the economic and social conditions of society. The Marxist interpretation, however, since it has largely lost its territorial base with the collapse of Communism in Eastern Europe, is now in some — if not complete — disarray.[61] Social history, however, still very much alive, has contributed much to our understanding of the age. Nevertheless, it too manifests a tendency to focus on the revolutionary aspects of the Anabaptist movement, a tendency that can be seen even in the English Fabian Baptist historian, Richard Heath, whose 1885 study was entitled: *Anabaptism, From its Rise at Zwickau to its Fall at Muenster 1521-1536.*[62] His American friend and founder of the "Social Gospel," Walter Rauschenbusch, demonstrated a similar predilection for the revolutionary over the nonviolent wing of the Radical Reformation.[63] At times combined with a kind of popular cultural approach that seeks to understand Anabaptism as the religion of the "poor" or "common" person, these interpretations have also sought to reverse the sixteenth-century judgments, especially with respect to value judgments about revolutions. Consequently, they have made no attempt to defend Anabaptism against the accusations of sedition and revolution, as insiders have attempted to do. Instead, like Karl Kautsky in his 1894 *The Forerunners of the Newer Socialism,*[64] social and Marxist historians, too, have sought — in open or more veiled terms — to legitimate their intellectual[65] positions by discovering the "origins" of their movements in the radicals of the sixteenth century.

It would seem, therefore, that writing history from a "Whig" perspective is not limited to nineteenth-century liberals; defenders of religious as well as secular ideologies have, at all times, exhibited a strong tendency to fall prey to the temptation to validate their current beliefs by mining history. Christian humanists, interested in the reform of the church, did less of this. Nevertheless, even they, like Erasmus, found themselves caught in a dilemma: on the one hand, they were drawn to return to a purer ideal of Christianity in the primitive church; on the other, however, they felt compelled — for a variety of reasons — to uphold the authority of the sixteenth-century

Catholic Church.[66] Having rejected the church's authority, the Anabaptists could devote themselves with greater singleness of purpose to the attempt to restore that primitive church. Since they shared this impulse with the Hussites, Waldenses, and Christian humanists, it might be more rewarding to approach the birth of Anabaptism from an earlier period rather than from some predetermined "modern" position — be that religious or secular.[67] For the writings of the Anabaptists demonstrate only too clearly that they were overwhelmingly concerned with returning to the teachings of Christ, and the apostles' interpretation of these teachings, though they too did so from within a context that had changed dramatically since the time of Christ and his apostles.[68]

In this book I will argue that it was indeed the impact of Christian humanism in general, and that of Desiderius Erasmus in particular — only partially mediated by Ulrich Zwingli — that gave rise to Anabaptism. The approach used will be twofold. In the next chapter I will attempt to delineate the broader context of Erasmian thought, and some of the more general areas in which that thought influenced the birth of Anabaptism. In the third, fourth, and fifth chapters, however, we will turn our attention to one very specific, concrete, and critical aspect of Erasmian influence — indeed, an influence that shaped the direction of both Anabaptist thought and practice. It is an aspect that led the Anabaptists to attempt to integrate the various aspects of Christianity and derives from Erasmus's paraphrases of Christ's Great Commission as interpreted through the baptismal passages in Acts — precisely those passages which Luther and Cochlaeus attempted to use in their debate over the extent of the authority of the Catholic Church.

2

Erasmus and the Anabaptists[1]

Erasmus of Rotterdam said, This Word was God. It was
Almighty, out of the Almighty, brought forth from the Father,
not in time but before all time; coming forth from the heart
of the Father, but in such a way as never to become separate
from Him. Moreover he says that the Father begot Him from
eternity and will beget Him forever. And in his *Ecclesiastae,*
Christ is the Word of God, Almighty, who proceeds without
beginning and without end from the heart of God.

Menno Simons, *The Incarnation of Our Lord* (1554)

In a recent book on the Copernican revolution of the sixteenth century, Thomas Kuhn argues that scientific advances, rather than moving
forward in an evolutionary linear progression, come in the formulation of new models, new paradigms, that make better sense of existing
evidence.[2] An established interpretation of the universe, such as the
one proposed in the ancient Ptolemaic model, adopted and Chris-
tianized by the medieval church, was therefore by its very nature
limited in the amount of new scientific data it could absorb. When
the weight of the new evidence began to strain its credibility, scientists
began to cast about for alternative models that might better integrate
the data. Nicholas Copernicus proposed such a new model in his *De
Revolutionibus* of 1543, but it was not until Isaac Newton's *Principia* of
1687 that a fully integrated version of the heliocentric universe ap-

20

peared. So striking was Newton's accomplishment that Alexander Pope wrote:

Nature and nature's laws lay hid in night:
God said: "Let Newton be," and all was light.

Kuhn's argument may also apply to theological or philosophical systems. Loose ends and tensions in such systems tend to irritate us, make us uneasy and uncertain of ourselves. We feel a need to have them integrated. At least some sixteenth-century thinkers appear to have recognized this. With respect to life and theology in the late medieval church, Thomas More wrote: "But preachers, who are indeed clever men, seem to have followed your counsel. Seeing that men will not fit their ways to Christ's pattern, the preachers have fitted His teaching to human customs, *to get agreement somehow or other.*"[3] And Erasmus, writing in his *Enchiridion,* noted: "Too many theologians only make matters worse by adapting the words of Scripture to the justification of their own crimes. It is indeed a sad state of affairs when we have given to vices the names of virtues, when we are more diligent in defending our vices than in correcting them, and when we even turn to Scripture to condone them."[4] Luther himself, as Philip Watson has observed, was not simply seeking, in his reform work, "to correct an error here and there, but his task, in his view, was such as to 'alter the whole religion of the Papacy.' The Christian faith is a unity, and if 'one little error' corrupts the whole, then the correction of error in any part cannot leave the rest unaffected."[5] It is from within this perspective, as well as from that of direct or indirect influence, that I wish to treat the problem of the relationship of Erasmus to the Anabaptists.

The theme, "Erasmus and the Anabaptists," is an old one. As early as the 1530s friends warned the prince of humanists that his name was being associated with the arch-heretics of the sixteenth century.[6] Later generations have picked up the theme, but in a more positive vein. Ludwig Keller, propounding the ancient Dutch Mennonite thesis that the Anabaptists were the sixteenth-century heirs of the Waldenses,[7] asserted in 1885 that Erasmus and his Basel circle were also Waldensian in their orientation; the clearest expression of this fact, he said, was Erasmus's 1519 *Annotations* on the New Testament.[8] Some years later Walter Koehler asserted more categorically that Erasmus "was the spiritual father of the Anabaptists."[9] And in his 1938 discussion of the origins of Anabaptism Leonhard von Muralt, the editor of the first volume of the *Quellen zur Geschichte der Taeufer in der Schweiz,*[10] wrote,

> In any case, certain intellectual preconditions were also present, as in a number of goals set by Christian humanism, above all by Erasmus of Rotterdam. In the same way that this scholar, through certain of his ideas, prepared the ground for the coming of the Reformation, he also — to a certain extent through the same ideas, to a certain extent through others — prepared the way for Anabaptism and provided material for the construction of their teachings; obviously first of all through his important work on the Bible, through his repeated references to its unique importance for the Christian faith, through his call to a *militia Christi,* to an immediate and active Christianity, and especially through his outspoken religious pacifism. Above all it was Erasmus who mediated the fundamental context of an older pietistic movement, that of the *Devotio Moderna* especially in the form of Thomas a Kempis' *Imitatio Christi,* to the later leaders of Anabaptism.[11]

In the last thirty years or so the theme of Erasmian influence on the early Swiss Anabaptist movement has grown exponentially, sometimes expressed in quite general terms,[12] at other times in more specific terms. Thus it has been argued that the Anabaptists were dependent upon Erasmus for their views on the freedom of the will,[13] their pacifism,[14] their ethical sincerity,[15] and the spiritualism of a Hans Denck.[16] Whereas some Mennonite scholars, such as Harald S. Bender,[17] have denied a direct influence, a Catholic scholar of the stature of John P. Dolan has said: "There can be little doubt of the perduring influence of Erasmus of Rotterdam on the early development of Anabaptism and his efforts to interpret it as a religious rather than a social revolutionary movement. . . . As an independent movement originating in the immediate circle of Zwingli at Zurich, Anabaptism found its roots in the spiritualism of the Rotterdam priest."[18] Yet, with the exception of direct Anabaptist dependence upon Erasmus in the area of free will,[19] the connections remain conveniently vague, lying too much in the nebulous realm of the "spirit of the times," of vague possibilities of influence, of tenuous connectedness. It is in the hope of providing a more convincing argument that I seek a larger framework from within which to test the hypothesis of Erasmian influence on the beginning of Swiss Anabaptism.

Renaissance humanism is probably best defined in Paul Oskar Kristeller's terms as consisting of a set of disciplines called the *studia humanitatis:* the humanizing disciplines, or the humanities, consisting of grammar, poetry, history, rhetoric, and moral philosophy.[20] Derived from the ancient rhetoricians, these disciplines had come to be seen as a unit. As early as the mid-fourteenth-century Francesco Petrarca, the titular father of Renaissance humanism, criticized Aristotle from this perspective, all of whose "moral books" he claimed to have read, some of them also "heard commented on." Through the study of these books, he said, he had "perhaps become more learned," but "not better, not so good as [he] ought to be." Therefore the promise made by the philosopher at the beginning of the first book of his *Ethics,* namely that "we learn this part of philosophy, not with the purpose of gaining knowledge but of becoming better" had not been fulfilled. Aristotle had taught what virtue was, "but his lesson lack[ed] the words that sting and set on fire and urge toward love of virtue and hatred of vice." He who looked for such powerful words of persuasive eloquence would find them "in our Latin writers, especially Cicero and Seneca."[21]

This passage in Petrarch's "On His Own Ignorance" points unmistakably to the humanists' central concern for moral reform. In that context, the moral philosophy of an Aristotle had to be combined with the power of rhetoric, with the art of persuasion, which, as Coluccio Salutati observed, "acts upon the will,"[22] otherwise knowledge would never be transformed into action. Persuasive eloquence, as important as it was,[23] was to be combined with history, which provided moral philosophy with its examples, and grammar, "which laid down the rules of composition."[24] Poetry, too, had its role in this scheme of things, presenting humans, in a more pleasurable form, with the lofty goals they were to pursue.[25] Combined in this fashion, the *studia humanitatis* constituted a program of moral reform designed to motivate people to aspire to that dignity uniquely theirs as beings created in the image of God.[26]

Along with a preference for the *studia humanitatis* over Scholasticism, most humanists would have preferred Plato over Aristotle. Here the context was the classical and patristic definition of *sapientia* as the knowledge of things human and divine.[27] Once again, it was Petrarch

23

who made the point. In the above mentioned treatise he observed that Plato and Aristotle had "come as far in natural and human matters as one can advance with the aid of mortal genius and study. In divine matters," however, Petrarch continued, "Plato and the Platonists rose higher, though none of them could reach the goal he aimed at. But, as I have said, Plato came nearer to it." Petrarch's reasons for preferring Plato over Aristotle, then, were clearly religious.[28] In another passage he asked who had assigned this principate to Plato, answering: "Not I, but truth, as is said — that truth which he saw and to which he came nearer than all the others, though he did not comprehend it." The authority for this assertion was no less a person than Augustine, the greatest saint of the Latin church. For, Petrarch proclaimed, "No Christian and particularly no faithful reader of Augustine's books will hesitate to confirm this."[29]

How close had Plato come to this truth? In his *Confessions,* the source of Petrarch's assertion,[30] Augustine had given quite an explicit answer. There the great saint had remarked,

> And Thou, willing first to show me how Thou "resistest the proud, but givest grace to the humble," and by how great an act of mercy Thou hadst pointed out to men the way of humility, in that Thy "WORD was made flesh," and dwelt among men — Thou procurdest for me, by means of one puffed up with most unnatural pride, certain books of the Platonists, translated from Greek into Latin. And therein I read, not indeed in the very words, but to the very same purpose, enforced by many and divers reasons, that "In the beginning was the Word, and the Word was with God, and the Word was God: the same was in the beginning with God: all things were made by Him, and without Him was nothing made that was made: that which was made by Him is 'life', and the life was the light of men, and the light shineth in darkness and the darkness comprehended it not." And that the soul of man, though it "bears witness to the light, yet itself is not that light"; but the Word of God, being God, "is that true light that lighteth every man that cometh into the world." And that "He was in the world, and the world was made by Him, and the world knew Him not." But that "He came into His own, and His own received Him not; but as many as received Him, to them gave He power to become the sons of God, as many as believed in His name"; this I did not read there.[31]

The argument that Plato had anticipated, though not reached, Christ's teachings gave both the Church Fathers and the Renaissance humanists access to Plato and justified their immersion in his writings. And through Plato the door was opened to other writers of classical antiquity as well. Nonetheless, it was from Plato that the humanists drew their basic categories, or models, of thinking on issues dealing with the relationship of things human and divine. Peter Brown has demonstrated the significance of this for Augustine's view of the church:

> Augustine, however, was a man steeped in Neo-Platonic ways of thought. The world appeared to him as a world of "becoming," as a hierarchy of imperfectly-realized forms which depended for their quality on "participating" in an intelligible World of Ideal Forms. This universe was in a constant, dynamic tension, in which the imperfect forms of matter strove to "realize" their fixed, ideal structure, grasped by the mind alone. It was the same with Augustine's view of the Church. The rites of the church were undeniably "holy," because of the objective holiness of a Church which "participated" in Christ. The "true church" of Augustine is not only the "body of Christ," the "heavenly Jerusalem," it is also deeply tinged with the metaphysical ideas of Plotinus; it is the "reality," of which the concrete church is only an imperfect shadow. Thus, the men who received and administered these rites merely strove imperfectly to realize this holiness, according to a certain shadow of reality.[32]

Neoplatonism therefore provided Augustine, and through him Petrarch and many of the Renaissance humanists, with the basic model within which they thought.[33] That model posited a realm of perfection, of archetypal ideas, of "Ideal Forms" that emanated from the mind of God. Man "participated" in these ideas, but his formulations of them were at best shadowy reflections, imperfect images of the Ideal Forms. Christians could justify such constructs with the words of St. Paul, who had said that now we see as through a glass darkly. They could give a Christian justification for the Platonic distinction between the Ideal Forms and their shadowy reflections in the world by citing the passage where St. Paul argued that the things that are unseen are eternal, while those seen are transitory. Within this setting Platonism could prove most useful.

25

Rather than posit a sharp break between things human and things divine, between the kingdom of God and the kingdom of man, the Platonic model argued in favor of a continuum between the two. After all, human realities, no matter how distorted, how corrupt, nevertheless remained shadows of the Ideal Forms. Seen through Platonic eyes, the temporal church remained a reflection, a shadow, of the ideal no matter how corrupt it might become. Brown speaks of Augustine's church as always in a state of becoming; it could never be a church "without spot or wrinkle" here on earth. While the church could therefore never be perfect, Plato's analogy of the cave gave all of this a decidedly pessimistic turn, for that analogy made it palpably apparent that the great mass of humanity in such a church was quite content to accept the shadows as true reality; they showed no interest in moving beyond them. This being so, did not the Platonic context work at cross purposes with the *studia humanitatis* in matters of reform? If, under even the best of circumstances, the real world had of necessity to remain a shadow of the ideal, how much could eloquence accomplish? Perhaps Pico's famous words, recorded in his *Oration on the Dignity of Man* — "Thou shalt have the power out of thy soul's judgment, to be reborn into the higher forms, which are divine"[34] — should be taken with more than just a few grains of rhetorical salt! Even with these cautions, however, the *studia humanitatis* were still of considerable importance, for without them there was little hope of any moral improvement. It was within this tension-filled model that Erasmus lived, moved, and had his being.[35]

As Petrarch the Christian noted, not even Plato had seen the Ideal Forms with anything resembling absolute clarity. Christian Platonists, however, could argue that Christ had come directly from the Father, the very fount of truth itself, to reveal the Ideal Forms to humankind. In a Platonic context Christ became the teacher of archetypal wisdom, indeed, he became the archetype itself. Witness the following passage from Erasmus's *Enchiridion:*

> From among the many thoughts that have entered my mind since I began this letter to you, I think it would be fitting to choose a sixth rule that, incidentally, is observed by too few who claim to be followers of Christ. If we would be holy, we must go to the sole archetype of godliness, Christ himself. Anyone who refuses to do this is outside the pale. Plato in his *Republic* points out that no man

can defend virtue unless he has trained his mind in opinions regarding the true nature of good and evil. We can see then how dangerous it is if false opinions of those things that pertain to wellbeing should sink deeply into the mind.[36]

No wonder he could say, in the preface to his New Testament, that we should "ponder within ourselves" this new and wonderful philosophy since, "in order to transmit it to mortals, He who was God became man, He who was immortal became mortal, He who was in the heart of the Father descended to earth."[37] Since Christ was to be the goal of the Christian's life, Erasmus sought to clarify and emphasize the teachings of Christ, his counsels of perfection, as applicable to all. He did this as early as his *Epistola de contemptu mundi.* There, as also Ernst-Wilhelm Kohls has remarked, Erasmus revived the original monastic ideal and asserted that it applied to everyone who would be a Christian.[38] Because they did the very same thing, sixteenth-century Anabaptists were called "new monks" by the Reformers.[39] Ambrose Pelargus, one of Erasmus's most persistent critics, saw similarities between Erasmus and the Anabaptists on this issue and wrote to the former,

> So that you may defend yourself, how do you extricate yourself from this charge . . . that you mix up monastic poverty, counseled by Christ, with the precepts of Christ which apply to all equally? For it is not so uncertain that you may do so designedly. Your words in the *Enchiridion* go thus: "You believed that only to monks was property forbidden and poverty imposed? You have erred, for it pertains to all Christians." But if monastic poverty (namely that disengagement which is even now permitted to be undertaken by a soul prepared for it so that it may renounce and give up all inheritance just like the primitive church) is enjoined upon all Christians the consequence would be that as many are true Christians, as have professed monasticism. Is there not danger in those words of yours that the Anabaptists may also find support for their falsehoods?[40]

Erasmus saw these teachings of Christ and the idealized world, where all Christians would be monks, as being in tension with the Christian world in which he lived.[41] He made the point quite explicitly

27

in the *Enchiridion:* "Yet we are living in a world that has grown alien to the world of Christ both in doctrine and in practice. There are too many who think that the expression 'world' refers only to those who have embraced the monastic state. In the Gospels, and for the Apostles, and for Augustine, Ambrose, and Jerome, the expression means the infidel, enemies of the faith and the Cross of Christ."[42]

Erasmus labels his world as one that has grown alien to Christ. Once upon a time, in the age of the apostles and Church Fathers, the tension had been far less. Not that it had ever been totally absent. Yet, whereas Erasmus could castigate his age as being "alien to the world of Christ," he chided the Anabaptists, who sought to recover that pristine purity of the primitive church of which he was so fond of speaking:

> Look at these unhappy Anabaptists, whom I call unhappy, because it is error rather than wickedness that carries them on to their own destruction. Are they not satisfied with baptism as it was practised in the Church for fourteen hundred years,[43] which in the time of Augustine was so ancient that no one knew its origin, and which the Apostles probably extended to children. Their refusal to obey princes is quite at variance with Christ's command to render unto Caesar the things of Caesar; and the communism they attempt was only possible when the Church was small, and then not among all Christians. As soon as the Gospel spread widely, it became quite impossible. The best way towards agreement is that property should be in the hands of lawful owners, but that out of charity we should share with one another.[44]

The juxtaposition of these two quotations should help to highlight the problem of Erasmus for us, for even though he argued that his world had grown alien to the world of Christ, his concern was not, apparently, to reestablish Christ's ideal teachings among Christians, but simply to move the shadowy reflections of the Ideal Forms of his day somewhat closer to their archetypes, to bring the individual Christian closer to Christ, his archetype, to have him move from the visible ritual to the invisible, spiritual worship. And so Erasmus can, at the same time, criticize his own age for having departed from the ideals of Christ and chide the Anabaptists for being too rigid in their attempt to restore them. As the rhetorician that he was, Erasmus could encourage his fellow Christians in the following manner:

> Therefore, my brethren, put on Christ. Take as your rule that you no longer wish to crawl upon the ground with the beasts, but to rise upon those wings that sprout in the minds of those who love. Advance from the body to the spirit, from the visible to the invisible, from things sensible to things intelligible, from things compound to things simple. If you come near to the Lord, He will come near to you; if you make a sincere effort to escape from the chains of blindness with which the love of sensible things has bound you, He will come to you, and you, no longer chained to the things of the earth, will be enveloped in the silence of God.[45]

The realist in Erasmus, however, saw the obvious obstacles to accomplishing this ideal, for he said on another occasion: "The great mass of the people are swayed by false opinions and are no different from those in Plato's cave, who took the empty shadows as the real thing."[46]

No matter how elusive a thing reform might be, it was nevertheless important for Erasmus, given his Platonic context, to elucidate the teachings *of* Christ — not the teachings *about* Christ that so preoccupied Luther — as much as possible.[47] For Erasmus was, after all, concerned with moral reform. He therefore held Christ's teachings up to the world as the ideal, as the archetypes to be opposed to the corrupt practices, the ritualistic shadows of these forms within the Catholic Church.

What were these ideals Erasmus saw as being in tension with a corrupt Christian society? We have already heard him say that he was living in a world that had grown alien to Christ "both in doctrine and practice." In a letter to Julius Pflug of 20 August 1531 in which he bemoaned the wicked conditions in church and state, Erasmus observed that there were few sheep in his day, "that is those who simply find themselves on the wrong path rather than sinning from a hardened, wicked disposition." No age, he said, was as mad as his own.[48] His repeated references to Plato's analogy of the cave added weight to his assertion that the masses admired "only what is corporeal and hold all else as being almost lacking in existence."[49] This was, he said in a letter of 1517, an age worse than iron.[50]

Much of the problem for Erasmus lay in the fact that the "world" had crept into the church, and the distinctions now made between "world" and "Christendom" were all wrong. The rejection of the world did not only apply to monks: "In the Gospels," we have heard him say, "for Augustine, Ambrose, and Jerome, the expression means the infidel, enemies of the faith and the Cross of Christ." How much more consonant with Christ's teachings, he argued, it would be "to regard the entire Christian world as a household, as a single monastery."[51] The counsels of perfection applied to all Christians, and the latter were to separate themselves from the world. As he wrote a friend in 1502: "Associate with those in whom you have seen Christ's true image; otherwise, where there are none whose society can improve you, then withdraw from human intercourse as far as you can, and take for company the holy prophets and Christ and the Apostles."[52] In effect, Erasmus was saying that the church ought, ideally, to follow Christ and be separated from the world like a monastery, though he, like the later Anabaptists, rejected the sixteenth-century monastic version of these Christian ideals.[53] The reality of the situation seemed somewhat more bleak to Erasmus, however, for he said there would only be few who "are truly converted from evil habits."[54]

Erasmus was convinced that the early church had been very different from the church of his day. In his attack on Luther in *Freedom of the Will* he wrote: "But if Paul in his time, in which the gift of the Spirit was in full force, orders spirits to be tested whether they be of God, what ought to be done in this carnal age?"[55] In a 1519 letter to Eberhard von der Mark he wrote: "Paul speaks somewhat more fully about the gift of tongues, of interpretation, of prophecy and other matters, in whose place congregational singing, the Scripture lesson, and the sermon later appeared. For the gifts of healing and revelation departed from us long ago, especially since our love has grown cold, our faith weak, and we have become more dependent upon human than divine help."[56] In his *Praise of Folly* he contrasted popes and cardinals to Christ and his apostles, concluding that the church had no greater enemies "than these charlatan popes who encourage the disregard of Christ, who depict Him as a mercenary, who corrupt His teachings by forced interpretations, and who scandalize Him by their infamous lives."[57]

In the process of increasing corruption from the primitive church and estrangement from the counsels of perfection, the Catholic Church had moved further and further away from the spiritual, the invisible ideals, substituting in their place visible rituals. The visualization of spiritual phenomena, however, led ineluctably to superstition, to placing one's trust in the visible transaction of the sacrament. Erasmus wished to reverse the trend. Not that he rejected the visible transaction entirely. It was, after all, a shadow of the ideal. Rather, he desired to move the Christian beyond it to the spiritual reality. And so Erasmus could write about baptism:

> Do you really think that the ceremony of itself makes you a Christian? If your mind is preoccupied with the affairs of the world, you may be a Christian on the surface, but inwardly you are a Gentile of the Gentiles. Why is this? It is simply because you have grasped the body of the sacrament, not the spirit. The ceremony consists of washing the body with water, but for you this is not a cleansing of the soul. Salt is placed upon your tongue, but your mind remains uncured. The body is anointed with oil, but the soul remains unanointed. You have been sprinkled with holy water, but this accomplishes nothing unless you cleanse the inner filth of your mind.[58]

Or consider the following passage from his *Education of a Christian Prince:*

> Do you think that the profession of a Christian is a matter to be lightly passed over, entailing no responsibilities unless, of course, you think the sacrament which you accept along with everything else is nothing. And do you think you renounce just for the once the delights of Satan which bring pain to Christ. He is displeased with all that is foreign to the teachings of the Gospel. You share the Christian sacrament alike with all others — why not its teaching too? You have allied yourself to Christ — and yet you slide back into the ways of Julius and Alexander the Great? You seek the same rewards as others, yet you will have no concern with His mandates?
>
> But on the other hand, do you think that Christ is found in ceremonies, in doctrines kept after a fashion, and in constitutions of the church? Who is truly Christian? Not he who is baptized or anointed, or who attends church. It is rather the man who has embraced Christ in the innermost feelings of his heart, and who emulates Him in pious deeds.[59]

31

Erasmus complained that such an emphasis on the visible ritual resulted from a false set of values and "brought more ruin than any other because in appearance it was very close to godliness."[60] The rituals and ceremonies of the church fell into this category. Yet they were at best "signs, supports of piety."[61] They might be necessary "for children in Christ," perhaps until they became more mature. And so even those "more advanced in perfection" should not scorn them, "lest their scorn work great harm among the simple and uninstructed. *My approval,*" Erasmus continued, "*rests on the assumption that they are steps, gradations, that lead to more appropriate means of salvation*" (my emphasis). But "to place the whole of religion in external ceremonies" was "sublime stupidity." To do so amounted to "revolt against the spirit of the Gospel and [was] a reversion to the superstition of Judaism."[62]

Given this position, even the Eucharist was better interpreted in a spiritual sense, as Zwingli and the Anabaptists interpreted it. Writing to Willibald Pirckheimer on 6 June 1526, Erasmus stated that the spiritual interpretation of Oecolampadius would not displease him "if the unanimous opinion of the Church were not against it." He did not understand, he said, "what good it was for the Eucharist to be considered a physical eating of the body when the elements contain a spiritual grace."[63] But he could not oppose the tradition of the church. And his Neoplatonism allowed him to hold the visible and the invisible together, though in considerable tension. This tension Erasmus hoped at least to lessen — as it had been perhaps, in the primitive church — by moving people away from their reliance upon the visible and drawing them to the invisible, the spiritual.

Primarily because of his emphasis on the teachings of Christ unadulterated as the ideal to be pursued, Erasmus stressed Christian pacifism, more so than all of the major sixteenth-century intellectuals. In his *Complaint of Peace* he made as good a case for it as has been made. There he wrote: "Men who are not ashamed to be called Christian act in total disagreement with what is most important to Christ. Consider His life. What is it other than a doctrine of concord and love? What do His commandments and parables teach? Peace and charity. Did the prophet Isaiah, when he foretold of the coming of Christ, promise that He should be a ruler of cities or a warrior? No! What then did he promise? A Prince of Peace."[64] In this matter of peace Erasmus found the greatest disparity between the ideals of

Christ and the practice of his sixteenth-century followers. "All Christian doctrine in both Old and New Testaments calls for peace, yet Christian life is filled with warfare. What evil is there that cannot be overcome? Let them either relinquish the name of Christian or give expression to the doctrine of Christ by concord. How long shall theory and practice disagree?"[65] Or again: "The celestial Jerusalem Christians desire is called the vision of peace. The Church on earth is its prototype. How is it then that the Church differs so greatly from its exemplar? Has industrious nature accomplished so little? Has Christ with His commandments and mysteries accomplished nothing?"[66] Perhaps in this most important instance Erasmus was unable to discover the continuum that connected Christ's ideal with the world of reality. There was not even a shadow of peace on earth. Not even baptism, that "sacrament common to all," by which all "are born again to Christ, cut off from the world and grafted as members of Christ" brought peace. "What can be as much itself as members of a body? There is neither bond nor free, barbarian nor Greek, man nor woman. All are identical in Christ, Who reduces all things to concord."[67]

> A little blood tasted on both sides joins Scythians so that they do not hesitate to die for their friends. Amity is a sacred and holy thing among pagans when a common table unites them. Shall not that Heavenly Bread and that mystical cup unite Christian men in charity when Christ has ordained it and they renew that sacrifice daily? If Christ has accomplished nothing, why these ceremonies? If He did something really important, why do we neglect it as if it were trivial? Does any man dare to be so bold as to come to that table, the banquet of peace, who prepares to war against fellow Christians, who prepares to destroy those for whom Christ died, who prepares to draw blood for whom Christ shed His?[68]

Like the Anabaptists, Erasmus regarded baptism as the most important of sacraments. He speaks of "swearing allegiance to Christ in baptism."[69] In the *Enchiridion* he wrote: "When you were baptized, you took an oath to do just that [suffer with Christ]. To my way of thinking there is no vow or promise that is more religious or sacred than this."[70] Real apostates to the faith, Erasmus wrote in his *Ratio*, "are those whose entire life stands in opposition to Christ . . . and the confession made at baptism."[71] Baptism was therefore of critical importance and Erasmus hardly ever spoke of it in terms of promises others made for a child. When he did, he came extremely close to advocating rebaptism, as in the preface to the third (1522) edition of his Latin New Testament, where Zwingli and his later radical followers must have read it and contemplated its meaning as they met to study the Bible. Taking his cue from the monastic movement itself, which had long since come to regard monastic initiation as a "second baptism,"[72] Erasmus suggested in that preface that something similar be instituted for all the other inhabitants of Christendom, for, nowadays, he argued, "there are many fifty-year-olds who have no idea what vows they undertook in the baptism ceremony, who never even dreamed of what the articles of faith demand of them, what Sunday prayers mean, or what the sacraments of the church imply."[73] But this ignorance was not only prevalent among laymen, for "many of us who are priests are also of this sort; we have never seriously considered what it is to be truly Christian."[74] They were Christian in name only, in customs, in ceremonies; their minds had remained unaffected. Therefore Erasmus applied the passages from Isaiah 56:10, Jeremiah 50:6, and Ezekiel 22:28 — which spoke of blind, ignorant, lazy, and greedy watchmen who sought only their own gain; of sheep having gone astray because the shepherds had turned into wolves — to the priests of his day.

To remedy the situation, Erasmus recommended a number of changes in the church. First, in order to get more people to read the Bible, he suggested that "every year the substance of our Christian faith and doctrine . . . be proposed, briefly, clearly, and with learned simplicity, to the entire population."[75] He also wanted the preaching "to be done, not from the defective inventions of human minds, but from the evangelical sources, from the apostolic letters, from the creed, which — though I don't know whether it was produced by the apostles — certainly carries on it the marks of apostolic majesty and purity."[76] In addition, Erasmus proffered a second proposal:

> I think it would help in no small degree toward the end we desire if children who have been baptized, when they reach the age of puberty, should be ordered to attend sessions in which it would be made clear to them what was actually involved in the baptismal ceremony. Then let them be carefully examined in private by men of authority, to make sure they know and recall what the priest has

taught them. If they have that material in hand, let them be asked further to give an account of what their sponsors promised in their name at their baptism. If they can give a good account of that, then let them renew their promises in public assemblies to the accompaniment of many solemn ceremonies — seemly, serious, chaste, and splendid, such as may befit that declaration of principles than which nothing can be more holy. What, after all, are human promises, but initiations, as it were, of this most sacred promise, recalls, so to speak, of Christianity's first fall into the world.[77]

In spite of the fact that Erasmus may have averred from time to time that infant baptism removed the stain of original sin,[78] this entire passage leads the reader almost ineluctably to the conclusion that infant baptism had — objectively speaking — accomplished nothing.[79] It was necessary, therefore, to "imitate" or reiterate baptism — much as the monks did — in public ceremonies where youngsters who had reached the age of puberty were instructed in "what their sponsors [had] promised in their name at baptism" and would dedicate "themselves to Jesus Christ [as so many] new recruits pledging loyalty to his cause."[80]

Erasmus spoke of these new recruits as "advancing from the holy feast," as though coming from baptism, having sworn allegiance to Christ in "very public" ceremonies. If this were done, he asserted, there would be "many more genuine Christians than we . . . now [have]." He recognized a difficulty in the above recommendation, however: that the "ceremony of baptism seems to be repeated, which is not right." But he thought the difficulty could be overcome "if things are so managed as to make clear that the ceremony does nothing but ratify the first." Though based, as this recommendation was, on the monastic initiation rites that were in fact consistently called "second baptisms," Erasmus apparently wished to avoid such terminology, probably because he was only too aware of the problem heretical baptism had caused in the patristic church and the decisions reached regarding the rebaptism of such persons. Nevertheless, his reference to the monastic precedent indicates clearly enough what Erasmus had in mind. It is little wonder, therefore, that when the doctors of the Sorbonne took a look at Erasmus's proposal in 1526, they censured it and wrote that to "rebaptize" children would be to open "the door to the destruction of the Christian religion."[81] For Erasmus, however, as

35

this passage makes plain enough, in ideal terms baptismal vows were something all individuals should take for themselves once they understood what the vows implied.

What we have in Erasmus, then, is an ideal world consisting of Christ's teachings, in which baptism is the most important sacrament, for it is here that the disciple swears an oath of allegiance to his Master. The real world of Christianity, however, the world in which Erasmus found himself, was a mere shadow of this ideal world. Indeed, the two seemed separated by a vast gulf, yet Erasmus's Neoplatonic paradigm allowed him to regard the visible as similar in kind to the ideal, no matter to what extent it had been corrupted. Nor would the tension between the two ever be eradicated; the temporal church would never become a perfect replica of the ideal. At best, it would always be in a process of becoming, never to reach the state of being.

Were one to read Erasmus without his Neoplatonic perspective one might nearly think him an Anabaptist. Some of his non-Anabaptist contemporaries read him from this vantage point; some modern scholars have done so as well. It should therefore not be surprising to find the Anabaptists doing the same. We have already seen a number of his Catholic contemporaries warn Erasmus that he was moving dangerously close to an Anabaptist position. Whenever he was attacked by such persons, however, he could always slip to the other end of his Neoplatonic scale and point to the fact that he had never rejected the rites and sacraments of the church; he had merely attempted to move people up the scale to a more profound, a more spiritual understanding of them. And so he could cling to a church he had himself repeatedly condemned as totally corrupt, rather than break with it. But he could do so only because his Neoplatonic model held the ideal and the real together, though in considerable tension. This tension the Reformation broke.

It was Luther who did so first by proclaiming the principle of *sola scriptura*. Upon this foundation Luther sought to remove all human speculation, all philosophical intrusions, from theology.[82] He derived this emphasis on Scripture and "right reason," which he proclaimed before Cajetan at Augsburg in October of 1518, at Leipzig in July of 1519, and at Worms before Charles V in April of 1521, from a letter of Augustine to Jerome.[83] With respect to Luther's desire to remove philosophy from theology, Erasmus made an interesting comment in a 1520 letter to the Augustinian monk. He recognized Luther's intention to separate the spiritual from temporal matters, philosophy from theology, but he cautioned him to proceed more slowly and chided him that if he wished to make a complete break with philosophy, he would also have to give up his beloved Augustine![84] It does not appear that Luther ever did so.

Zwingli adopted this same principle of *sola scriptura* in Zurich after his conversion in 1520. Yet Zwingli had been much more heavily influenced by Erasmus, especially in the years 1515-1520, than had Luther. The Erasmian impact in Zurich reached well beyond Zwingli, for Leo Jud, Zwingli's successor in Einsiedeln from 1519-1522 and partner in Zurich after 1522, became one of the main translators of Erasmus's writings into German, published by Froschauer in Zurich. Beginning in 1520 with Erasmus's *Enarratio in primum Psalmum,* Jud proceeded to translate the *Querella Pacis,* the *Institutio principis Christiani,* and the paraphrases of the New Testament.[85] Perhaps due to this Erasmian influence, Zwingli[86] — and through him his Anabaptist followers — took a broader view of biblical inspiration than did Luther. At the same time, as Robert Friedmann argued some years ago, the Anabaptists developed a very strong sense of the separation of the kingdom of God and the kingdom of the world.[87] Erasmus's Neoplatonic continuum between the shadows and the Ideal Forms was irreparably breached. Through Luther's reformation and Zwingli's legacy, the Anabaptists developed an interpretive model different from that of Erasmus. That model rejected the latter's Platonic interpretive scheme but not the ideals Erasmus had sought to establish as the ideal forms of Christianity. Indeed, these forms were affirmed in the strongest of terms in the Anabaptist model. Even some modern scholars, ignorant of Erasmus's Platonic context, have interpreted him in the way the Anabaptists must have. It is only by doing so that Walter Koehler was able to call Erasmus the spiritual father of Anabaptism, that Paul Wernle could describe his theology as embodying the "simple undogmatic morality of the Sermon on the Mount,"[88] and that Ernst Troeltsch could say of the *Enchiridion:* "This document marks the transition from St. Paul, whom none of these [humanists] understood, to the religion of the Sermon on the Mount with its simple faith in Christ."[89]

Aside from the strongly Erasmian context within which the Zurich Reformation took place, an even more important and specific link connected Erasmus with the birth of Swiss Anabaptism: Erasmus's

1516, 1519, and 1522 editions of the New Testament and the various editions of his *Annotations* that accompanied them. From Conrad Grebel,[90] Balthasar Hubmaier,[91] and Menno Simons[92] we know that they used Erasmus's New Testament, his *Annotations* and paraphrases. One may assume that other Anabaptist leaders did so as well.[93] The Grebel circle in Zurich studied the New Testament in the original Greek,[94] and, in Andreas Castelberger's bookstore, they had Erasmus's New Testament and *Annotations* for sale.[95] Modern scholarship appears largely to have overlooked this factor, even though a Louvain Carmelite monk in late 1520 accused Erasmus, in an open church service, of providing Luther with all his innovations from the editions of his New Testament. In the presence of Erasmus he advised his congregation to "avoid the new and abide by the old Gospel."[96] Ludwig Keller, some one hundred years ago, argued the same for the Anabaptists,[97] only he labeled this influence Waldensian.

Erasmus's influence in this regard is important for at least two reasons. First, it was precisely in these *Annotations* and paraphrases that Erasmus — in the process of clarifying the meaning of the Bible, which was for him the purest expression of the Ideal Forms — accented those ideals he had been advocating for some time.[98] For here there was little or no room for the shadowy reflections of the real world. Second, whether or not they derived their central emphasis on the Bible from Erasmus,[99] the Anabaptists regarded the Bible as normative in matters Christian.[100] Over a hundred and forty years ago C. A. Cornelius called the Anabaptists a "church of radical Bible readers."[101] And in 1925 Walter Koehler wrote, "This independence of the Zurich [Anabaptists] rests on a solid basis at their disposal: the Bible. They have drawn everything from it; this is an emphasis that must be placed prior to the influence of Karlstadt and Muentzer and considered the decisive criterion. This factor makes the movement autochthonous and it is therefore proper to place Zurich at the source of the Anabaptist movement."[102]

Confirmation of this assertion has come in a recent essay by Heinold Fast,[103] who discovered a little "book" by Hans Kruesi, an early Anabaptist of St. Gallen. Rather than being a theological treatise as one might expect, it was a collection of the relevant biblical passages on the topics of faith and baptism: the first, the central concern of the Protestant Reformation; the second, added to the first by the Anabaptists. This is the earliest-known example of many similar later lists.[104]

Fast contends that it has its source in Grebel himself, who wrote his brother-in-law, Vadian, on 3 September 1524: "In conclusion, I shall collect and arrange all [biblical?] passages pertaining to two themes and present them to the public, if someone else does not do so first."[105] In a subsequent letter to Andreas Castelberger, Grebel indicated that he was circulating such a list and that one had even been sent to Zwingli.[106] This list gave the ordinary reader and follower of the Anabaptist leaders a ready group of biblical citations to use before the authorities who arrested and interrogated them. No theological writings of any kind were included. The Bible alone had authority for the Anabaptists; and if the leaders used Erasmus's New Testament and his accompanying *Annotations,* then it is perhaps permissible to speak of a direct influence of Erasmus on the Anabaptists. In this biblical context, however, Erasmus's influence would have come to them largely bereft of its Neoplatonic overtones.

In the next chapter I will treat the most direct influence of Erasmus on the Anabaptists; here, however, I wish to note the other areas in which Erasmus's *Annotations* may have served the Swiss Anabaptists. The great humanist's notes on biblical passages dealing with communion could well suggest that he favored a symbolic or spiritual interpretation.[107] Some of his Catholic critics thought so, and Leo Jud, in a booklet published in Zurich in 1525, attempted to show "that Erasmus shared Zwingli's views on the symbolic nature of the Eucharist."[108] To the extent that Zwingli did indeed derive his views from Erasmus, the Swiss Anabaptists as followers of Zwingli were also dependent upon Erasmus in this area.

Other intriguing passages in Erasmus's *Annotations* are pregnant with possibilities for influence on the Swiss Anabaptists. One of these has to do with the oath, another with Christian pacifism. With respect to the former, Erasmus wrote in the 1516 edition of his notes on the New Testament, commenting on Christ's words in Matthew 5,

> Let your communication be yea, yea, nay, nay — whatsoever more than these comes from evil: It is amazing how the theologians twist these words. Some interpret "comes from evil" as meaning from the evil of disbelief, not from the evil of swearing, others interpret it as meaning from the evil of punishment, not from the evil of guilt. But, in my opinion, Christ simply meant that perfect men (for the words pertain to them) must not swear at all in matters

concerning which the common people swear. As for the rest, concerning of faith and piety even Christ and the apostles swear oaths.[109]

In 1519 Erasmus elaborated on his views, adding,

for [Christ] wished his people to be of such a character that there would be no need for oaths. For what is the use of swearing an oath if no one wishes to cheat anyone else even if he could do so with impunity, but each man, judging the other by his own intention, trusts everyone else? For a true Christian considers his neighbour's convenience, even at his own inconvenience. . . . In this manner we shall all be able to solve many knotty questions, if we realize that Christ did not forbid swearing oaths absolutely but only swearing in the vulgar manner of men.[110]

If, as Erika Rummel notes, Erasmus's words were "widely interpreted as a categorical denial of the legitimacy of oaths,"[111] the Swiss Anabaptist leaders studying his *Annotations* may also have done so. Menno Simons certainly did so, referring specifically to Erasmus's notes on the Matthew 5 passage.[112] Whereas the early Swiss Anabaptists, as John Howard Yoder observes, "were divided about the degree of thoroughness with which to apply Jesus' prohibition of the oath"[113] — perhaps reflective of Erasmus's comments on the passage — the 1527 *Schleitheim Confession* took a much more categorical position against the oath.

Erasmus's pacifism, too, was accentuated in the *Annotations*. In the 1519 edition he observed, commenting on a passage in Luke 3, "I think it is permitted to prefer the doctrine of Christ and the apostles to the views of Augustine. Yet he [Augustine] does not approve the type of war in which we now engage without end."[114] In another note, this time on Luke 22, he observed that, in the past, men who had rejected war completely had been branded as heretics, but to him, "no heresy seems . . . more pernicious, no blasphemy more wicked than . . . to turn the spiritual sense into a carnal one."[115] As Ambrose had said, "The arms of the church are its faith; the arms of the church are prayers which overcome the enemy."[116] Along with the German translation of Erasmus's *Querella Pacis* by Leo Jud, these notes on pacifism may also have had their impact upon the Swiss Brethren.

Finally, Erasmus's *Annotations* may also have impressed the Swiss radicals with their egalitarian view of a Christian society. As Rummel has asserted, "Erasmus believed in a brotherhood of men, a 'classless' society in Christ. 'In my opinion,' he says, 'the term *brother* applies to all men' (Matt. 5, note 18)."[117] This was an appropriate passage for a group that was to call itself the "Swiss Brethren." Even more so, Erasmus may have been at least one source for the emphasis on a community of goods among believers. This may well have been reinforced for the Anabaptists by Rothmann's tract on the two sacraments — which preceded the Münster Colloquy of 1533 and was largely republished verbatim by Pilgram Marpeck in his *Vermahnung* of 1542 — though without acknowledgment — where he wrote,

> These four things they practised with all earnestness in the breaking of bread, which they had in common, as Erasmus interprets the passage in his *Annotations*.[118] First, he presents the teaching of the Gospel; second, brotherly love, which caused them to have all things common; third. . . . This custom [community of goods] is not only to be found in St. Paul, but was also present in the early Church. See Acts 2:[42], Erasmus's *Paraphrases,* Sichard on the 4th epistle of Clement, for the kind of appearance and structure the first church had.[119]

From Rothmann's tract of 1533, this impulse may well have gone through Marpeck to the Hutterites who, as Robert Friedmann has pointed out, used the early church's example and Clement's epistle to justify their community of goods. Another source of Erasmus's views on these matters may have been the writings of Sebastian Franck.[120]

What I have provided in this chapter is at best a preliminary study of Erasmus's possible impact upon the early Swiss Anabaptists. A close analysis of the writings of Menno Simons, for example, might demonstrate that many of the latter's references to the Church Fathers came from Erasmus's editions of their works, or even from the latter's own citations of their writings in his *Annotations*. Furthermore, it does not appear that Thomas Müntzer made use of the Erasmian edition of the New Testament, continuing to use the Vulgate.[121] Perhaps at least some of the differences between Müntzer and the Swiss Anabaptists derive from this factor. Whatever the case, the Louvain Car-

41

melite monk who accused Erasmus of providing Luther with all of his heretical ideas through the edition of his New Testament — though an obvious exaggeration — was onto something that merits a much closer scrutiny. For in his *Annotations* Erasmus expressed the ideas he voiced elsewhere in connection with his philological prowess and the biblical passages in plain view. In that setting his arguments must have carried all the greater weight. Here, too, the Platonic paradigm that encased his thought and through which he expressed his Christianity was less intrusive and more easily overlooked, even though that paradigm allowed him, in succeeding editions, to protest his Catholic orthodoxy to his increasingly vocal Catholic critics.

3

Anabaptism and the "Great Commission"

Then Jesus came to them and said, "All authority in heaven and on earth has been given to me. Therefore go and make disciples of all nations, baptizing them in the name of the Father and of the Son and of the Holy Spirit, and teaching them to obey everything I have commanded you. And surely I am with you always, to the very end of the age."

Matthew 28:18-20

If, as I argued in the previous chapter, there were differences in the intellectual paradigms of Erasmus and the Anabaptists, this chapter will demonstrate the striking similarities between the two with respect to the context into which they placed the moral imperatives the great humanist had isolated in his *Annotations* on the New Testament. Erasmus developed this context in his paraphrases of the Gospels and the Acts of the Apostles; the Anabaptists absorbed it from him. And it was this context that gave meaning to these moral imperatives by placing them into a larger theological — indeed biblical — framework. Ignorance of this context has led scholars to speak of Erasmus's theology as "undogmatic," as the "simple Christianity of the Sermon on the Mount." Nothing could be further from the truth, as Craig R. Thompson already argued some years ago in his analysis of the

43

Erasmian colloquy *Inquisitio de Fide.* If this is true of Erasmus, it is equally true of the Anabaptists who — as I intend to demonstrate — absorbed this context from the prince of humanists. In this instance we have a case of direct influence.

The similarities and differences in the intellectual paradigms of Erasmus and the Anabaptists delineated in the previous chapter led to the conclusion that Erasmus's Neoplatonism was less apparent and less intrusive in his annotations on the Bible than in his other writings. In the biblical context he could concentrate on the ideal types, the archetypal wisdom that Christ had brought to earth "from the heart of the Father." This is probably even more true in his paraphrases of the various books of the New Testament. In his concluding remarks on the Great Commission (Matt. 28:18-20), in his paraphrase of that gospel, Erasmus observed: "Therefore, deliver to them [the believers] whatsoever I have commanded you, [teaching them] to obey everything. I have not commanded you to observe the ceremonies of the Mosaic law,[1] *which must now vanish away like shadows in the light of evangelical truth;* nor have I prescribed the constitutions of the Pharisees; but only those things that bring true innocence and godliness, and which make you truly happy and dearly beloved of God."[2] In his paraphrases of the Gospels, therefore, Erasmus believed himself to be dealing with the "light of evangelical truth." As a consequence, the Platonic "shadows" had to pass away.

It is precisely his discussion of this Matthean version of the Great Commission and the way he related it to the baptismal passages in the Acts of the Apostles that was to have a profound impact upon both the origin and the development of Anabaptist thought. But since such a connection would not normally — if at all — have been made in either the primitive or the modern church because of Luke's authorship of both the third Gospel and Acts, it is incumbent upon us — before we turn to the specific aspects of the above relationship — to explain how Erasmus could have arrived at such an association, as well as to reconstruct, as much as possible, the context within which Zwingli and his followers encountered the great humanist's paraphrases of the Gospel of Matthew and the Acts of the Apostles. I will address the last concern first.

Erasmus's impact upon Zwingli's intellectual development, which began no later than Zwingli's meeting with the Dutch scholar in 1515, has been well established elsewhere.[3] Given such an influence, it should not surprise us that the emerging Swiss Reformer — like Luther in the midst of his lectures on Romans — acquired a copy of Erasmus's 1516 edition of the Greek New Testament with the humanist's preface — the *Paraclesis,* Latin translation, and explanatory notes [annotations] — immediately upon its appearance.[4] Zwingli must surely have done the same with Erasmus's 1519 edition, an edition Heinz Holeczeck has rightly termed "the most important and, in its impact, most influential of Erasmus' editions."[5] It was the most influential because in it Erasmus departed much more freely from the wording of the ecclesiastically approved Vulgate text, returning to his own direct translation begun in 1505-1506 from the original Greek. This 1519 edition also contained Erasmus's *Paraclesis,* his *Ratio verae theologiae, Apologia,* and *Capita argumentorum.*[6] It was in the *Paraclesis,* his preface to the first and second editions, that Erasmus proffered the proposition that the Bible, especially the New Testament — not the church — alone contained the "eternal wisdom" from which one could derive a true theology.[7] And at the conclusion of the biblical text — later also published separately — Erasmus appended his ever-expanding annotations; in the second edition also giving the reasons why he had, on occasion, criticized — at times even rejected — the traditional Vulgate rendering.[8]

Erasmus's third edition of the New Testament appeared in 1522. Essentially a replication of the 1519 edition, it contained a new preface which, with its emphasis on the Christian instruction of the church's youth followed by what Erasmus himself referred to as a possible rebaptism, may well have made a powerful impression upon both Zwingli and his followers.[9] For if the Paris theologians, in 1526, felt compelled — with specific reference to this second preface — to censure Erasmus for the above suggestion and write that to "rebaptize" children would "open the door to the destruction of the Christian religion,"[10] it is perhaps not without foundation to suggest that Zwingli and his followers — being admirers of Erasmus — could have gained the impression that the great biblical scholar wished, in an ideal Christian world, for a baptism based upon an understanding of, and voluntary personal committment to, the Christian faith.

Close upon the heels of this 1522 preface came Erasmus's paraphrases of the Gospel of Matthew; the following year, 1523, his paraphrases of the Acts of the Apostles. Why Erasmus should have chosen to publish these two paraphrases in this particular sequence

— especially since he must have been as aware as anyone that Acts was an extension of Luke's Gospel — is not apparent. But it is of considerable consequence that he did so. Zwingli and his followers must have welcomed this sequence, especially since Zwingli had himself begun his preaching ministry in Zurich in 1519 with a series of sermons on the Gospel of Matthew followed immediately by another on the Acts of the Apostles. The Swiss Reformer is reported to have justified this sequence by saying that he

> wished to preach the history of our Savior Jesus [Christ] in order that the people no longer, as heretofore, should, to the great derogation of God's glory and the detriment of the souls of those called Christian who knew Christ in name only, remain ignorant of his history and work of salvation. Therefore he would preach through the entire Gospel of Matthew, verse upon verse and chapter upon chapter, relying only upon the Bible as source and the Holy Spirit as guide, through prayer and a careful comparison of the text, without tying himself to any human interpretive aids.[11]

From the Gospel of Matthew Zwingli had then immediately proceeded "to the Acts of the Apostles in order to enlighten his audience about the dissemination [and spread] of the gospel."[12] The above explanation implies that Zwingli chose the sequence he did for two simple reasons: first, because he wished to tell the story of Christ and the spread of Christianity; second, that Matthew just happened to be the first Gospel in the New Testament and Acts the only book that narrated the spread of Christianity. If he knew that Luke and Acts belonged together because they had been written by the same person, and for that reason might fit together better, it does not appear to have been important to him.

Erasmus followed this same sequence in the publication of his paraphrases in 1522-1523.[13] As I have already suggested, however, the primitive church would hardly have prefaced a reading of the Acts of the Apostles with that of the Gospel of Matthew. This is due to the fact that, of all the Gospel writers, Luke is the only one to have followed up his Gospel with a chronological sequel.[14] Therefore, the Acts of the Apostles, in the first few centuries, would invariably have been either physically attached to Luke's Gospel, forming a greater whole,[15] or closely linked to it by its opening sentence, which begins:

"The former treatise [Luke's gospel] have I made, O Theophilus."[16] It is thus highly improbable that the primitive church would have used the Acts of the Apostles as a sequel to the Gospel of Matthew as did both Zwingli and Erasmus. This is of some consequence since Luke's Gospel does not contain Christ's Great Commission in as explicit a form — if at all — as do the gospels of Matthew and Mark.[17] Thus it is highly unlikely that anyone in the primitive church — after the time of the apostles when the oral traditions had been supplanted by written texts — would have been led to make the associations between Matthew and Acts that Erasmus did. The apostles, however, coming directly out of the school of Christ, would not have been influenced by the later Luke/Acts continuity, or the Matthew/Acts discontinuity! In other words, the Luke/Acts sequence should not mislead us into thinking that the association Erasmus postulates did not, or could not, exist in the minds of the apostles. Nevertheless, given Luke's lack of emphasis upon Christ's Great Commission, when Luke/Acts came to dominate the way in which this continuity was viewed in the second and third centuries, the emphasis on the Great Commission may have been lost as well. A number of scholars of early Christianity have made just that assertion.[18]

Thus it was not until the wake of the Arian controversy in the third and fourth centuries that the Great Commission in its Matthean formulation — with its singular emphasis upon a trinitarian baptismal formula — came to be associated with the Acts of the Apostles, and that through its baptismal passages. It may well have been Tertullian who prepared the way for such an association when he spoke of a baptismal "formula" with reference to the Matthean version of the Great Commission, saying: "For the law of baptism has been imposed, and the formula prescribed: 'Go,' He says, 'teach the nations, baptizing them into the name of the Father, and of the Son, and of the Holy Spirit.'"[19] This emphasis upon a trinitarian baptismal formula appears to have been picked up by the Church Fathers during the Arian controversy and associated nearly exclusively with the quarrel over the correct baptismal formula, that is, with whether one had to be baptized in the name of the Father, the Son, and the Holy Spirit, or if it was sufficient to have been baptized only in the name of the Father. The Council of Nicea, for example, commanded that if someone requested admission to the church from a heretical background and had been baptized "into the Father, and the Son, and the Holy

Ghost," he needed only to have a hand laid on him so that he might receive the Holy Spirit. However, had he been baptized with a formula that had not employed the words "Son" and "Holy Spirit," his baptism was to be considered invalid.[20] To justify this position, the proponents pointed to Christ's command in Matthew 28:19 to baptize "in the name of the Father and of the Son and of the Holy Spirit." But when these same advocates turned to the apostolic examples of baptism contained in the Acts of the Apostles they discovered that Peter, in Acts 2:38, commanded that converts be baptized "in the name of Jesus Christ for the forgiveness of . . . sins." Though the example of Philip's baptism of the Ethiopian eunuch (Acts 8) made no mention of whose name the eunuch had been baptized into, the Centurion Cornelius (Acts 10) was baptized only in the name of Jesus. The same was true of the disciples of John who, having been baptized only with John the Baptist's baptism, were rebaptized in the name of Jesus by the apostle Paul (Acts 19).[21] How was the command of Christ to baptize in (into) the name of the Father, Son, and Holy Spirit (the Trinity) to be reconciled with the apostolic practice of baptizing only in the name of Jesus?[22] The debate over this issue appears to have dominated the discussion of Christ's Great Commission from the time of the Fathers to the present, as Bernard Henry Cuneo has shown. So much has this been the case that around the turn of the last century, F. C. Conybeare suggested that the last section of Matthew 28 was a later — after the pronouncement of the Council of Nicea — interpolation.[23] A cursory study of the Church Fathers' interpretation of the Matthew 28 passage only confirms Cuneo's findings. One possible exception is that of Tertullian in his *On Baptism,*[24] written well before the Arian controversy[25] but nevertheless also in the context of controversy over heresies. One of the consequences of this discussion was that the baptismal passages in Acts came to be intimately associated with the Matthean version of Christ's Great Commission in contrast to the conventional connection between Luke's Gospel and the Acts of the Apostles. Had it not been for this development it is highly improbable that Erasmus likewise would have associated Christ's Great Commission with the baptismal passages in Acts.

Nevertheless, while retaining the association between the Matthean version of the Great Commission with the baptismal passages in Acts, Erasmus broke decisively with the interpretive tradition emanating from the Church Fathers. And he did so because, as a Christian humanist, he attempted to read the Great Commission not from a presentist but from a historical perspective.[26] Not only did he see Christian history from a vantage point different from that of the Catholic Church, his method of interpreting the Bible also differed from the one validated by the church. And it was the latter that led to his radically different approach to the interpretation of Christ's Great Commission.

The sixteenth-century Catholic Church, as I noted in the opening section of Chapter 1, understood its development in terms of an advancement from a primitive to a modern, more perfect, structure. Also formed in the crucible of heretical attack, this Catholic interpretation of church history was first clearly enunciated by Vincent of Lerins in his *The Commonitory* of 434.[27] Arguing that the Catholic faith had to be established in opposition to heretical attacks by the "authority of the Divine Law, and then, by the Tradition of the Catholic Church," Vincent addressed the question why the canon of Scripture, "complete and sufficient of itself" for everything else, was not sufficient in this instance. His answer was because "all do not accept it in one and the same sense, but one understands its words in one way, another in another; so that it seems capable of as many interpretations as there are interpreters." This being so, "the rule for the right understanding of the prophets and apostles should be framed in accordance with the standards of Ecclesiastical and Catholic interpretation."

Whereas Vincent could still argue that such an interpretation was based on that faith "which has been believed everywhere, always, [and] by all,"[28] by Erasmus's time the church was arguing that the Bible had to be interpreted through the writings of those "teachers accepted and approved by the Christian Church."[29] But then, in accordance with its belief that the institutional church was guided by the Holy Spirit, it argued that the latest teachers — the great Scholastic theologian/philosophers of the Middle Ages — were the best interpreters. Erasmus and the Renaissance humanists, however, asserted that the earliest interpreters were the best.[30] In opposition to this "Whig" interpretation of the Roman Catholic Church in the age of the Renaissance and Reformation, which in effect sought to justify the religious and theological status quo, Erasmus, critical of the abuses and immorality within the church and in order to effect change, sought to challenge the church by cutting through the institution and its dogma and returning to first historical principles. That is, he sought to return to the "pure," or primary sources of Christianity, and to interpret them with the help of their earliest interpreters, in effect to get beyond the interpretation of those teachers "approved by the Church."[31] In order to interpret Christ's Great Commission as closely as possible to Christ's intended meaning, Erasmus therefore asked himself three important questions: first, what had Christ intended to say with those words; second, how had his most intimate followers — his apostles — interpreted those words; and, third, to what extent had the second meshed with the first? Thus, whereas the church's first formulation of its interpretation of these passages had been driven by the Arian controversy and its struggle with other heretical groups, that is, by contemporary issues in the fourth and fifth centuries, Erasmus sought to determine, as nearly as he could, Christ's own meaning.[32] That interpretation, as we shall see in a moment, was passed on to the sixteenth-century Anabaptists. The evidence for this is nothing less than overwhelming, as I will demonstrate.

Erasmus began his interpretation of the Great Commission, found in his paraphrases on Matthew and the Acts of the Apostles, by asserting that Christ had informed his disciples that all nations belonged to him; they were therefore to win as many of their inhabitants as possible for his cause, beginning with the Jews and then moving on to the Gentiles and the entire world. This was not to be accomplished by war but by wholesome doctrine and a life worthy of the gospel. Thereupon Erasmus turned his attention to the first aspect of the Commission: the initial command to "teach." What was it the apostles were to teach at the very outset of their mission? Erasmus was anything but vague in his answer, stating that the disciples were to teach that which all of humankind should know about Christ.[33] He went even farther, describing in considerable detail what they were also to teach about God the Father and the Holy Spirit, as well as the essentials about the church and the resurrection of believers after death. And then he observed:

> After you have taught them these things, and they believe what you have taught them, have repented[34] their previous lives and are ready to embrace the doctrine of the gospel [in their life], then immerse them in water, in the name of the Father, the Son, and the Holy Ghost, so that by this holy sign they may believe that they have

been delivered freely through the benefit of my death from the filthiness of all their sins and now belong to the number of God's children.[35]

Rejecting circumcision and the "ceremonies of Moses" or of anyone else as a means of salvation, Erasmus therefore focused on the teaching of the "good news" of the gospel in the first part of the Great Commission.

The great Christian humanist did not stop here. He proceeded to argue that lest any person should "think it sufficient for salvation to have professed the faith of the gospel and been baptized," believers had to be taught how they might retain the purity just acquired — by what means they might continue to move forward toward the "perfection of evangelical godliness." For Christ had omitted nothing that was conducive to eternal health. Nor would the Holy Spirit, whom they were about to receive, permit them to forget what Christ had taught them. Therefore, the disciples were to teach their converts to obey whatever Christ had taught them. Once again Erasmus reminded his readers that Christ had not commanded his disciples to place their trust in Mosaic ceremonies or Pharisaical constitutions — all of which were now, like the Platonic shadows they were, to vanish in the bright light of evangelical truth — but only in those things which led to true purity and godliness. They were to do this in deeds as well as words, just as Christ had both taught and lived.

Erasmus's elaboration of Christ's Great Commission appears to have been based, at least in part, on his conviction that the apostles had, in their earliest sermons, sought to put into practice what Christ had commanded them in this his last will and testament. For in virtually every passage in the Acts of the Apostles that deals with baptism, Erasmus proceeded to set the sermon or event into the context of the Great Commission. Thus, with respect to Peter's Pentecost sermon recorded in Acts 2, Erasmus wrote:

> For this is what the Lord commanded them [his disciples]: go forth, he said, and teach all people, baptizing them, and teaching them to keep everything I have commanded you. Teach them that must be baptized, the rudiments and first beginnings of the gospel. For if a man will not believe these rudiments and principles, his baptism will avail him nothing. And teach those who have already been

51

baptized that they must live in accordance with my teachings, proceeding always to greater perfection.[36]

The passage in Acts 8 dealing with Philip's baptism of the Ethiopian eunuch provided Erasmus with an even better opportunity to focus on what was to be taught people at the very outset, before baptism. On this occasion he focused principally on Christ since, as the text stated: "Then Philip began with that very passage of Scripture [from Isaiah] and told him the good news about Jesus." This allowed Erasmus to conclude that Philip had expounded the principal points of the gospel to the eunuch: that Christ was the son of God born of a virgin and the Holy Spirit; that he was the true paschal lamb who had died for the sins of humankind; that he had ascended to the heavens and would come again to judge the quick and the dead; that he had sent the Holy Spirit who had so "inspired the apostles' hearts and tongues" that they had begun fearlessly to proclaim Jesus of Nazareth to be the chief author and fountain, through faith and baptism, of life and bliss to all the world. Upon spying a spring of water, the chamberlain immediately requested to be baptized. If he steadfastly believed everything he had been told, Philip answered, and intended, with all his heart, to keep Christ's commands, he could be baptized. Such a promise of obedience, Erasmus observed, was made only at baptism.

At various points in his paraphrases of these baptismal passages in the Acts of the Apostles, Erasmus drew the reader's attention to the sudden and often dramatic conversions of the persons involved. Such conversions, he asserted, were the work of the Holy Spirit. With respect to Peter's Pentecost sermon, for example, he spoke of the "sudden change" toward "great purity and cleanness of life" of the many persons converted. He regarded this to be the work of some "celestial power."[37] He made a similar observation in regard to Paul's baptism (chap. 9), where one reads: "they marvelled at what had happened to the man who had so suddenly and completely changed."[38]

All of these passages — Acts 2, Acts 8, Acts 10 (the story of the conversion and baptism of Cornelius the Centurion) and Acts 19 (the story of Paul's rebaptism of the twelve men from Ephesus baptized only with John the Baptist's baptism) — Erasmus very consciously placed into the context of Christ's Great Commission. With regard to

Peter's message to Cornelius and his household he remarked: "And before he went into heaven, he [Christ] commanded us [Peter is speaking], whom he had chosen for this office earlier, that we should openly preach and bear witness to every man that he was the one whom God had exalted, and that, in the end of the world, he should judge both the quick and the dead."[39] And in connection with Paul's rebaptism of the disciples of John the Baptist from Ephesus, Erasmus wrote: "This tradition, that those who believed in the gospel should be baptized in the name of the Father, of the Son, and of the Holy Ghost, the apostles had received from their lord."[40]

It is little wonder, therefore, that Balthasar Hubmaier could write in his *Old and New Believers on Baptism* (1526):

> He [Erasmus] recounts all the articles of faith as they are contained in the *Symbolo Apostolorum* [the Apostles' Creed][41] and adds these words: "After you have taught the people these things and they have believed what you have taught them, have repented of their prior life, and are ready henceforth to walk according to evangelical doctrine, then immerse them in water in the name of the Father and the Son and the Holy Spirit." Here Erasmus publicly points out that baptism was instituted by Christ for those instructed in the faith and not for young children.[42]

Hubmaier then turned from Erasmus's paraphrase of Christ's Great Commission to his paraphrase of the Acts of the Apostles, saying:

> He [Erasmus] writes further about the Acts of the Apostles: "The Lord commanded the evangelical shepherds: Go forth and teach all peoples, baptize them, teach them to hold all things which I have commanded you. Teach those who are to be baptized the most important evangelical truths. If one does not believe these [truths] he is baptized in vain." Dear reader, read his paraphrase of the 8th chapter of the Acts of the Apostles and many other places.[43]

Hubmaier further couples Erasmus's paraphrase of Christ's Great Commission with Peter's Pentecost sermon as well as with the other passages in the Acts of the Apostles to demonstrate how the apostles had interpreted Christ's command.

Some fifty years later, in his 1577 *Artikelbuch,* the Hutterite mis-

53

sionary Peter Walpot could still cite Erasmus's paraphrase of Matthew 28:18-20 as authoritative in his argument in favor of believer's baptism. But he also cited Erasmus's *Annotationes in Novum Testamentum* on the parallel passage in Mark 16:15-16, observing: "Here Erasmus says: 'The apostles are commanded that they teach first and baptize later. The Jew was brought to a knowledge [of God] through ceremonies; the Christian is taught first.' And one could cite other passages, but we shall let this suffice in order to save time."[44]

These two examples demonstrate the enduring importance of Erasmus's interpretation of Christ's Great Commission for the Anabaptists. It is not accidental, therefore, that Matthew 28:18-20 became the *locus classicus* for the Anabaptist argument in favor of believer's baptism. Its critical importance can be seen in Hubmaier's writings where it repeatedly stands at the head of all other biblical references cited in favor of adult baptism.[45] Its central importance can also be seen in the role that it played in Felix Mantz's *A Declaration of Faith and Defense,* written in December 1524, about one month prior to the first believer's baptism, which took place on 21 January 1525. There, referring to the baptism of Cornelius as recorded in Acts 10, Mantz observed:

> From these words one can clearly see *how the apostles understood the command of Christ as above related from Matthew,*[46] namely that as they went forth they should teach all nations that to Christ is given all power in heaven and in earth, and that forgiveness of sins in his name should be given to everyone who, believing in his name, does righteous works from a changed heart. After the receiving of this teaching and the descent of the Holy Spirit which, by speaking in tongues was evidenced to those who heard the words of Peter [Acts 10:40ff.], water was then poured over them. This meant that, just as they were cleansed within by the coming of the Holy Spirit, so they were also poured over with water externally to signify the inner cleansing and dying to sin.[47]

Mantz probably used this particular example of baptism, rather than the ones cited by Hubmaier and Walpot, because he wished to highlight the role played by the Holy Spirit in the conversion of Cornelius in particular, and of all believers in general.[48] But he nevertheless used Matthew 28:18-20 in precisely the same manner as

54

had Erasmus. The Great Commission also provided him with the larger context within which he interpreted virtually every other passage on baptism.[49]

This assertion is confirmed in innumerable other documents, not only of the Swiss Brethren. Johannes Kessler reported in his *Sabbata* that approximately one year prior to writing his chronicle (sometime prior to January 1524), while he was expounding the famous Pauline baptismal text in Romans 6, Lorenz Hochruetiner interrupted him, saying: "I note from your words that you think infants should be baptized." Taken aback, Kessler enquired why they should not be baptized. Hochruetiner replied: "On the basis of the saying and command of Christ in Matthew 28: He who believes and is baptized will be saved, etc."[50] Hans Denck based his argument for believer's baptism on the same passage,[51] and Valentin Gredig, almost immediately after the first adult baptisms had taken place in Zollikon in early 1525, said that "nothing else has motivated us to take this step than the plain Word of God which states very clearly: 'Go to all nations, teach and baptize them; whoever believes and is baptized will be saved.' "[52]

Emil Egli, whose 1878 and 1887 studies of the Zurich and St. Gallen Anabaptists respectively were based on extensive original research in the two archives, makes apparent that these essentially Erasmian arguments — heretofore enunciated primarily by the leaders — penetrated deeply into the movement as a whole. Not long after the movement had taken hold in Zollikon, for example, Georg Blaurock submitted a written brief to the Zurich civic authorities to justify "believers' baptism and the 'holding of all things common' through the apostolic example (contained in Matthew 28 and chapter 2 of the Acts of the Apostles)."[53] Blaurock also offered to prove that "Zwingli falsified the Scriptures more than the old pope"! Several years later, in August of 1527, a number of Gruenningen Anabaptist families themselves submitted a *Darlegung ihrer Standpunkte* — a "Presentation of their Views," as Egli terms it — to the local *Landtag* (representative body) to explain and justify their proselytizing in the region. They did so with the Erasmian argument, citing the Mark 16 version of the Great Commission; Acts 2, Peter's Pentecost sermon; Acts 8, Philip's encounter with the Ethiopian eunuch; and then Acts 19 to justify their rebaptism. To clinch their argument they cited Romans 6:4 to establish the proper relationship between the inner baptism of the Holy Spirit and the external baptism with water.[54] They concluded by accusing Zwingli of being a "false prophet" who, "since he can find no proofs in the New Testament, reaches back into the Old to justify [his argument] regarding the similarity [between baptism] and the covenant God made with Abraham." But, they argued, God had established such a covenant only with the Jews, not with the heathen. That being the case, why did the preachers insist on baptizing their children? They were descendants of the heathen, not of the Jews. Moreover, girls, every whit as much as boys, had been included in God's promise even though they were not, like the latter, circumcised. What was more, these families concluded, the law had come to an end with Christ and they were now living under the gospel.[55]

This same argument is found among the Anabaptists of St. Gallen. There, on 25 August 1525, Wolfgang Schorant (called Uolimann), a Grebel disciple, was cited to appear before the city council for creating a disturbance at a church service. While the minutes of the meeting, duly recorded by the secretary, refer to two central aspects of the discussion — baptism and the Lord's Supper — only Uolimann's argument with regard to the former is given. Claiming to have been instructed by none other than God himself, Uolimann asserted that infant baptism was a later innovation of the church, and that without warrant of Scripture. He justified believer's baptism with Matthew 28:18-20, saying that after Christ had fulfilled every aspect of his Father's will, he commanded his disciples to teach (the gospel), encourage faith and baptism. Such a believer's baptism, based upon faith in the risen Christ, entailed the commitment to die to sin and live in the resurrection, obeying everything Christ had commanded. For the first two hundred and some odd years, until the time of Cyprian and Tertullian, this had been the practice in the church. The latter had, however, begun to concede baptism to sick children, and then to baptize those who could recite the Lord's Prayer. But even then, baptisms took place only at Easter and Pentecost.[56]

Even Zwingli in his *Taufbuechlein* inadvertently pointed to the importance of this passage for his rebellious followers when he wrote:

> For those who say that they [infants] should not be baptized are the ones who raised the issue. They should also show where it is written that infants should not be baptized. Otherwise, they are adding to the Word. For we are not adding to it: we include the children in "people" and "men." But when they counter with

Matthew 28, "teach and baptize them," the consequence will be that they do violence to the Word, for baptism was not instituted at that place.[57]

The influence of Erasmus's interpretation reached well beyond Zurich, for even Bernhard Rothmann reflected the importance of the Matthew 28 passage in his 1533 tract on the two sacraments. There, arguing that the first and foremost evil to grow out of infant baptism was that the baptism instituted by Christ was destroyed, he remarked that Christ had left his apostles and all his "subsequent sincere servants" with a prescribed method of how to lead people to the kingdom of God and a command; to begin with, everyone who wishes to be saved must have a personal faith from an understanding of Christ.

> Since faith and knowledge of Christ comes from instruction and through hearing the Word of God, therefore Christ first commanded and instituted that all people be instructed and the Gospel be proclaimed to all creatures, that is, to proffer them forgiveness of sin in his name. Then, those who believe in the Gospel are given the power to become children of God, nor can one become a child of God in any other way. . . . Once it is certain that a person has accepted and believes the Gospel . . . then this other can follow, that is then it is time that a person be baptized, that he forsake himself and trust in Christ.[58]

Rothmann used the same argument in the same central manner in the colloquy, observing:

> As one takes up the arguments of Hermann Busche previously touched upon, one can prove that infant baptism is forbidden by Scripture. This can be proved, first of all, by the Words of Christ in the last chapter of Matthew [28:19-20]. "Go forth," Christ said to his apostles, "teaching all people, baptizing them" — that understand the teaching — "in the name of the Father," and so on, "teaching them to observe all that I have commanded."
>
> Here Christ commands that all be baptized who have been instructed, and the baptized are commanded to observe all that he ordered.
>
> Now, since infants cannot be instructed, Christ therefore ex-

cluded them from baptism, since he expressly commands who is to be baptized.[59]

As time passed, the intimate connection that Erasmus had posited between Christ's Great Commission and the apostles' interpretation of it in the Acts of the Apostles appears to have been somewhat obscured, with an ever greater emphasis placed on the sequence of Christ's words rather than the interpretation given them by the apostles. This is already the case with Rothmann in the above passages. In 1542 Pilgram Marpeck, an early leader of the South German Anabaptists, published Rothmann's tract on the two sacraments under his own name as the *Vermahnung,* not indicating to his readers that it derived, essentially, from the man who came to be so intimately associated with the Münster rebellion of 1534-1535.[60] Wherever Rothmann derived his emphasis on Christ's Great Commission, it came through Marpeck's *Vermahnung* to permeate South German Anabaptism, where it probably confirmed the emphasis coming from Hubmaier and the Swiss Brethren.[61]

The Hutterites, although perhaps stimulated by Marpeck's tract and the writings of the Swiss Brethren, appear — as we have seen from Peter Walpot's *Artikelbuch* — to have gone back directly to the original Erasmian passages. And in their confessional writings, the Great Commission received the highest priority, as Robert Friedmann has written:

> All seventeen versions [of one of the Hutterites' most important confessional pamphlets] open the first article on baptism with the words of Matthew 28: "Christ our Lord says, 'All power is given unto me in heaven and in earth. Go ye therefore, and teach all nations, baptizing them in the name of the Father, and of the Son, and of the Holy Ghost. . . .' He (therefore) first commands to teach, thereafter to baptize." And then follow the familiar Scriptural proofs for the sole rectitude of adult baptism.[62]

The same emphasis on the sequence of Christ's words "teach and baptize" is found among the Anabaptists in the lands of Philip of Hesse, where, though at a somewhat later date,[63] the Matthew passage played an equally important role. Repeatedly it was the center of discussion,[64] so important in fact that in one such discussion of 1538 between Anabaptists and Philip's theologians, Theodor Fabritius was brought in to assist in the debate because he had informed the duke that the Greek text of the passage had "baptism" come before "teaching." As Valentin Breul reported to the duke,

> When Your Grace commanded me a few days ago that I should notify Fabritius of Altendorf of the time when Noviomagus [Gerhard Geldenhauer] and I wished to be in Wolckstorf [to debate] the Anabaptists, in order that he might accompany us since he was the Greek [scholar] who had informed Your Grace that the Greek text of Matthew, the last chapter [28:19], is supposed to have baptism stand first — we have, as your obedient [servants], informed him that we wish to be in Wolckstorf next Thursday, August 8. But Magister Adam [Kraft], pastor here in Marburg, Noviomagus and other learned scholars have told me that Fabritius is in error, and that he could not prove, nor get anyone to support him [in the attempt to prove] that the correct Greek text has, as he says, baptism stand first, but that to teach stands before and after baptism, as both the Latin and German texts also demonstrate. Nevertheless, in spite of the order in the text, there are good reasons to hold that the apostles were supposed to teach and baptize or baptize and teach, so that, in sum, the text has been interpreted more often against than for the Anabaptist [position], and that all their arguments are without foundation.[65]

Not all second-generation Anabaptists failed to refer to the examples of apostolic baptisms when citing the Great Commission as their proof text for adult baptism, however. Menno Simons, for example, in his major theological tract, the *Fundamentboek* of 1539, wrote concerning baptism:

> Christ commanded his disciples after his resurrection, saying: "Therefore go and teach all nations, and baptize them in the name of the Father, and of the Son, and of the Holy Ghost; and teach them to observe everything that I have commanded you. For behold, I am with you always, even to the end of the earth." Matt. 28.
>
> Here we have the Lord's command regarding baptism, who shall receive God's ordinance, and when and what it is to serve; that is

that the Gospel must first be preached and then baptize those who [accept and] believe it, as he [Christ] says: "Go into all the world and preach the good news to all creation. Whoever believes and is baptized will be saved, but whoever does not believe will be condemned."

Somewhat later Menno continued:

Christ's holy apostles taught and practised [baptism] in accordance with Christ's commandments, as one can readily understand and note from many passages of the New Testament. Thus Peter says: "Repent and be baptized every one of you in the name of Jesus Christ for the forgiveness of sins, and you will receive the gift of the Holy Spirit." And Philip said to the [Ethiopian] eunuch: "If you believe with all your heart, you may be [baptized]." Acts chapter 8. For faith does not follow upon baptism, but baptism follows from faith. (Matt. 28, Mark 16.)

This is the kind of baptism Christ commanded, and he himself accepted it in the following manner. As the time drew near, the hour in which he was to fulfill the command to preach the Word of his Father and proclaim his holy name, he sought out John the Baptist on the Jordan River and requested to be baptized by him in order that he might fulfill all the obligations of righteouness. He prepared himself for temptation, misery, the cross and death, and placed himself at the disposal of the will of his Father as an obliging, obedient child, just as he himself says that he had not come to do his own will, but the will of him who had sent him. Thus he was baptized by John, confirmed by the Holy Spirit, and accepted by the Father as a son pleasing to him. (Matt. 3:13-17.)

Behold, that is how Christ's own commandment reads: Christ was himself baptized in accordance with it; and in accordance with it the Apostles both taught and baptized. Who would then wish to oppose the Lord and say: it shall not be done in the above manner? Who would dare to teach and instruct this wisdom? Who would wish to accuse the apostles and evangelists of lying?[66]

With the possible exception of the passages cited from Hubmaier's *Old and New Believers on Baptism* and Rothmann's *Confession Concerning the Two Sacraments,* Menno's presentation replicates the

Erasmian argument more clearly than any other within the corpus of Anabaptist writings. This may well indicate that, as in the above instances, Menno too encountered the argument in its pristine form in Erasmus's paraphrases. The possibility does exist, however, that he may first have seen it in Rothmann's *Confession,* written in preparation for the Münster Colloquy of early August 1533, and only later sought it out in the paraphrases of his fellow countryman.[67] Since Menno never mentions Hubmaier's name and appears not to have read any of his writings, and since the argument is not to be found in the writings of Melchior Hoffmann or any of his Melchiorite followers at this time, the above would appear to be the only two alternatives available. If Menno first discovered the argument in Rothmann's *Confession,* it would add to the persuasiveness of the argument I made some years ago that Menno, who appears to have plagiarized a short passage from this first tract of Rothmann's in his 1535 *Against the Blasphemy of Jan of Leiden,*[68] came to see the Münsterites as false prophets who, as he remarked, had "desert[ed] the pure doctrine of Christ and [begun] to traffic in strange doctrine."[69] For if Menno, like the other Anabaptists — and this appears clearly to have been the case — came to see Erasmus's interpretation of the Great Commission to constitute the heart of the "pure doctrine of Christ," then the Münsterite departure from it in their ill-advised pursuit of the "visible kingdom" must have struck Menno as apostasy of the worst kind.[70] That this "pure doctrine of Christ" was indeed subverted by the arrival in Münster of Jan of Leiden and Jan Matthys in January and February 1534 respectively even Rothmann conceded in his *The Restitution of the True Christian Doctrine* of 1534.[71]

The fact that Rothmann succumbed to the rationalized Melchiorite teachings of a van Leiden and Matthys while Menno clearly and decisively rejected it — when both had taken their point of departure from the same Erasmian interpretation of the Great Commission — points to something of great importance for the history of Dutch Anabaptism. Before ever Menno came into contact with the peaceful Melchiorites Dirk and Obbe Philips, he had — on the basis of the Erasmian interpretation — rejected Melchiorite ideology as it was reflected in the teachings of the Münsterites. As in the case of the relationship between Zwingli and the Swiss Brethren, the fact that both Rothmann and Menno began with an Erasmian interpretation recasts the entire question of intellectual influence. In the former case,

61

the discussion has revolved around the question whether Zwingli changed his mind and turned on his earlier, "correct," insights, as his radical followers repeatedly charged and later Mennonite historians have argued; or did he retain, consistently throughout, his views on these matters, especially with regard to the Christian society, as Robert Walton and others have argued?[72] But if both Zwingli and his followers were responding to a position that had already been articulated — indeed articulated in the biblical paraphrases of the intellectual giant both admired — their *Auseinandersetzung* is placed into an altogether different light. And the same is true of Menno's relationship both to the revolutionary Münsterites and the more pacific Melchiorites.[73] In the latter case, however, the implications are much more dramatic than in the case of Zwingli's relationship to the Swiss Brethren.

In the first place, if Menno and the Rothmann of 1533 both stood under the influence of Erasmus's interpretation of the Great Commission, then, as we have already argued, Menno can hardly have come under the influence of radical "Münsterite" ideology as Rothmann did. His *Blasphemy* is the best evidence for this. But, perhaps even more important, it separates Menno theologically even from the pacific Melchiorites like Dirk and Obbe Philips. While Menno in his 1539 *Fundamentboek* developed this Erasmian position at length and more clearly than did most other Anabaptists, Obbe Philips left the movement in 1540 and later wrote a poignant "Confession" in which he despaired of overcoming his Melchiorite origins.[74] Nor did Dirk Philips write any theological tracts during this early period of association with Menno in which he presented a pacific Melchiorite perspective; rather, Menno did all the writing, begining with his 1535 *Blasphemy*, his *Meditation on the 25th Psalm*, his 1536 *The Spiritual Resurrection*, his 1537 *On the New Birth*, and his 1539 *Fundamentboek*. These are not the works of a man seeking to find himself — as Dirk and Obbe appear to have been attempting to do — but of a man who has come to rest spiritually and intellectually and knows where he is going.

There is, however, one problem in Menno's relationship with pacific Melchioritism that demands clarification if we are fully to establish Menno's spiritual and intellectual independence[75] — and that is his "Melchiorite" doctrine of the incarnation. For is not the fact that he shared this doctrine — and defended it throughout his life — indication enough of their influence upon him? Not necessarily, for in *A True Confession and Spiritual Demonstration of the Most Holy Incarnation,* Menno wrote:

> When the matter of the incarnation of our beloved Lord Jesus Christ *was first mentioned by the brethren* [the Philips brothers], *on hearing it I was terrified at heart, lest I should err in the matter and be found, before God, in pernicious unbelief.* On account of this article I was often so troubled at heart, *after receiving baptism,* that for many days I abstained from food and drink, by the overanxiety of my soul, beseeching God and praying in extreme necessity that the kind Father by his mercy and grace would disclose unto me, poor sinner, who, although in extreme weakness, desired to do his will and pleasure, the mystery of the incarnation of his blessed Son, to the extent necessary to the glorification of his holy name to the consolation of my afflicted conscience.[76]

This passage may well hold the solution to two problems in Menno's biography: first, how and when he adopted the Melchiorite interpretation of the incarnation; and second, why he withdrew into seclusion for a time after his baptism.

Menno is here saying that he first heard of the Melchiorite doctrine of the incarnation from the "brethren," undoubtedly a reference to Dirk and Obbe Philips. At this late date, 1544, he would most certainly not have addressed the Münsterites as "brethren." When did he encounter these brethren? Certainly not before the collapse of Münster in June of 1535; probably not before he left the Catholic Church in January of 1536. That is, it was long after he had begun his intellectual journey into Protestantism with his first doubts about the doctrine of transubstantiation in 1525. More important, however, the words Menno employs to express his feelings vis-à-vis the Melchiorite doctrine when he first encountered it exude extreme anguish of soul. He speaks of being terrified, troubled at heart, of extreme necessity, and of being overanxious and having an afflicted conscience. He is afraid of falling into pernicious unbelief. These are not terms, used with reference to this doctrine, that express the joy of a person discovering, or having revealed to him, a new truth. Menno's language stands in marked contrast, for example, to Luther's in his 1545 retrospective where he explains the thrill of his discovery of Paul's understanding of the "righteousness of God." Luther's discovery led him from an afflicted conscience to a serene peace; Menno's discovery of the Melchiorite doctrine of the incarnation led in a reverse direction. And the question must be asked: Did he ever move into serene peace with respect to the doctrine? It appears not, for every time he broaches the subject he does so most defensively. Lawrence Mosheim, the great eighteenth-century church historian, already noted this, but also argued that Menno at times explained the incarnation in ambiguous terms.[77]

If Menno is forced to confess such sentiments about his reception of the Melchiorite doctrine of the incarnation, he must have been pressured to accept it under difficult circumstances. What might these have been? He gives us some indication when he states: "On account of this article I was often so troubled at heart, *after receiving baptism. . . .*" Was Menno informed about the doctrine only after baptism? If he felt negatively about it, would he have allowed himself to be baptized by Obbe Philips had he known about it beforehand? I think not. And if not, one must conclude that Menno was informed about the doctrine only after his baptism. And if this is the case, then he was placed in a nearly untenable position. No wonder he was constrained to speak of an afflicted conscience: he did not agree with the doctrine but could not undo his rebaptism after he was told of it.

Now it is only with respect to the above event that Menno speaks of "abstaining from food and drink." He refers to the latter in connection with his baptism, indeed he states: "after receiving baptism." This must surely refer to that period of time — thus far inadequately explained[78] — during which he withdrew from everyone for some time after his baptism. Such an event as described above would have been reason enough to withdraw from society for a time in order to fast and pray and beseech God "in extreme necessity that . . . by his mercy and grace [he] would disclose unto me, poor sinner . . . the mystery of the incarnation of his blessed Son."

The above issue is not without relevance to the story of Menno, Erasmus's interpretation of the Great Commission, and the transformation and spread of Dutch Anabaptism. Rather, it lies at its very heart. What is more, it answers that vexing question posed by Johan Huizinga some years ago when he asked, "How is it that a religion whose zealots were responsible for fanatical excesses in Amsterdam and Muenster should have subsided so gently into decorous piety, and that many disciples of Menno[79] in the northern provinces, in Haarlem and in Amsterdam, became the most peaceful citizens of all?"[80]

With the exception of Rothmann's *Confession,* the Erasmian interpretation of Christ's Great Commission is nowhere to be found in Dutch Melchioritism; yet after Menno's first exposition of it in his 1539 *Fundamentboek* it gradually came to constitute the theological heart of the movement. It is most clearly expressed in Thomas van Imbroeck's 1558 "Confession Concerning Baptism"[81] and in the early pages of Dirk Philips's1564 *Enchiridion,*[82] which is well after Menno first laid out the interpretation in the pages of his *Fundamentboek.* It is also found in the confessions of innumerable Dutch Anabaptist martyrs, most of whom were assuredly not highly educated.[83] This would indicate that not only did Menno's theology displace that of Melchior Hoffmann in the minds of the leaders of the movement; it transformed the movement itself down to its rank and file followers. This obviosuly did not take place without a struggle — not only between Menno and radicals such as Jan Battenburg and David Joris — but also between Menno and the peaceful Melchiorites. This latter struggle is clearly reflected in Menno's dilemma regarding the Melchiorite doctrine of the incarnation. In the latter case, however, Menno did not win.

The other element of this transformation of Dutch Anabaptism that derives from Menno is the powerful emphasis upon conversion that runs through the pages of the *Martyrs' Mirror.* Menno's own conversion experience, which probably took place at the height of the Münsterite crisis and the execution of his own brother, Pieter, around Easter of 1535,[84] resulted in the publication of two early tracts on the subject, his "The Spiritual Resurrection" (1536) and "On the New Birth" (1537). Having experienced a conversion, Menno in typical fashion sought to explain it in biblical terms. And these two tracts, along with Menno's repeated preaching that "ye must be born again," obviously had their impact upon those who heard him. For the pages of the *Martyrs' Mirror* are filled with the evidence.

Erasmus's interpretation of Christ's Great Commission and Menno's emphasis on the "new birth," then, were the twin pillars upon which post-revolutionary Dutch Anabaptism was built. And it was clear to the members of this church that they were not the descendants of the Münsterites, though the inquisitors made the charge often enough in the interrogations. Rather, they referred to themselves as "Menno's people,"[85] and they argued that Menno had first introduced their church.[86] The inquisitors themselves repeatedly noted Menno's importance. He it was who had a price placed upon his head as early as 1542. Dirk Philips hardly gets a mention in the pages of the *Martyrs' Mirror*.

Menno's *Fundamentboek,* which was of critical importance in redirecting the Dutch Anabaptist movement after the Münster revolution, played an important role elsewhere as well. In 1575 it was translated into German. Beginning in 1582,[87] there are repeated references in volume one of the *Quellen* for Württemberg to persons possessing Menno's *Fundamentboek.*[88] From these references, it would appear that the authorities — who demanded its confiscation — regarded it as of the first importance in the justification and spread of believer's baptism. As late as 1648 the dean of Schorndorf, near Stuttgart, M. Matthias Lanius, was ordered by the authorities "not to allow Menno's *Fundamnetum* to surface in Urach, but to make certain that it be destroyed so that people would not be led astray by it."[89] Wherever the authorities encountered it, they confiscated it. No other book appears to have received the same attention from them. Its importance can clearly be seen, for example, in the 1589 confession before the authorities of one Joerg Suesz of Dallau in Electoral Palatine. His confession includes the very words of the 1575 German translation of Menno's *Fundamentboek,* the first two paragraphs cited at the outset of our discussion of Menno and the Great Commission.[90]

Certain consequences must of necessity follow if Erasmus's interpretation of Christ's Great Commission played such a decisive role in Swiss/South German Anabaptism and the theology of Menno Simons. First, as I have already suggested, Zwingli's relationship to his "rebellious" followers must be rethought; the same applies to Menno's relationship to both revolutionary and pacific Melchioritism. For in both instances the central intellectual/theological position came to all parties involved from outside of their circles and in its pristine yet fully developed form; no one in either camp — or anyone else before and after Erasmus for that matter — improved upon his presentation. Thus, both Zwingli as well as his followers were constrained to grapple with Erasmus's formulation. Only to the extent that Zwingli may at first have been captivated by the argument could he later have turned his back on it. But it was *never his argument* in the sense that he first formulated it, or even had anything to do with its formulation. It must surely be easier to give up such a position than one that you have arrived at through personal study. Perhaps this is what Zwingli meant to say when, in his *Refutation of Baptist Tricks,* he asserted that he had never been so dogmatically of this opinion as were his followers. Zwingli did, however, for whatever reason, soon reject the Erasmian interpretation. This becomes apparent as early as his 1524 *Commentary on True and False Religion,*[91] about the time his relations with the radicals had reached a crisis, but still nearly five months before the irreparable breach of 21 January 1525.[92] At precisely what point in his theological development Menno appropriated Erasmus's interpretation is even more unclear. But if — as we have suggested — his argument about the Dutch movement having begun well only to have been subverted by "false prophets" rests on his reading of the Erasmian rendering in Rothmann's *Confession,* then it was already part of his theological arsenal before his 1535 *Blasphemy.* It is in any case fully developed in his 1539 *Fundamentboek.*

The fact that this interpretation of the Great Commission came to everyone who encountered it in a fully developed form from Erasmus's paraphrases is therefore a clear indication that neither Zwingli, nor Grebel, nor Mantz, nor Menno, nor Rothmann, nor anyone else contributed anything to its formulation. This is further confirmed by the fact that no one came even remotely close to explicating this interpretation as fully as Erasmus did. That being so, the individual character and social, economic, or political *Sitz im Leben* of anyone other than Erasmus can have had nothing whatever to do with its original formulation. Hence, calling Anabaptism the "religion of the common man," as some have done on occasion, at the least needs modification. Initiators of the Anabaptist movement accepted the argument as found in Erasmus because of its intellectual/theological cogency. Protestants and Catholics who opposed the Anabaptists indirectly at least conceded this cogency, for virtually all of them felt compelled to undermine the argument as made by the Anabaptists. The following chapter will demonstrate this. They all seem to have been convinced that they had to respond negatively to it.

But why? Perhaps in this respect a social and political analysis of motives might be in order, for from the 1526 response of the Parisian theologians to Erasmus's not-so-veiled recommendation of a second baptism in the 1522 preface to his New Testament, the primary argument has been that to "rebaptize" baptized children at a later age would "open the door to the destruction of the Christian religion."[93] Oecolampadius in the Protestant camp, responding to the

Anabaptist Carlin's argument based on the Great Commission, made a similar observation in 1527: "If anyone no longer baptizes children with our external sign," he informed the Basel authorities, "then the number of visible Christians will immediately decline. That is a very important consideration."[94] In both instances, the future of the Christian society — the *gemein christenheit* as Oecolampadius termed it — was at stake, not the correct interpretation of the passage in question. But the latter did become an issue once the decision was made in favor of the *gemein christenheit*.

The appropriation by both parties of the Erasmian argument also explains — with one stroke of the pen — the overriding similarities between the Swiss Anabaptists and their Dutch brethren after Menno. And it does so in spite of the at times very different set of economic, social, and political — not to speak of intellectual and cultural — conditions prevailing in the two regions. Indeed, once the interpretation had sprung full blown from the fertile mind of Erasmus it followed its own course irrespective of what lay in its path.

If the Erasmian interpretation helps to explain the above similarities, does it also explain — at least in part — the differences between the Swiss/South German Anabaptists and Menno, on the one hand, and those who came to the movement from the outside, on the other? It does — at least to a degree, since the Erasmian configuration is not present in the writings of Thomas Müntzer, Carlstadt, or Melchior Hoffmann, and only appears later — often in truncated form — in the writings of Melchior Rinck, Hans Hut, and even Hans Denck.

The only reference to Erasmus in Müntzer's writings are indirect — to his 1516-1518 edition of Jerome[95] and his 1519 edition of Cyprian, which he apparently possessed.[96] There is one reference to "believe and be baptized" in his *Prague Manifesto,* but this is of no consequence nor could it have been dependent on Erasmus since the *Manifesto* was written before Erasmus's paraphrases were published.[97]

The situation is somewhat different in Carlstadt's case. He appears to have been much more familiar with, and appreciative of, the great humanist's work.[98] Yet there appears to be no reference in his extant work to the above argument drawn from Erasmus's 1522 and 1523 paraphrases.[99] Perhaps because these were years of turmoil for Carlstadt, as well as years in which he temporarily turned his back on academia, he failed to take note of them. But he may also have been precluded from focusing on them because of his increasingly mystical orientation. This may be inferred from the one extended reference to the Great Commission cited by Pater. There Carlstadt writes:

> Take baptism for example, and note what one is to be told first, when one is to be baptized. Christ says, "ye shall baptize them in the name of the Father and the Son and the Holy Ghost," Matt. 28:19. He who allows himself to be baptized in the name takes the external baptism, because he wants to show before everyone that he confesses the triune God and accepts him as creator of heaven and earth, who can and will give him all things needful and good. Where this righteousness is not present in the Spirit, the sign is false and God does not heed it. Hence adults *(die alten)* cannot find consolation in their baptism if they do not feel the descent *(niderganck)* of their life. Thus the Spirit is not bound to an external thing, *nor does inner harmony have to be attested to or authenticated by the external sign.* Nor (should one assume) that the Spirit cannot perform his life and work without externals, John 4, 13f, but (it should be done) simply without comfort and trust in externals.
>
> Where, however, one knows some who think that eternal bliss *(selickeyt)* and true union depend on the external sign, *to them he shall denouce and condemn the external sign,* though fittingly and properly, as Paul did with circumcision.[100]

This passage has more in common with Müntzer's mystical views than with anything that might have come from Menno or the Swiss Brethren.

Like Carlstadt, Melchior Hoffmann on occasion cited Matthew 28:18-20, but never in conjunction with the baptismal passages from Acts as did Erasmus and the Anabaptists. He also employed the passage for purposes other than theirs. Thus, in his *The Ordinance of God,* Hoffmann cited the passage at the very outset, but his focus was on the "power" Christ had received from God.[101] Somewhat later he emphasized the covenantal nature of baptism, and that those baptized were no longer to sin.[102] In a third reference, after he had reiterated that Christ had enjoined his apostles to "baptize the *nations* who accept their word and preachment of the crucified Christ Jesus and give themselves *over to him of their own free will,*" he pointed out that the baptized should then be taught "only that . . . which the Lord commanded them *and otherwise nothing.*"[103] That all of this was to be seen from within a context other than that of Erasmus is made apparent by the fact that — like Caspar Schwenckfeld and Sebastian Franck — he could command baptism to be suspended once persecution set in with the execution of Sicke Freerks at Leuwarden in 1531.[104]

The same might be said of Hans Hut.[105] In the tract that Lydia Mueller attributed to him (edited in her *Glaubenszeugnisse oberdeutscher Taufgesinnter* and translated by Gordon Rupp in his *Patterns of Reformation* as "Of the Mystery of Baptism"),[106] Hut refers to the Mark version of the Great Commission. Here he observes that one must not leave "aside the form and devising of Christ and his apostles":

> First Christ says, "Go ye into all the world and preach the Gospel of all creatures." Then he says, "whoso believes," and thirdly, "and is baptized, shall be saved." This Order must be observed, if a true Christendom is to be set up, and though the whole world should be broken in pieces about it. Where it is not preserved, there is no Christian people of God, but of the devil, and the dregs of the whole world and of all false Christians who change it with their perverted Order and maintain that it is untrue.
>
> First then, Christ says, "Go into all the world and preach the Gospel of all creatures *[aller creaturen]*." Here the Lord shows how man shall come to the knowledge of God and himself, namely through the Gospel of all creatures. But we must first of all learn and know what is this "gospel of all creatures." For, God have mercy, the whole world is utterly ignorant of it, and it is also never preached in our age.[107]

Hut then proceeds to explain what this "gospel of all creatures" is. For it was upon faith in this gospel that one was to be baptized. Nor was this baptism, Hut insisted, "first instituted in the time of Christ, but it was from the beginning, and in it all the Elect Friends of God [a mystical/Müntzerian term] from Adam until now have been baptized."[108] Not exactly the Erasmian version.

Melchior Rinck, like Hut also early under Müntzer's influence, joined the Anabaptists after the Peasant War and soon became a leader in relatively tolerant Hesse. On 17-18 August 1528 he was captured and interrogated in Marburg. His reported confession exudes the spirit of Müntzer to the extent of arguing that although Luther had at first possessed the Holy Spirit, the latter had soon departed from him.[109]

70

It is informed throughout by a mystical perspective;[110] furthermore, it contains no reference to Matthew 28:18-20 or Mark 16:15-16 in the passage dealing with baptism, though it does cite three of the Acts passages.[111] By 1531 this had changed, for in an interrogation of Rinck's followers in Vach on 11 November, the authorities were told that Rinck had taught his captured followers baptism on the basis of the Great Commission.[112] There is nothing to indicate, however, that the command of Christ to baptize was to be interpreted through the baptismal passages in Acts. It would appear that Rinck and his followers had heard the interpretation from Anabaptists coming from the south — perhaps seeking sanctuary — but did not ever come to a full understanding of the Erasmian argument. In any case, had the interpretation come from Müntzer, Rinck must surely already have employed it in 1528, if not sooner.

Thus, though Rinck and his followers may well have cited Matthew 28:18-20 in their defense of believer's baptism after 1531, it does not appear from its later use among them that they ever came to understand it from within the larger Erasmian framework. Certainly, as the Hutterites discovered from Rinck's disciple, Hans Bot, in 1535, the former was not orthodox — from their perspective — in the matter relating to Word and Spirit either. Having its roots in mysticism's Neoplatonic understanding of the soul,[113] this separation of "inner" and "outer," of "spirit" and "creature" can be seen in virtually everyone coming to Anabaptism from a mystical orientation. Even the earlier passage on baptism from Carlstadt is clear evidence of this. Along with the very different interpretations of Matthew 28:18-20 presented by the above individuals, the reader is led to conclude one of two things with respect to the use of the Erasmian argument among them: either they never encountered it in its pristine form or, if and when they did, their prior mystical intellectual committments precluded them from understanding it in the way other Anabaptists did. This is exemplified even in the writings of Hans Denck, whom Clarence Bauman has recently called an "ideal" Anabaptist.[114]

Of all the Anabaptists influenced by mysticism, Hans Denck was perhaps the most nearly integrated into the movement emanating from Zurich. But even he appears to have rejected it just before his death.[115] The reason for this would seem to lie, on the one hand, in the greater individualism implicit in the mystical orientation, which gave rise to a far greater variety of theological perspectives in the

71

aforementioned personalities than among the Swiss Brethren and the *Mennists* after Münster; and, on the other hand, in that major difference between these individualists and the other groups, which also derived from mysticism, and to which Johannes Bader, Reformer of the free imperial city of Landau referred in his 1527 *Brotherly Warning against the Idolatrous Order of Anabaptists*.[116]

Bader asserted that he wrote his book primarily for one reason: because he believed that Zwingli had, in his writings against the Anabaptists, missed the salient aspect of their teaching.[117] That aspect, he observed, was "their strange opinion concerning the relationship of Spirit and holy Scripture which I have learned from him [Hans Denck], for it leads them, ultimately, to regard the Bible as utterly useless and [therefore] to reject it, [thereby] diverting the people's attention from it to the lying spirit of his baptismal order (in keeping with Muentzer's method)."[118] Bader wished to make it exceedingly clear that Denck, whom he called the foremost Anabaptist and "abbot" of the new order, had himself informed him of this "strange opinion."

Bader's assertion that Zwingli had missed this most important aspect of Anabaptist thought did the Zurich Reformer an injustice. For if the latter had encountered it among the Swiss Brethren he would most assuredly have exploited it to the full, as Calvin was to do in his famous letter to Jacopo Sadoleto of 1 September 1539, only one year after coming to Strasbourg where mystical Anabaptists were numerous.[119] Though Bader was therefore not mistaken about Denck's views on the "inner" and the "outer" Word, he was in error if he assumed this to have also been the position of the Swiss/South German Anabaptists and that Zwingli had missed it. That Bader was in error on this last matter is confirmed by the 1527 Nicolsburg encounter between Hubmaier and Hut,[120] by the 1536 rejection of Hans Bot — Melchior Rinck's emissary to the Hutterites — when he began to speak of the "well of living water" within him,[121] and the 1538 rejection of Hoffmann's teachings by the Swiss Brethren at the Bern disputation of that year.[122] Already the *Schleitheim Confession* of 1527 appears to reject this mystical position,[123] as does Pilgram Marpeck in his 1530 *A Clear Refutation* directed against Caspar Schwenckfeld. There Marpeck wrote in the opening lines:

First, certain spirits are advocating [as Hoffmann, Schwenckfeld and Franck did] that the children of God should no longer use the ceremonies of the New Testament such as baptism, the Lord's Supper, and the Scriptures. These spirits think that such ceremonies are to be shunned because they have been abused and destroyed by Antichrist, who imitates them without a mandate and without the witness of the heart. Therefore the ceremonies are misunderstood, abused, and stained. This abomination will remain to the end.[124]

These repeated confrontations between the various parties must be taken seriously. They indicate that, on the one side are those who had adopted Erasmus's interpretation of the Great Commission; on the other, those influenced by mysticism and apocalypticism who, even though they may at some point have encountered that interpretation, continued to read the Great Commission through mystical eyes. In particular, it was that aspect of mysticism Bader highlighted in Denck — and Müntzer — which influenced how they read Matthew 28:18-20.

This is true even of Denck. For in the very document in which Bader accused Denck of separating Word from Spirit and then boasting of the spirit within, he also addressed Denck's argument from Matthew 28:18-20 as the latter's first response to Bader's defense of infant baptism. But though Denck employed the same Matthean passage to argue in favor of believer's baptism, he made no reference whatever to the baptismal passages in Acts. Neither Denck, nor Bader for that matter, appears to have been familiar with the problem posed by the passages in Matthew and in Acts. And there is no hint anywhere in the document that either man had read Erasmus's paraphrases on the passages.

At the very outset, Bader asserted, Denck had informed him that Christ had sent him out to "attack and reject holy infant baptism as an abomination before God."[125] And his heart had confirmed this mission! He justified such an attack with a unique grammatical analysis of the Great Commission, asserting

that if the *relativum eos* [sic], which is found in the baptismal text of Matthew 28 *(baptisantes eos),* were not there, then my reasoning would be right, but the *eos* alone stands in the way. Thereupon he took his Greek testament to hand and read the text, from which he concluded that the substance and most important aspect of Christian baptism was the oral confession of faith. The reason for this [he said] was the fact that the words *docete omnes gentes* stood before the words *baptisantes eos;* this *docete* in the Greek, as he asserted — for I do not understand the Greek language — is comparable to saying: to make disciples of Christ or to accept them as followers of Christ. Furthermore, he says that the intent and command of Christ is the same as if he had said: go and teach all people and only those who accept my teaching and who, because of this have become my disciples, baptize in the name of the Father etc. Thus Denck concluded that a personal confession makes a person into a disciple of Christ and therefore it is the most important aspect of baptism; without it no one may be [properly] baptized before Christ. Since children cannot fulfill this requirement they are not elligible for Christian baptism. He also added that the meaning might be made even clearer were one to resolve Christ's statement in another way and express it in individual terms as follows: go and teach, or make disciples, of Peter, Paul, Cuntz, Heyntz etc., baptizing the same in the name of the Father etc. In such a formulation, he says, one sees clearly why the *docete* (teach) must precede the *baptisantes*.[126]

If, as Bader argued, Denck made no distinction between the first and second command to teach — even though Bader himself recognized that the two Greek words were spelled slightly differently[127] — then Denck was clearly not influenced by the Erasmian interpretation. This conclusion is given further credence by the fact that Denck does not use the baptismal passages in Acts to illuminate the Great Commission. Nor, at least not in Bader's telling of it, does Denck address the issue of repentance and conversion. Instead, he emphasizes "making disciples." Were one to question Denck as to how this might be done, he would probably respond by describing what mystics called the "baptism of the Holy Spirit," which instantaneously transformed the "scribe" into a person enabled to live his faith.[128]

From the perspective of the interpretation of Christ's Great Commission, then, there are clearly two distinct parties. On the one hand, Erasmus's interpretation of Christ's Great Commission becomes normative for the vast majority of Swiss/South German Anabaptists as well as for Menno and post-Münsterite Dutch Anabaptism. On the other hand, the Erasmian interpretation is absent in all the rest, even in the majority of those individuals who, after they had joined the movement through rebaptism, might also be called Anabaptists. However, unlike the magisterial Protestant and Catholic opponents of the Anabaptists, whom we shall treat in the next chapter, these mystically inclined Anabaptists did not oppose the Erasmian interpretation — or consciouly seek to reinterpret it if and when they encountered it.[129] Rather, they read the Great Commission through eyes already prejudiced by mystical — or other — preconceptions. The Swiss Brethren and Menno, however, came to be persuaded by the Erasmian argument and developed their theology from within this framework.

4

Protestant and Catholic Responses

> Their third objection is this: "He who believes and is baptized
> shall be saved; but he who believes not shall be damned"
> [Mark 16:16]. Faith must therefore be present first, or one
> might just as well baptize a raven. I answer: This verse cannot
> be applied to children, for just before these words, he said,
> "Preach the gospel to every creature" [Mark 16:15], and then
> "he who believes" — that is, when he has heard the gospel.
> But since it can neither be preached to infants nor heard by
> them, it clearly follows that they were not meant by this
> admittedly very important passage, but only those who hear
> the preaching and then either believe it or evade it.
>
> Ulrich Zwingli, Letter of 1524 to Franz Lambert

The Anabaptists were not the only ones who grappled with the Erasmian interpretation of Christ's Great Commission during the early
years of the Reformation; the magisterial Reformers did so as well.
More important, however, both Protestants and Catholics had eventually to confront this interpretation in its Anabaptist formulation
where it bore fruit undermining the *corpus christianum*. That they did
both the following discussion will demonstrate.

There are indications that Zwingli's earlier, more accepting views
of believer's baptism may have been stimulated by Erasmus's annotations on the Great Commission, his 1522 preface to the New Testa-

76

ment, and his paraphrases on the Gospel of Matthew and Acts. For as early as his letter to the Bishop of Constance of 2 July 1522, Zwingli wrote:

> We are aware that our life [in this instance with regard to priestly celibacy] differs all too widely from the pattern of the Gospel, but is the Gospel on that account to be abolished and done away with? Ought we not rather to devote ourselves vigorously to correcting our faults according to its standards and to subduing our feebleness, since it is the one thing, could we only believe it, from the inspiration of which salvation will come to us, according to the commandment of Christ when he sent forth his apostles to preach the Gospel with these words: "Preach the Gospel (not your own theories or decrees or regulations which some chance shall happen to dictate) to every creature." And he added: "Whoever believeth" (when the Gospel has been preached, of course), "and is baptized, shall be saved," and on the other hand, "Whoever believeth not, shall be damned."[1]

As the disciple of Erasmus after 1515, Zwingli may well have himself been the mediator of the great humanist's interpretation of this passage to his early followers. That Zwingli believed that the earliest church had not baptized children is made apparent in the 18th article of his January 1523 *Basis and Exposition of the Conclusions,* where he wrote:

> The rite of confirmation became customary only after a general beginning had been made to baptize the children in their infancy, or immediately after birth. Confirmation was introduced that the faith which was confessed for them by their fathers and mothers through their godfathers might not be unknown to them [since they were instructed previous to confirmation]. Although I know, as the ancients indicate, that from the earliest times infants were sometimes baptized, it was nevertheless not so common a custom as it is in our time, but the general practice was, as soon as they arrived at the age of reason, to form them into classes for instruction in the word of salvation (hence they were called catechumens, i.e., persons under instruction) and when they steadfastly believed in their hearts and confessed with their mouths, they were baptized.[2]

Nor did Zwingli fail to realize that the Anabaptists justified their practice of believer's baptism with the words of the Great Commission. Therefore, after he had changed his mind on the matter,[3] he attempted to deflect their argument by saying: "But then when they counter with Matthew 28 'teach and baptize them,' the consequence will be that they do violence to the Word, for baptism was not instituted at that place."[4]

By the time Zwingli came to write his 1524 *Commentary on True and False Religion,* he had already changed his position and begun to attack his former followers. He knew intimately the biblical passages upon which they based their opposition to infant baptism; indeed, his counterargument was based on the very same passages. This would appear to indicate that he, too, had been forced to deal with the Erasmian argument.[5] But the perspective from which Zwingli read these passages was no longer — if it ever had been — that of the great Christian humanist. Rather, it was now clearly the traditional Catholic definition of a sacrament as the external sign of an inner, spiritual reality. More specifically, he viewed this relationship from the perspective of the Catholic doctrine of baptismal regeneration, which asserted that the application of the external sign assured the interior spiritual reality.[6] This assumption, Zwingli had become convinced, had no validity. For although everyone in Christendom had received the external sign of water baptism, the spiritual reality — the interior spiritual renewal or regeneration — was only seldom found.[7] Thus he could contend:

> For if we become new men, that is to say, if we love God and our neighbor, we shrink from sin, put on Christ and daily grow more and more into the perfect man, are changed by the action of the Holy Spirit. *But who would not feel this change?* If, however, pleasing ourselves for a time with the freedom from guilt we have acquired, presently, when the hallucination has worn off, return to the old life, like a dog to his vomit [cf. Prov. 26:11], *it is evident that we have not felt any change of heart, but only the awe of the water. Many are baptized therefore, who during baptism feel nothing beyond awe of the water, and not also remission of sins, that is deliverance of the heart.*[8]

Zwingli called this "deliverance of the heart" the baptism of the Holy Spirit.[9] He described this baptism, interestingly enough, with reference to Acts 2, Peter's Pentecost sermon, which had served Erasmus as the prism through which he had interpreted Christ's Great Commission. Thus Zwingli wrote:

> The baptism of the Holy Spirit, then, is twofold. First, there is the baptism by which all are flooded within who trust in Christ, "for no man cometh to him, except the Father draw him," John 6:44. "And all shall be taught of God," Isa. 54:13. Second, there is the external baptism of the Holy Spirit, just as there is the baptism of water. Drenched with this, pious men at once began to speak in foreign tongues [Acts 2:4-11]. This was a sign to others rather than to the speakers, for the speakers felt within themselves faith and enlightenment of soul, but the others did not know this of them. It, therefore, turned their tongues into foreign speech, that others might know that what was taking place was done by the divine Spirit. And this latter baptism of the Holy Spirit is not necessary, *but the former is so very necessary that no one can be saved without it; for no one is saved except by faith, and faith is not born save at the instance of the Holy Spirit.*[10]

For Zwingli, this baptism of the Holy Spirit, even in biblical times — as demonstrated by those baptized by John and "those who after the ascension of Christ at the preaching of the Apostles and disciples received baptism before they were sure of salvation through Christ or were fully taught in regard to it" — had not been tied to the external sign of water baptism. To confirm this assertion, he employed another two baptismal passages from Acts that also were central to Erasmus's argument: Acts 19:2-6 and Acts 10:44. The first dealt with Paul's rebaptism of twelve Ephesian disciples of John the Baptist because they had not received the Holy Spirit at baptism; the second, with the baptism of Cornelius who had received the Holy Spirit before baptism. The first, Zwingli argued, demonstrated that water baptism had not conferred the Holy Spirit; the second, that the baptism of the Holy Spirit had preceded water baptism and was therefore clearly unconnected to it. For that reason Zwingli concluded that it was wrong to assume "that the sacraments are signs of such a kind that, when they are applied to a man, the thing signified by the sacraments at once takes place within him."[11] From Zwingli's perspective, then, Acts 19:2-6 and 10:44 clearly demonstrated that there was no necessary connection between conversion — the baptism of the Holy Spirit — and water baptism; any attempt to bind the Spirit to the external sign therefore limited it and constrained "the liberty of the divine Spirit which distributes itself in individuals as it will, that is, to whom it will, when it will [and] where it will. For if it were compelled to act within when we employ the sign externally, it would be absolutely bound by the signs."[12] This was a manifest impossibility.

Zwingli did concede that his interpretation seemed "to be opposed by what is written in Acts 19:1-10 and Matt. 28:19." For the first "plainly [bore] witness that twelve men were baptized over again."[13] He sought to get around this apparent conclusion, however, by arguing that the difficulty was semantic and, therefore, more apparent than real. For like Christ in Matthew 21:25, Paul had employed the word "baptism" for "teaching."[14] The Matthew 28:19 passage seems to have appeared perhaps even more problematic to Zwingli, for he did not return to it until later.

Between his *Commentary* of late 1524 and his *Of Baptism* of May 1525, Zwingli wrote to Franz Lambert and others in Strasbourg regarding the quarrel with his followers. Apparently among friends, he reiterated that he made "no distinction . . . between the baptism of John and that of Christ," for although each was "performed with different words, it was still the same sign or sacrament."[15] He also argued now that baptism, in the New Testament, simply took the place of circumcision in the Old.[16] He used this argument to shore up his contention that "those who were only about to become believers had already received water baptism, as, for example, the disciples who had been baptized by John — assuming that we agree that they were indeed baptized." If the latter were correct, one could also baptize children who were only to be brought up in the faith at a later date.[17]

Finally Zwingli came to the Great Commission, but in its Markan formulation. To the Anabaptist belief derived from this passage that "faith must therefore be present first," Zwingli answered that "this verse cannot be applied to children, for just before these words, he said, 'Preach the gospel to every creature,' and then 'he who believes' — that is, when he has heard the gospel." But since the gospel could neither be preached "to infants nor heard by them," it had to follow that they could not have been addressed by this "*admittedly very important passage,* but only those who hear the preaching and then either believe it or evade it."[18] The Matthean version did not pose the same problem for him, for there he could argue that the "teach all nations" now included children.

Zwingli addressed the Matthean version more fully in his *Of Baptism*. As he did so, he also returned once more to the "sacramental" context of his argument. And he conceded that he had himself earlier believed — because of the traditional definition of a sacrament — that it would be better not to baptize infants until they had reached years of discretion. But the "fact" of infant baptism had changed his mind, for baptism — having failed to regenerate persons even in the first years of the church — could not produce faith in children either. Therefore, the Holy Spirit had to be completely loosed from every form of water baptism.

Zwingli knew well enough that the Anabaptists "alleged [Matt. 28:18-20] against infant baptism."[19] He was also very much aware that the order of the words, "teach and baptize," was important to them. But if he was aware of the Erasmian context of their argument he gave no indication of it, for he made no attempt to distinguish between the first and second command to "teach" in the Commission. Quite to the contrary; he sought to oppose such an Erasmian distinction and conflate them.[20] And he did so by arguing that the first "Teach all nations, baptizing them," was followed by another command to teach somewhat later, the "Teaching them to observe whatever I have commanded you." From this dual command to teach, and the fact that one was to keep all things Christ had commanded *only after* baptism, Zwingli concluded — as he had already done many times before — that baptism was a mere sign of initiation.

Unlike Erasmus and the Anabaptists, therefore, Zwingli refused to distinguish between the two commands to teach. Did he not know of Erasmus's argument? Hardly. He must have known of it; but if he did, he had now clearly rejected it. Did this influence the Zurich theologians' decision not to translate Erasmus's paraphrases on Matthew and Acts at this time, waiting until 1535, four years after Zwingli's death? Was Zwingli avoiding the implications of Erasmus's interpretation by consciously attempting to obfuscate the issue? Or was he sincere when he wrote that the literal sense of the passage was "'Go ye and make disciples of all nations'; then there follows the initiation with which they are to make disciples: 'Baptizing them in the name of the Father, and of the Son, and of the Holy Ghost'; and after the initiation: 'teaching them to observe all things whatsoever I have entrusted to you.'"[21] With such a formulation Zwingli could justify his position, but was this a rationalization that he developed in response to his followers' reading of the passages in Erasmus's paraphrases, or the consistent outgrowth of his struggle with the Catholic interpretation of the baptismal sacrament? It could be the latter; but it could also be the former. Until there is conclusive evidence one way or the other, Zwingli should be given the benefit of the doubt.

If Zwingli and his Anabaptist followers received their inspiration for believer's baptism from Erasmus's exegesis of Christ's Great Commission, then it is quite probable that Oecolampadius and the other Swiss/South German Reformers were also influenced by Erasmus. And this does indeed appear to have been the case, for in his *Exposition of the Epistle to the Romans* (1524), Oecolampadius referred to the parallel passage in Mark 16, saying: "But the Lord, when he says in the last chapter of Mark: He who believeth and is baptized, etc., *demands* of us confession through baptism and *requires* unconditional faith. For he who would not be baptized, will neither confess Christ."[22] And even Bucer wrote Luther as late as 1524:

> Although the baptism of adults alone would probably be far more in accord with the practice of the early church and also with the teachings of Scripture which *order* that those who know Christ should be baptized, confessing Christ in baptism after they have been taught the doctrine of godliness; and by baptizing adults only would also be destroyed a deceptive trust in baptism. . . . nevertheless [and then Bucer proceeds to accept infant baptism but to argue that] arrangements should be made for instructing them [the children] in religion.[23]

Besides Oecolampadius and Bucer, Capito, Vadian, Ulrich Hugwald, and Sebastian Hoffmeister of Schaffhausen were also early opposed to infant baptism.[24] As late as 14 August 1525, Hoffmeister was expelled from Basel for having taught there what he had taught from the pulpit in Schaffhausen: "dy erschrecklichen artickel, das heylig hochwuerdig sacrament, dy heylig mesz und kindertauf, by uch offentlich an der cantzel verkundt."[25]

In Wittenberg the situation was more ambiguous, but even here the same biblical passages appear to have been at work in the discussion of baptism. Historians and theologians alike have consistently taught that the opposition to infant baptism was first raised in Wittenberg by the Zwickau Prophets, who appeared in the city on 27 December 1521 while Luther was absent at the Wartburg. However, this does not appear to have been the case. On the latter occasion, the Prophets challenged Melanchthon, Luther's junior partner in the cause of reform, to prove to them from *sola scriptura* — one of Luther's fundamental principles — that infant baptism could be substantiated by that authority. Melanchthon had consequently — as Elector Frederick the Wise observed — "written His Grace in such an emotional manner"[26] concerning the Prophets' challenge of infant baptism. Not only did Melanchthon write to George Spalatin and Frederick the Wise in this manner, he also wrote to Luther at the Wartburg in like fashion.[27] Why should this challenge, coming from essentially unlearned men, have troubled Luther's young reform partner to such an extent that even Elector Frederick was taken aback by the emotional tone of Melanchthon's letter? Could it be that this was not the first occasion on which the problem of infant baptism was broached in Wittenberg? Spalatin's notes on the exchange between Melanchthon, Nicholas Amsdorf, and the Elector, which took place on 2 January 1525, deserve to be quoted in this context.

> To begin with, the matter that moves me [Philip Melanchthon] happened as follows: On the day of St. John the Evangelist [27 December] there came to me in Wittenberg Claus Storch with two companions, who informed me than an uprising had occurred in Zwickau.[28] The issues involved had been *baptismi parvulorum* [sic] and *fides aliena*. And they had done so on the authority of Doctor Martin.
>
> In a separate discussion later with Marcus Thome, one of the three, I was told that he, as well as Storch, had received revelations from [spoken openly with] God. Nor did any of them preach anything except that which God commanded.
>
> So much I have noticed from him, that, in the most important articles of faith, he has interpreted the Scriptures correctly, even though he speaks in a strange manner.
>
> Half a year ago I also debated this Marcus, but at that time he did not say anything about his conversations with God. [Had he said anything about infant baptism?]
>
> And so I have mulled the matter back and forth over in my mind,

83

especially because they told us about the unrest it had created in Zwickau and might create elsewhere. I thought since such unrest cannot be quieted by force, but primarily through Scripture and the judgments of spiritual men, it would be essential to get Doctor Martin's judgment [on the matter], especially since they call on him as their authority.

Two questions especially are not to be dismissed [despised] lightly by persons, [questions] that may well agitate the common people as well as myself.

I also thought the devil wished to attack us at a weak point.

Augustine and others of his time disputed about infant baptism, but accomplished little.[29] Augustine rested his case on [the doctrine of] original sin and an old custom.

Doctor Martin well knows the import of this issue.

And that, in sum, was then, and still is, my concern.

I was not particularly perturbed by the fact that they claimed to have spoken with God, and the like. For such matters must rest on their own merits *and are not of great import,* except that under this guise other problematic matters might be undertaken.

But the question de baptismi [sic] *has perturbed me, and in my view, justifiably so.*[30]

The above notes contain a number of indicators that all point to a prior discussion of infant baptism in Wittenberg between Luther and his reform colleagues. The first is Melanchthon's statement that "Doctor Martin well knows the import of this issue." Would Melanchthon have made such a statement had the matter of infant baptism not been discussed — and that fairly thoroughly — in Wittenberg prior to Luther's appearance at the Diet of Worms in April 1521 and his going into hiding at the Wartburg? Second, Melanchthon observed that the issue of *baptismi parvulorum* — and the last sentence of the passage makes it abundantly apparent that it was this issue alone that perturbed him — was a "weak point" in their theology where the devil was now attacking them. Surely, he had not come to this conclusion suddenly without having thought about the problem earlier, and that at some length. That he had — and not he alone — thought about the issue earlier is further indicated by his observation that "Augustine and many others of his time disputed about infant baptism, but accomplished little." No doubt, Melanchthon had not pulled his annotated Augustine from the bookshelf after the arrival of the Prophets to check what the learned Church Father had said on the subject; he, together with his Wittenberg colleagues, had already had occasion to do this earlier.[31] Not only had they investigated what Augustine had said on infant baptism, they had apparently concluded from their study of Augustine — and the other Church Fathers — that these great teachers had "accomplished little" with respect to the problem. In other words, Augustine and the others had not resolved the issue for them. This would appear to be confirmed by Melanchthon's subsequent observation that "Augustine rested his case on [the doctrine of] original sin and an old custom." The reference to "an old custom" was probably made to contrast Luther's emphasis on *sola fide* and *sola scriptura*.

As intriguing as the above is Melanchthon's observation that the Zwickau Prophets, with respect to their rejection of *baptismi parvulorum* and *fides aliena,* appealed to Martin Luther — not Thomas Müntzer! — as their authority. Melanchthon made the point at least twice. Nor did he make any attempt to deny that Luther was indeed an authority for such a position! Surely he would have done so had there been no reason to justify the Prophets' appeal to the authority of Luther. Rather, what he did say was: "Doctor Martin well knows the import of the issue."

The assumption that infant baptism was discussed in Wittenberg well before the arrival of the Zwickau Prophets on 27 December 1521 would appear to be confirmed by Luther's own writings on baptism published before that date. He addressed the question of the relationship between faith and baptism on a number of occasions, at least one of these with reference to the same passages emphasized by Erasmus. In a sermon of November 1519, for example, Luther spoke of baptism in terms of the original meaning of the word — immersion in water — and the oath taken by the baptizand. The latter is reminiscent of Erasmus's argument in the *Enchiridion*. There was "no loftier, better, greater oath than the oath taken at baptism," he argued.[32] In the *Babylonian Captivity of the Church* (1520) he dealt with the subject more fully and in the context of Christ's Great Commission, but as given in Mark 16:16: "He that believeth and is baptized shall be saved." It is significant that Luther does not, as had Erasmus, set this command to baptize into the larger context of the Commission. For he began by asserting that "Unless faith is present, or comes to life in baptism,

85

the ceremony is of no avail; indeed, it is a stumbling block not only at the moment we receive baptism but for all our life thereafter."[33] In line with his emphasis on the necessity of faith, Luther also spoke of baptism as "a sign;" its effectiveness, he continued, lay "in faith, and not in anything that is done."[34] He repeated this emphasis, saying: "baptism justifies nobody; rather, faith in the word of the promise to which baptism was conjoined, is what justifies, and so completes that which the baptism signified."[35] Again he returned to Mark 16:16, saying: "Christ said: 'He that believeth and is baptized shall be saved; but he that disbelieveth shall be condemned.' Here He points out that, in the sacrament, faith is necessary to such a degree that it can save even apart from the sacrament; that is why He did not add, after 'He who disbelieveth', the words *and is not baptized*."[36]

In the wake of these considerations Luther conceded that "it may be objected that, when infants are baptized, they cannot receive the promises of God; are incapable of accepting the baptismal faith; and that, therefore, either faith is not a requisite, or else it is useless to baptize infants."[37] He rejected these arguments, however, saying that he agreed with "everyone" in holding that "infants are helped by vicarious faith; the faith of those who present them for baptism."[38] Here Luther himself raises the question of *baptismi parvulorum*, probably because it had been discussed in the circle of the Wittenberg Reformers and was considered a problem. He resolved the problem by arguing in favor of a *fides aliena*.[39] The Zwickau Prophets raised these two issues when they came to Wittenberg in late December 1521, and they must have derived both from Luther's early writings.[40]

In the process of making his case, Luther also addressed the apparent conflict between the Markan and Matthean passages, on the one hand, and the Acts passages, on the other, regarding the correct baptismal formula. But he did not do so from an Erasmian perspective, for he wrote:

> I am glad to adopt this point of view because it gives a very complete support to our confidence and a real incentive to faith, to know that we are not baptized by human hands, but by the Holy Trinity itself through the agency of man who performs the rite in Their name. This puts an end to that tiresome dispute about the words employed, and which are called the "form" of baptism. The formula of the Greek Church is: "May a servant of Christ be baptized"; and

that of the Latin: "I baptize." Others again, sticking rigidly to their pedantry, condemn the use of the words, "I baptize thee in the name of Jesus Christ," *although it is certain that the Apostles used that form in baptizing,* as we read in the Acts of the Apostles. They refuse to regard any as valid except: "baptize in the name of the Father, and of the Son, and of the Holy Spirit, Amen." . . . *Pointless disputes about questions of this kind are raised for us by those who lay no emphasis on faith, but all on works and the proper rites; whereas we lay all the stress on faith alone, and none on a mere rite;* and this makes us free in spirit from all these scrupulosities and distinctions.[41]

Whereas, according to Luther, placing the "stress on faith alone" made irrelevant the quarrel over the correct baptismal formula, it did raise other questions, as Luther conceded — questions about the validity of infant baptism because of the inability of children to believe. In 1520 he still chose to resolve this problem by arguing in favor of a *fides aliena,* precisely the kind of faith attacked by the Zwickau Prophets.

Would Luther have raised the question of infant baptism in such a public document had it not been discussed in Wittenberg before the arrival in that city of the Zwickau Prophets, indeed before he wrote the *Captivity*? Melanchthon's observation that Augustine had not resolved the issue for them may have derived from some of Erasmus's own statements to that effect, but it may also rest on their own investigations into the writings of that Church Father. In any event, it also points, as noted above, to a prior discussion of the issue. But nowhere in these Wittenberg discussions can we detect the larger context of Erasmus's interpretation of the Great Commission, even though Luther, in the *Captivity,* deals with the problem in the context of the same biblical passages.[42] He does so again in his *Grund und Ursach* of March 1521. Here he is, if anything, even more insistent on the presence of faith before baptism, stating:

The same meaning is contained in the words of Christ, Mark 16:16, "He that believeth and is baptized, shall be saved." He sets faith before baptism. For where faith is not in evidence, baptism is of no avail, as he himself says afterwards: "He that believeth not shall be condemned," even though he has already been baptized. For it is not baptism but the faith added to baptism that saves. It is for that reason that we read in Acts 8:37 that St. Philip would not baptize the eunuch before he had asked him whether he believed. And still today we see daily that in all the world, wherever one baptizes, the infant, or the godparents in his stead, is first asked whether he believes, and on the faith and confession [of the godparents] the sacrament [of baptism] is administered.[43]

This time Luther brings the Great Commission into connection with one of the baptismal stories in Acts, the story of Philip and the Ethiopian eunuch, in order to emphasize the importance of faith being present before baptism can be administered. Even so, he once again proceeded to justify infant baptism. Nevertheless, in all of these instances — in this last one even more so than the previous ones — Luther was concerned to stress the importance of faith, as one would expect him to do given his doctrine of *sola fide*. Nowhere, however, does he approach these passages from within Erasmus's context.[44]

The Wittenberg story does not end at this point, however. In the course of his conversation with Frederick the Wise, Melanchthon informed his prince that the issue of *baptismi parvulorum* was important enough to merit a full discussion in a public forum not unlike that of the famous Leipzig Disputation of 1519. Frederick, not called the "Wise" and the "cautious" for nothing, refused to be persuaded. For at least several months he had attempted to prevent the Wittenberg Reformers from introducing innovations into their eucharistic services, specifically forbidding Andreas Bodenstein von Carlstadt from performing an "evangelical eucharist" on 1 January 1522 in the Wittenberg Castle church. A man obedient to the letter of the law but not its spirit, Carlstadt celebrated an evangelical eucharistic service on Christmas day, several days earlier — not without tension in the church and social unrest in the city. Nor had Frederick been happy with the aftermath of Leipzig — the disputation had drawn far too much attention to Luther and his reform. And now Melanchthon was suggesting that infant baptism be debated in a public university forum before all Christendom! If such a discussion, on a much smaller scale in Zwickau, had led to social unrest, what might happen in this larger context? And — worst of all possible scenarios — what if infant baptism were to be rejected? What innovation might replace it? Therefore, despite the fact that Melanchthon had asserted that Augustine and his allies had "accomplished little" in the matter, Frederick refused

Melanchthon's request. Instead, he inquired of the young Reformer whether Augustine was not held in high esteem by the Wittenberg theologians. Receiving an affirmative response, the Elector proceeded to ask Melanchthon what form of baptism Augustine had practiced. Informed that it had been infant baptism, Frederick in effect told Melanchthon that what had been good enough for the great Church Father would have to be good enough for the Wittenberg Reformers. And so it was. Obviously, there were political limits beyond which religious reform, without the universal approbation of the church, would not be allowed to go in Saxony.

The investigation of the political opposition to infant baptism in the other regions will have to await another study. But it may be suggested that Frederick's opposition was not an isolated instance. Rather than the presumed Anabaptist involvement in the Peasants' War of 1524-1525, it was political opposition that turned Reformers against believer's baptism. When that happened, "Magisterial Reformers" were forced to find reasons to oppose it. They were also forced to attempt to refute the Erasmian argument. That they attempted to do so can be seen not only in the writings of these Reformers, but also in some Catholic writers, which only confirms how widespread the Erasmian argument had been among the Anabaptists.

Luther also addressed the Great Commission in Mark's version in three later sermons, the first two preached in 1522 and 1523, and the third well after the rise of Anabaptism. All three sermons are directed, like the above documents, against the "papists," though the Anabaptists are mentioned in the last. As a consequence, Luther, in his 1522 sermon, stresses the fact that Christ desired his followers to believe not only "that they had a gracious God . . . , [but] they must believe also the resurrection of Christ. For this cause Christ became man and took upon himself our sins and also the wrath of the Father, and drowned them both in himself, thus reconciling us to God the Father. Without this faith, we are children of wrath, able to do no good work that is pleasing to God, nor can our prayers be acceptable before him."[45] According to Luther, however, only a few Christians had this faith, for the vast majority of people ran to cloisters and convents seeking to be saved through good works. This demonstrated only too clearly that they did not believe their sins to have been taken away through Christ's death and resurrection.

Luther, like Erasmus, also stressed the fact that the apostles had been commanded by Christ at the outset to preach the gospel: that Christ had been raised from the dead and had "overcome and taken away sin and all misery."[46] In the sermons Luther was quite obviously more concerned with the issue of faith and works, but he did eventually arrive at the question of baptism, saying, "God has always accompanied his Word with an outward sign to make it more effective to us, that we might be strengthened in heart and never doubt his Word, nor waver."[47] Without faith, baptism was "worth nothing." It would be no more than a "seal affixed to a letter in which nothing is written." Anyone who had the sign without faith, possessed "only seals upon a letter of blank paper."

Luther's 1523 sermon on the same text also was directed against the "papists." As a consequence, he reiterated his earlier arguments; but he also went somewhat further, asserting that baptism was "to be coupled . . . with faith, because God would not have faith to be hidden in the heart, but would have it burst forth and manifest itself to the world." For this reason God had ordained "such outward signs, by means of which everyone may show and confess his faith, to the end that we may come to the holy cross. For, if faith were to be kept a secret, hidden in the heart, we would be pretty sure of not having to bear the cross or to follow Christ; if the world knew not that we believed, we would not be persecuted."[48]

Luther's third sermon was still directed primarily against the "papists," but it also emphasized, more overtly, the Matthew version of the Great Commission. In connection with the last part of this version — "teaching them to obey all that I have commanded you" — the "papists" had argued that "this text must be interpreted to mean that it demands not faith alone, but also good works."[49] Such an argument, Luther insisted, only demonstrated Catholic ignorance with respect to the question of the relationship between faith and works. And then he continued:

> We also confess, and have always, better and more forcibly than the papists, taught that good works must be done; that they must follow faith, and that faith is dead if good works be absent. Therefore, this doctrine of faith does not denounce good works; it does not teach that they should not be performed. Nor is it the question here, whether or no good works are requisite. But faith and good works differ, and it must be taught with discrimination what is the value

of each for and by itself. Each must be considered in its proper relations that we may understand both what faith accomplishes and receives, and why good works are necessary. This distinction is everywhere taught in the Gospel and was preached by the apostles. It is, therefore, but blindness, if not intentional malice, that these papal sophists, without here making any distinction, in a swine-like manner misconstrue and pervert these passages so that neither of them can be clearly understood.[50]

Because of this Catholic misrepresentation, Luther insisted that the passages in Matthew and Mark had to "be properly interpreted in the light of their *actual wording and arrangement.*"[51] The sequence was important, for the apostles were

to preach to them [the Jews and heathen] the teaching of the Gospel, how they must be saved — which, as yet, neither the Jews nor the heathen knew — and in this knowledge to baptize them, making the people disciples or Christians. These are the first essentials and thereto the words agree: 'He that believeth and is baptized' etc. *Then comes the other part, which must follow the teachings of the Gospel, namely, what those who believe and are baptized shall do. These, Christ says, ye shall teach to observe all things that I commanded you,* so that all things may be according to my Word, and not according to Jewish law and ceremonies, or any man-made laws pertaining to self-chosen works or religious services.[52]

At this point Luther finally turned to the Anabaptists. It is significant that he had not done this either in his 1522 or 1523 sermons on the same passages. Had either the Zwickau Prophets or Thomas Müntzer based their arguments against infant baptism on Erasmus's interpretation of Christ's Great Commission, as the Swiss Anabaptists did, Luther must surely have addressed them in his earlier sermons. But there is no mention of them in this context. When he does mention them in this his last sermon on the passages in question, he asserted he had already written "against this error of the Anabaptists in former postils and elsewhere."[53]

As he asserted, Luther faced in the Anabaptists, unlike the Catholics, a group intent on abolishing infant baptism. Their agenda was therefore different from that of the Catholics, and so the arguments

91

he had used against the "papists" were not applicable here. More important, in order to attack the Anabaptist argument he was forced to muddy precisely those waters he had sought to clarify in his attack against the Catholics. Thus rather than stressing the "order and sequence of Christ's words" in this context, Luther sought to distinguish between "teaching and baptism." The latter was to be administered only once; "teaching and preaching," since they were more important, had constantly to be done. Nor did he emphasize in this context "whether baptism should be granted before or after teaching."[54] Gone, too, was the emphasis on baptism as the outward sign of faith; and unspoken was his emphasis on the preaching of the gospel as the prerequisite of faith and baptism. Yet he had said earlier,

> Believing means: To hold to be true, and with all the heart to depend on, that which the Gospel and all the articles of faith say about Christ; that he has been sent to us by God the Father, that he suffered, died and rose again and ascended into heaven for the sole reason that we may obtain from God the Father forgiveness of sin and life eternal in his name. That our faith may grasp and hold this the more firmly, he gives us holy baptism, by this visible sign to prove that God the Father will accept us and unfailingly give us that which is offered to us in the Gospel.[55]

No wonder he labeled the Anabaptists a "troublesome . . . sect."[56]

Zwingli, as noted, faced the Anabaptist challenge in a more overtly Erasmian context. He was therefore forced to circumvent the logical inferences of the Erasmian interpretation of the Great Commission that he may himself have drawn earlier in his 1522 letter to the Bishop of Constance. Thus, in his 27 May 1525 treatise on *Baptism, Rebaptism, and Infant Baptism* he wrote: "But then when they counter with Matthew 28 'teach and baptize them,' the consequence will be that they do violence to the Word, for baptism was not instituted at that place."

A few years later, in June of 1527, a written disputation took place in Basel between an Anabaptist by the name of Carlin, Oecolampadius, and Augustin Marius, a Catholic theologian. In that written exchange, Carlin had argued, citing Matthew 28:19-20: "Christ has commanded to preach the gospel and to believe it, thereafter to be baptized. . . . Therefore it is written throughout the histories of the apostles that only the mature people [die alten], who have faith, were baptized, and no child."[57] Here, once again, we see the two aspects of the Erasmian interpretation — the words of Christ as given in Matthew 28, and the interpretation given these words by the apostles. However, Oecolampadius responded to this argument by asserting, as Zwingli had before him, that Christ had not instituted baptism at this place, but in the fourth chapter of the Gospel of John. There one reads: "The Pharisees heard that Jesus was gaining and baptizing more disciples than John, although in fact it was not Jesus who baptized, but his disciples." Oecolampadius attempted to use this passage to prove that the apostles "had gathered a people [volck] for Christ through baptism," clearly signaling that his interpretation was predetermined by his view of a Christian society. He confirmed this by speaking of "einer gemeinen christenheit,"[58] and asserting that "should it come to pass that one no longer baptizes children with our external sign, then the number of visible Christians will immediately decline. That is a very important consideration."[59] His other arguments, as even the Catholic Marius pointed out, were not biblically based either, for the Bible was too severe even for them![60]

Marius, though critical of Oecolampadius's argument, also attempted to refute Carlin's argument in favor of believer's baptism drawn from Christ's Great Commission. He did so by rejecting the word "only" in Carlin's assertion that the apostles had *only* baptized mature adults upon their confession of faith. The case of Cornelius in Acts 10 clearly indicated, at least for him, that the apostles had baptized whole households, among which there must surely have been children.[61]

How widespread the awareness of the Anabaptist use of this argument was can be seen even from John Eck's *Enchiridion*. He, too, argued that in response to all of the Protestant and Catholic attacks on the Anabaptist teaching of believer's baptism, the latter responded by citing Matthew 28 and Mark 16, and then citing the examples of apostolic baptisms in the Acts of the Apostles — Eck citing the passage in Acts 10 dealing with Cornelius the Centurion.[62] Eck was also aware that the Anabaptists argued that infant baptism had begun with Pope Nicholas. But he countered all of their arguments essentially on the authority of Dionysius the Areopagite, whom even he, despite the skepticism of a Lorenzo Valla, deemed to have lived at the time of the apostles![63] Thus he could argue:

93

St. Dionysius, in [his book] on Church Leadership and Rule, writes concerning infant baptism: as our gracious captains (that is how he called the apostles) thought about the issue, they came to the conclusion that it would be good to admit children to baptism, but in this fashion, that the natural parents of the child turn the child over to a master [teacher] of spiritual things, from whom the bishop — once he has promised to train the child in a godly life — requires that he respond to the [baptismal] questions and also confesses the faith. Behold, already at the time of the apostles there were godfathers who confessed in the place of the child: I reject, I believe, etc.[64]

Dionysius, as the presumed contemporary of the apostles, was therefore an unimpeachable witness to the apostolic origin of infant baptism and the practice of having godparents answer for the mute child. The authority of Augustine, Jerome, and others was simply icing on the Catholic cake.

Like Marius and Eck, Protestant theologians, as we have already noted, were forced to come to grips with the Anabaptist argument derived from Erasmus; and that argument continued to trouble them for years to come. This can be seen in the writings of both Henry Bullinger and John Calvin, to name only two of the most important. And like Marius and Eck, they felt compelled to attempt to refute this interpretation when they discussed Christ's Great Commission. Bullinger did so in the following manner:

Now on the contrary part the anabaptists do contend, that none is to be baptized, but he alone which both is able to be taught, and to believe, yea, and make confession of his faith also. And for affirmation of this thing they bring these sayings of our Saviour: out of St. Matthew, 'Go ye therefore, and teach all nations, baptizing them in the name of the Father,' Ec.: out of Mark, 'Go ye into the whole world, and preach the gospel to all creatures: he which shall believe and be baptized, shall be saved,' Ec. Behold, they say, teaching goeth before baptism; therefore they that are not able to be taught ought not to be baptized. Furthermore, to believe goeth before, and to baptize followeth after: infants do not believe, therefore they are not to be baptized. Upon all these they heap up out of the Acts of the Apostles examples, which prove that the faithful, that is to say, they that confess the faith, were baptized of the apostles. They reckon up also the newly-instructed Christians of the old time, to whom, say they, there had been no place given, if they had baptized infants.[65]

Even John Calvin drew attention to this Anabaptist argument in his at times *ad hominem* commentary on the *Schleitheim Confession,*[66] in his commentaries on the harmony of the Gospels of Matthew, Mark, and Luke, as well as in his commentary on the Acts of the Apostles. In the harmony he wrote: "But as Christ enjoins them [the apostles] to teach before baptizing, and desires that none but *believers* shall be admitted to *baptism,* it would appear that *baptism* is not properly administered unless when it is preceded by faith. On this pretence, the *Anabaptists* have stormed greatly against infant baptism."[67] Calvin did not refer to the Anabaptists in his commentary on Peter's Pentecost sermon, but he did so on the passage in Acts 8 dealing with Philip and the Ethiopian eunuch, the passage in Acts 10 dealing with Cornelius, and the passage in Acts 19 dealing with the rebaptism by Paul of the twelve Ephesian disciples of John the Baptist.[68] Only in his *Institutes of the Christian Religion* does he appear to refer to the manner in which the Anabaptists, following Erasmus, interpreted the Great Commission through the baptismal passages in the Acts of the Apostles. There, arguing that scriptural statements referring to adults should not automatically be applied to children, Calvin wrote:

Now they come to the practice and custom of the apostolic age, where they find that no one was admitted to baptism who had not previously professed his faith and repentance. For when those who had a mind to repent asked Peter what they should do, he advised them first to repent, then to be baptized for the forgiveness of sins [Acts 2:37-38]. Similarly, Philip, when the eunuch asked to be baptized, answered that he could be, provided he believed with all his heart [Acts 8:37]. From this they seem able to make their point that baptism, unless preceded by faith and repentance, is unlawfully granted to anyone.[69]

But even here Calvin did not refer to the manner in which the Anabaptists, following Erasmus, interpreted the Great Commission through the baptismal passages in the Acts of the Apostles, or read the latter passages in the light of Christ's Great Commission, as did Bullinger and Eck.

The evidence is ample to indicate that believer's baptism in the age of the Reformation originated from Erasmus's 1522 preface to his New Testament, his paraphrase of Christ's Great Commission, and his annotations to the New Testament, though doubts regarding the validity of infant baptism were clearly raised by Luther's writings and by his mystical "followers." This evidence comes from Erasmus, the Anabaptists, and their Protestant and Catholic opponents. What is more, if Cuneo is right in his assertion that the Matthew 28 passage was cited nearly exclusively with reference to the correct baptismal *formula,* that is, the trinitarian formula, prior to and even after the Reformation, then the interpretation we have been discussing could have come only from Erasmus.[70] And the fact that the argument can be found among the Swiss Brethren, the South German Anabaptists, the Hutterites, Rothmann, and Menno Simons, as well as the Hessian Anabaptists after 1531, indicates that it was regarded by this wing of the Anabaptists as the most important evidence for their position. It was in all probability mediated to the followers of Zwingli by the latter himself and was viewed as persuasive by both Swiss and South German Reformers before 1525. It may also have played a very important role in Wittenberg. One must therefore regard the Erasmian argument as the primary, if not the sole, source of the intellectual impetus for the Reformation debate about adult baptism as opposed to the rejection of infact baptism and, therefore, also of Swiss and South German Anabaptist origins.

This fact broadens the issue far beyond the "sectarian" confines of the relatively small dissident group in Zurich. It also puts into serious doubt the recent "polygenesis" argument, for it is not as though there were three different strands that fed into Anabaptism. What happened was that persons or groups from different traditions reacted in somewhat different ways to this one intellectual stimulus — if they encountered it — that had its origin in Erasmus. The polygenesis thesis, the outgrowth of James Stayer's, Werner Packull's, and Klaus Deppermann's historiographic analysis of the studies dealing with the problem of the origins of the Radical Reformation, is in fact the product of the attempt to make sense out of the conflicting schools of thought that have sought to use the history of Anabaptism to interpret the movement for their own ends or to vilify it. Thus

Bullinger and the age of the Reformation focused on Thomas Müntzer as the father of the movement and Münster as the natural outcome; Marxist and social historians have simply reversed the sixteenth-century value judgments. Baptist historians, aside from those tinged with socialist leanings, have chosen Hubmaier as the most authentic Anabaptist. Liberal Dutch and North German Mennonites of the nineteenth century preferred Hans Denck or even Adam Pastor to Menno Simons. Conservative American Mennonites have favored the Swiss Brethren and Menno Simons as the "normative" Anabaptists. The polygenesis thesis has appeared to legitimate this "Whig" approach to Anabaptism so that even some Mennonites, who run the gamut from conservative to liberal in their theology, have taken solace in the theory.[71]

5

Implementing the "Great Commission"

Hence the words of Christ [in the Great Commission] declare, that teaching must take place before and after baptism, in order that the person baptized may use diligence to observe, after baptism, the Gospel (which was presented to him before baptism), and all things commanded him; for he is no more lord over himself; but, as a bride surrenders herself to her bridegroom, so he, after receiving baptism, surrenders himself to Christ, and loses his will, is resigned in all things, without name, without will, but leaving the name to Christ, and letting Him reign in him. For this is the signification of baptism, that the Christian's life is nothing but pure dying and suffering; because we are like unto the image of Christ, and baptized with Him, must die and suffer, if we would reign and live with Him. Rom. 6:4.

Thomas van Imbroeck, *Confession,* 1558

Not only is the Great Commission as interpreted by Erasmus the key to the problem of the *intellectual origins* of Anabaptism; it is also the key to understanding the movement as a whole. As early as 1952, Franklin Littell asserted that "no texts appear more frequently [than Matt. 28 and Mark 16] in the confessions of faith and court testimonies of the Anabaptists, and none show more clearly the degree to which Anabaptism was different in conviction and type from the intact and stable ways of magisterial Protestantism."[1] This is a clear indication that Anabaptists held the Great Commission to contain the essence of Christ's legacy to his disciples. In this last will and testament, the sequence of Christ's words was, as even Luther had observed in opposition to the "papists," of determinative importance.

Christ had prefaced his remarks in the Great Commission with the assertion that *all authority in heaven and earth* had been given him. Combined with Psalm 24:1 ("The earth is the Lord's, and everything in it, the world, and all who live in it"), which the Anabaptists cited nearly as frequently as Matthew 28 and Mark 16,[2] these assertions indicated to them, as they had to Erasmus, that Christ wished his followers to go forth in his power to reconquer what rightly belonged to him. Because the earth belonged to Christ, the apostles had been commanded to go forth into all the world to preach Christ's gospel. At the very inception of the Anabaptist movement, Valentin Gredig based their missionary activity on this command of Christ. "Nothing else has motivated us to take this step [baptize believers] than the plain Word of God which states very clearly: 'Go to all nations, teach and baptize them; whoever believes and is baptized will be saved.'"[3]

A number of scholars have emphasized this connection between the Great Commission and the missionary activity of the Anabaptists.[4] In this respect the Anabaptists differed from the magisterial Reformers with their territorial churches. The earth, said the Anabaptists, did not belong to the temporal rulers, nor even to the established churches. It belonged to Christ and he had commanded his followers — not merely the professional clerics — to proclaim his teachings. As Menno Simons put it: "But after it had all been accomplished according to the Scriptures, and had been made new in Christ, He did not send out the scribes and Pharisees with Moses' law, but His disciples with His own doctrine, saying: Go ye into all the world."[5]

As the apostles went out "into all the world," they were to "preach the good news to all creation." What was to be subsumed under the term, "good news"? According to Erasmus, as we have seen, the "good news" consisted of the essentials of the Christian faith; and Hubmaier was therefore correct in asserting that Erasmus had, in essence, enunciated the doctrines contained in the *Symbolum Apostolorum* — the Apostles' Creed. But within these teachings, Erasmus could also isolate the teachings about Christ, as he did in his paraphrase of the Acts 8 passage dealing with Philip and the Ethiopian eunuch.

Only when the listeners had accepted these tenets of the Christian faith could they be baptized. Erasmus, as well as his Anabaptist interpreters, knew full well that Christian dogma was an essential aspect of the apostolic message. And his paraphrases would appear to indicate that when he spoke of eliminating the "non-essentials" of the faith, he was referring to Catholic ceremonies, human additions to the gospel, and the like.[6] This was not an "undogmatic" Christianity that either Erasmus or the Anabaptists preached;[7] nor, therefore, was the Anabaptist emphasis primarily on the "existential" aspects of the Christian faith, as Robert Friedmann has argued.[8] Neither was the emphasis simply on the ethical and nonviolent imperatives of Christ's teachings that Bender emphasized in his classic essay. We should reject such arguments as half truths at best; at worst, as false.[9]

For no matter where one looks in the early writings of the Anabaptists, it is not the theology of the Reformers that is criticized, though, like Erasmus, they did not wish to go beyond those clear doctrines needed *ad salutem* into abstracted theological formulations. What they objected to was that Reformation theology did not lead to reform — that is, it was not implemented. They wished to provide the transformation of the institutional church and Christian life in order to complement the new theology — to bring them into conformity with the new "apostolic theology." They began with the observations of Erasmus and Thomas More that, over the centuries, the Catholic church had "accommodated" its teachings to justify and rationalize people's wicked ways, because humans — as More put it in his *Utopia* — would not conform their life to Christ's teachings.[10] If, however, Christ's teachings had once again been resurrected in all their purity — as Luther repeatedly asserted — should not the life, the ceremonies, indeed the very institution of the church itself be brought, once again as in apostolic times, into conformity, into congruence with those apostolic teachings? Surely, one could not simply pour this new theology into liturgical forms that had gradually emerged out of an accommodation of Christ's teachings to the evil customs of humans. This is an aspect of sixteenth-century radical Christianity common not only to Swiss/South German Anabaptism, but also to Menno Simons and even Thomas Müntzer, though the latter assumed Luther's theology to be — like his own — mystical in nature.

The following passages would tend to confirm the assertion that

Anabaptists assumed the renewal of theology through the Reformers. The *Hutterite Chronicle* observed: "But because God wanted his own people separated from the others he desired to bring back the true morning star, the light of his truth in all its brilliance, in the best age of this world, especially in the German nation and other lands, through his Word."[11] Menno Simons wrote in his *Fundamentboek* of 1539, specifically with respect to Luther and baptism: "It appears to me, to be a great error in this learned man, through whose writings at first the Lord effected much good, that he maintained that children, without knowledge and understanding, had faith, while the Scriptures teach so plainly. . . ."[12]

To a degree, at least, the Reformers recognized the legitimacy of the radical position. In the debates between Anabaptists and Reformed theologians in Switzerland in the 1530s, the Reformers remarked: "You are one with us in your belief that there is only one holy and Christian church, that is, one fellowship of the saints; and where one teaches repentance, remorse, conversion of life, castigates sin, etc., there is the true church. But that you declare that no unclean thing, no sin nor filth shall be found in it, we cannot accept."[13] Therefore, the Reformers recognized the essentially Protestant position of Anabaptist theology, aside from that held by individuals such as Hans Denck, Hans Hut, and Melchior Rinck and Menno's ideas on the incarnation.[14] What may have given rise to the assumption that Anabaptists were more "undogmatic" than the Reformers, or that they focused more on Christ's teachings than on the teachings about Christ, is a characteristic that can be seen in many of the later Anabaptist debates with Reformers.

Although Anabaptists knew their Bibles exceptionally well, they were not, with few notable exceptions, sophisticated or trained theologians, unlike many of their opponents. Therefore, one of the striking elements of both the Frankenthal Disputation (1571) and that of Emden (1578) is the unwillingness of the Anabaptists to allow themselves to become involved in any discussion of theology that could not be specifically proven by reference to Scripture. Repeatedly they turned back arguments that seemed intended to lead them beyond the explicit and apparent meaning of the biblical text. Repeatedly they would say that they were content to rest their case on the apparent meaning of the scriptural texts and not go beyond them. This does not mean that they had no theology, that theirs was an "undogmatic"

Christianity, or that they emphasized only the life of the Christian —
as the *Schleitheim Confession* might appear to do. What it does mean is
that they were hesitant, indeed afraid, to stray beyond the apparent
biblical meaning into abstracted theological positions reached by reason. Perhaps, unlike Luther who borrowed the phrase "Scripture and
right reason" from Augustine, Anabaptists settled for *Scripture alone*
and refused to follow the rationalized theological formulations of the
Reformers.[15]

One more aspect of Anabaptist thought deserves mention in the
above context. In his attempt to discover how the apostles had interpreted Christ's Great Commission, Erasmus had turned to such passages as Acts 2, 8, 10, and 19. Those passages not only provided
examples of believer's baptisms; they also presented examples of what
the apostles had taught. We have already noted that Erasmus set these
passages into the context of Christ's Great Commission. This meant
that what the apostles had preached on those occasions had constituted
the essential Christian message mandated by Christ. What, then, had
St. Peter taught in his Pentecost sermon recorded in Acts 2?

Peter began by quoting Old Testament prophecies that appeared
to be in the process of being fulfilled before their very eyes.[16] Then
he proclaimed to them Jesus as "a man accredited by God . . . through
miracles, wonders and signs," which had been performed in their
midst. By God's predestined purpose, they had crucified this Christ.
"But God raised him from the dead, freeing him from the agony of
death, because it was impossible for death to keep its hold on him."
After citing King David's predictions regarding these things, Peter
declared that the apostles were all witnesses to the fact that God had
raised Christ from the dead. This Christ had now been exalted to the
right hand of God and from him "had received the promised Holy
Spirit and has poured out what you now see and hear." All of the
other Acts passages that Erasmus cited carried essentially the same
message, Acts 8 in Erasmus's paraphrase more clearly than any of the
others. This, then, according to the Erasmian view, had to be the heart
of the Christian message.

Menno Simons appears to have echoed both the Erasmian argument about the relationship between the Great Commission and
the apostles' interpretation of it, together with the message it contained, in the following striking passage taken from his *Meditations on
the 25th Psalm* (1537):

Thou didst send thy beloved Son, the dear pledge of thy grace, who preached thy word, fulfilled thy righteousness, accomplished thy will, bore our sins, blotted them out with his blood, and brought about reconciliation; conquered the devil, sin and death, and obtained grace, mercy, favor and peace for all who truly believe on him; his command is eternal life; he sent out his messengers, ministers and apostles of peace, who spread this grace abroad through all the world; who shone as bright, burning torches before all, that they might lead me and all erring sinners to the true way. O Lord, not unto me, but unto thee be praise and honor; *their words I love; their usages I observe.*[17]

This was the message brought by the apostles. What had they expected their listeners to do about it? In his paraphrase of the Great Commission Erasmus had said: "After you have *taught* the people these things and they have *believed* what you have taught them, have *repented* of their prior life, and are ready henceforth to *walk according to evangelical doctrine,* then immerse them in water." What Erasmus was referring to was the very thing Peter had emphasized in his Pentecost sermon. When his listeners, convicted of their complicity in Christ's crucifixion, asked: "Brothers, what shall we do?" Peter replied, "Repent and be baptized everyone of you, in the name of Jesus Christ for the forgiveness of your sins." Whereupon the writer remarked: "Those who accepted [Peter's] message were baptized."

It is apparent from his paraphrase, however, that Erasmus elaborated on Peter's insistence upon repentance from his hearers, for he inserted the words: "and are ready to walk according to evangelical doctrine." Clearly, Erasmus was talking in terms of conversion — repenting of one's previous life and then conforming it to Christ's teachings, turning around and walking in the opposite direction. Such a conversion, however, quite apparently was not based on Christ's ethical teachings; it was rather based on faith in Christ as God's sacrifice for sin and the implication this had for the sinner; it was based on the message and fact of Christ's death and resurrection and, as can be seen from Mantz's *Protestation,* was effected by the coming of the Holy Spirit.

This emphasis on conversion is quite apparent in the Erasmian passages dealing with the examples of baptism in Acts. Repeatedly, as we have seen, Erasmus remarked on the radical transformation of the people being baptized, arguing that such transformations could only be the result of some "celestial power." This emphasis, so similar to that in early monasticism,[18] can be seen throughout Anabaptism. Felix Mantz wrote in his *Protestation:* "and that forgiveness of sins in his name should be given to everyone who, believing in his name, does righteous works from a changed heart."[19] The *Schleitheim Confession* observed: "Baptism shall be given to all those who have been taught *repentance and amendment of life* and [who] truly believe that their sins are taken away through Christ, and to all those who desire to walk in the resurrection of Jesus Christ and be buried with him in death, so that they might rise with him."[20] The reference to Romans 6:4 is unmistakable. Here conversion is spoken of in terms of dying to sin and being raised to "newness of life." And in the Swiss debates of the 1530s the Anabaptists, citing John 3, remarked: "Unless a man be born again he cannot enter into the kingdom of God."[21] Conrad Grebel wrote, as early as his September 1524 letter to Thomas Müntzer: "The Scripture describes baptism for us thus, that it signifies that, by faith and the blood of Christ, sins have been washed away from him who is baptized, changes his mind, and believes before and after; that it signifies that a man is dead to sin and walks in newness of life and spirit, and that he shall certainly be saved if, according to this meaning, by inner baptism [conversion] he lives his faith."[22]

The practical consequences of this emphasis can perhaps best be seen in Menno Simons's own conversion. In his autobiography he speaks of his intellectual development: his initial doubts about the Catholic mass in 1525; his questioning of infant baptism in 1531. Not able to resolve these doubts, even with the help of his spiritual superior or the Reformers, Menno turned to the Bible, studying it diligently until, by 1534, he knew it exceptionally well. He became adept at debating opponents, especially the Münsterites. He acquired a great deal of biblical and theological knowledge. But at the height of the Münsterite crisis, at the time when his own brother was executed as a result of the revolt at the Old Cloister, and he had just denounced — or was in the process of denouncing — Jan of Leiden in his "Against the Blasphemy of Jan of Leiden," Menno called to mind Christ's story of the person who readily recognized the "mote" in the brother's eye but remained oblivious to the "beam" in his own, and was convicted of his own hypocrisy. He knew better than all the rest, but for his ease and convenience he had remained in the Catholic

Church: When he realized this — and it must have struck him with considerable force — he submitted his volition, his will, not only his mind, to Christ. He brought practice into conformity with profession and cast his lot with the despised followers of Münster and took upon himself, as he put it, the cross of Christ, suffering persecution for the rest of his life.[23] In the words of Felix Mantz, Menno had received a "changed heart."

Teaching, acceptance, conversion, and transformation — then baptism. As Erasmus outlined the process: "have believed what you have taught them, have repented of their prior life, and are ready henceforth to walk according to the evangelical doctrine, then immerse them in water." The candidate for baptism was to have integrated faith and practice, to walk in accordance with evangelical doctrine, already before baptism. It was not enough to know and give intellectual assent to a creedal statement; one had to be raised to "newness of life." Hence the *Schleitheim Confession* observed: "we have no fellowship with [the evil ones in the world] and do not run with them in the confusion of their abominations."[24]

This emphasis on the correct sequence to be observed in the process of becoming a disciple of Christ is made explicit in the writings of a considerable number of Anabaptist leaders. Like Erasmus, and Luther when opposing the "papists," they were agreed that the first injunction to "teach" in Christ's Great Commission entailed teaching the "good news" of the gospel. Luther had argued that it meant to teach "how they [the heathen and the Jews] must be saved." Once they believed this "good news" of the gospel and had repented their previous life, he continued, they were to be baptized, "making them disciples or Christians." Only then was it proper for these new followers of Christ to be taught that "which must follow the teaching of the gospel" — namely, that believers were to "obey everything I have commanded you."[25] For, Luther concluded, where "faith is absent, all our good works . . . count for naught before God." Indeed, without faith in Christ, good works were impossible.[26] Before Luther encountered the Anabaptists, therefore, he opposed calling people to "obey everything I have commanded you" before they had accepted the gospel message. Even Erasmus observed in his paraphrase of the passage: "Teach them that are to be baptized the rudiments and first beginnings of the gospel. For if a man does not believe these, he is baptized in vain. Those who have been baptized you must teach to

105

live in accordance with my teachings, [so that they may] constantly proceed to ever greater perfection."[27]

This same distinction is also clearly evident, sometimes explicitly so, in the writings of the Swiss, South German, Dutch, and Hessian Anabaptists.[28] In their debates with representatives of the Swiss Reformed Church in the 1530s, for example, the Swiss Brethren repeatedly made the case for such a distinction, emphasizing the preaching of the gospel before conversion and baptism.[29] And Bernard Rothmann, in his *Confession Concerning the Two Sacraments* (1533), written before he came under the influence of Hoffman's disciples in February of 1534, observed:

> Therefore one must also note in this connection, that one is told to teach before and after, and that baptism is correctly placed between the two. The meaning of this is as follows: because everyone, in his natural state, is ignorant of spiritual matters, people must be brought to an understanding of the gospel and to faith in it — as the Scripture indicates — before they are able to accomplish anything in spiritual matters. Therefore a person must first be taught the gospel and, through its illumination, be brought to an understanding of Christ and the will of God. This, then, constitutes the first teaching: that the gospel is proclaimed to all creatures and salvation offered to everyone. This is included in the words: "Teach all nations." Wherever the Holy Spirit thereupon touches a human heart, so that he believes the gospel, there a child of God is born. Such a birth is witnessed to and confirmed in baptism, as shall yet be noted.
>
> Now that other teaching which follows baptism, that is that the born again and baptized children of God be taught to "observe everything Christ has commanded them . . ." may follow.[30]

Dirk Philips, Menno Simons's closest co-worker, made the same distinction in his confession of faith, stating:

> This is our Lord's true and immutable institution and order with respect to baptism, as Christ's words in the passages cited from both gospels [Matt. 28 and Mark 16] clearly indicate and attest, namely: that the teaching of the gospel must take place before and after baptism, in order that everyone may arrive at a true faith in the

teaching of the gospel through the grace of God and be baptized upon his confession of faith (Acts 2, 8); even then he must thereafter be constantly exposed to God's Word and seek to obey all of Christ's commands. For thus Christ spoke to his disciples: teach them (namely those who believe and are baptized) to obey everything I have commanded you.[31]

And Thomas van Imbroeck, in his 1558 confession of faith — which along with Dirk Philips's confession must have had a wide circulation among Dutch Anabaptists — said virtually the same thing.[32]

As we noted earlier, this differentiation between what was to be taught before baptism and what was to be taught after could be legitimately emphasized by Luther and the other Reformers in their attacks on the Catholic Church's teachings. But when the Anabaptists challenged them on the matter of infant baptism in this connection, they often attempted to blur the distinctions, arguing, as did Valentin Breul, that "there are good reasons to hold that the apostles were supposed to teach and baptize or baptize and teach, so that, in sum, the text has been interpreted more often against than for the Anabaptist [position], and that their arguments are without foundation."[33] Even Luther, who had been so careful in his analysis in opposition to the "papists," when dealing with the Anabaptists, said: "It is not stated here whether baptism should be administered before or after teaching, but may God grant that the office of preaching should be exercised above everything else; then baptism will follow."[34] If, like Zwingli, the Reformers conceded that the Great Commission did indeed mandate baptism upon confession of faith in the gospel, they either argued that Christ had not instituted baptism at this point in time, or like Bullinger and Calvin, contended that the passage only referred to the early period of the church when there were as yet no Christian families. They did not explain, however, why it was that many Christians had refused to have their children baptized for centuries after the foundation of the church.[35]

The Anabaptists may have regarded baptism as a significant milestone in the process of becoming a disciple of Christ; it was not its culmination, however. As we have seen, the Christian still had to be taught to "obey everything [Christ] had commanded." Christ had commanded his disciples to go out to preach, baptize, and make disciples. The latter entailed, according to the Great Commission, getting the baptized members to obey everything Christ had commanded. Such total obedience was not to be taken for granted, nor would it take place over night; it was a gradual process in which the apostolic church played a significant role as it gathered converts into fellowship with itself. The message before baptism contained the "good news" of the gospel and concentrated on the work of Christ; the teaching that followed baptism concentrated on getting believers to obey everything that Christ had commanded. Those baptized on their faith in Christ were now to be taught to fulfill all of Christ's commands. Seen within the context of the Great Commission, discipleship — *Nachfolge Christi* — could not be based on an "undogmatic" Christianity. Nor could it consist merely of an ethical view of the Christian life, with Christ as the great teacher. On the contrary, discipleship — entailing obedience to all of Christ's commandments — was based on a life-transforming experience resulting from faith in the risen Christ. It encompassed living a nonviolent life of Christian love in which even the "sword" and "retaliation," swearing an oath, and other "worldly" actions were to be sacrificed to "the way of the cross."[36]

At the heart of this interpretation of Christ's Great Commission lay the Anabaptist premise — perhaps also a legacy derived from Christian humanism, though without the latter's Neoplatonic overtones — that a necessary congruence existed between beliefs and actions. Erasmus implied as much when he wrote in his *Enchiridion* that "too many theologians only make matters worse by *adapting* the words of Scripture to the justification of their own crimes. It is indeed a sad state of affairs when we have given to vices the names of virtues, when we are more diligent in defending our vices than in correcting them, and when we even turn to Scripture to condone them."[37] Instead, one was to act in accordance with what Zwingli, with reference to the Great Commission, wrote to the Bishop of Constance on 2 June 1522: "We are aware that our life differs all too widely from the pattern of the Gospel, but is the Gospel on that account to be done away with? Ought we not rather to devote ourselves vigorously to correcting our faults according to its standards and to subduing our feebleness . . . ?"[38] Since the gospel had been restored, Christian life had to be brought into conformity with its teachings. The Catholic Church, More asserted in his *Utopia,* had turned the process on its head, for "seeing that men [would] not fit their ways to Christ's pattern, the preachers [had] fitted his teaching to human customs, to get agreement somehow or other."[39] Under these circumstances, the teachings of the "modern" church could in no way be the criteria by which one judged Christian truth. Instead, life and church had once more — as in apostolic times — to be brought into conformity with Christ's teachings.

Enunciated with considerable clarity by Grebel in his letter of September 1524 to Thomas Müntzer,[40] this principle of congruence between faith and practice, indeed apostolic faith and apostolic practice, became the guiding principle of the entire movement. On a personal level it led to an emphasis on Christian discipleship; on an institutional level, to an emphasis on the recovery of the practices of the apostolic church. Thus Menno could say of the apostles: "Their words I love, their practices I follow."[41] And he could continue: "I have taught no other baptism, no other supper, no other ordinance than that sanctioned by the unerring word of our Lord Jesus Christ, and the declared example and usages of the holy apostles, to say nothing of the superabundant evidence of the historians and learned of both the primitive and the present church. . . . *Does not the whole Scripture teach, that Christ is the truth, and shall abide forever? Is not the apostolic church the true Christian church?*"[42] Based on the assumption that the apostolic church was the true Christian church, Zwingli's radical followers came to him shortly before their final break with him, as he himself reported, saying:

> It does not escape us that there will ever be those who will oppose the gospel, even among those who boast in the name of Christ. We therefore can never hope that all minds will so unite as Christians should find it possible to live. For in the Acts of the Apostles those who believed seceded from the others, and then it happened that they who came to believe went over to those who were now a new church. *So then must we do:* they beg that we make a deliverance to this effect — *they who wish to follow Christ should stand on our side.*[43]

But Zwingli countered with the argument that "the example of the apostles was not applicable here, for those from whom they withdrew did not confess Christ, but now ours [their followers] did."[44] What was applicable, Zwingli contended, was Augustine's or the church's interpretation — or misinterpretation — of the Parable of the Tares.

And so he informed his erstwhile followers that Christ had addressed such "new beginnings" as theirs, commanding them "to let the tares grow with the grain until the day of harvest." This reflected Augustine's argument that the "field" into which the tares had been sown was the church. But already the Donatists, who had confronted him on the issue at the 411 Council of Carthage, asserted that Christ had himself said — in response to his disciples' query — that the "field" signified the "world." Almost immediately Augustine had begun to seek to convince his audience that the church had, at least to a large extent, become the world and so the parable now also applied to it.[45] Like Augustine, Zwingli too rejected the model of the apostolic church because of his desire — perhaps even his perceived necessity — to accommodate his concept of the church to the present reality. Anabaptists rejected this accommodation. As far as they were concerned, the apostolic church was the norm established by Christ and his apostles for all time. Times might change, but never Christ or his church.

6

Conclusion

Every elector, prince, prelate, count and other estate of the realm shall, with all due diligence, so order and decree that all preachers in his territory are justly and equitably advised to avoid everything that might lead to disobedience, dissension and revolt in the holy empire or that might cause Christians to be led astray [in their faith]. Instead, they are to preach and teach only the holy Gospel and that in accordance with the interpretation of the Scriptures as approved by the holy Christian Church.

The Edict of Nuremberg, 1523

If nearly all of those interested in the reform of the church read Erasmus's paraphrases of the last chapter of Matthew and the Acts of the Apostles, and understood the manner in which he related the baptismal passages in the latter to Christ's Great Commission, and if those who read them were initially persuaded of the validity of his approach, why did many change their minds during the years 1523-1525? The answer would appear to lie in a passage from the Edict of Nuremberg (6 March 1523), which reflected the reform policy of Frederick the Wise.[1]

I noted earlier that whereas Frederick was unwilling to allow Luther to be muzzled or the preaching of the "holy Gospel" to be inhibited, he refused to allow Carlstadt's introduction of an evangelical

111

mass on Christmas day 1521 to stand or to accommodate Melanchthon's desire to discuss the issue of infant baptism in a Leipzig-like disputation. Any visible changes in the church's ritual, he feared, would result in imperial intervention in his internal affairs — as indeed happened on 20 January 1522 with the empire's response to Carlstadt's innovations. Only if such changes were to be recommended by a universal church council would Frederick allow them.

Through Hans von der Planitz, his representative on the Imperial Governing Council established by the Diet of Worms, and the proto-Lutheran Hans von Schwarzenburg, Frederick saw his reform policy become the policy of the realm in the Nuremberg Edict, issued on 6 March 1523. It proclaimed "that every elector, prince, prelate, count and other estate in the realm shall, with all due diligence, so order and decree that all preachers in his territory are justly and equitably advised to avoid everything that might lead to disobedience, dissention and revolt in the holy empire or that might cause Christians to be led astray [in their faith]. Instead, they are to preach and teach only the holy Gospel and that in accordance with the interpretation of the Scriptures approved by the holy Christian church."[2]

It merits mention at this point that the assumption behind the promulgation of this edict was the belief that the political authorities were to exercise control over both what was preached and what was practiced in the Christian faith. Having exercised such de facto control for some time already, the political powers of the empire — through the promulgation of the above edict — legalized the exercise of religious powers by the political authorities. When Martin Bucer, in 1530 at the Diet of Augsburg, sought to justify the implementation of the Reformation in Strasbourg on the basis of this edict,[3] however, John Eck responded for the Catholic Church: "As is obvious from the statutes of the holy church which have come down to us from the time of the twelve apostles, such an order [as contained in the edict of 6 March 1523] does not lie within the jurisdiction of the secular power, but belongs to the bishops who have been ordained by God as shepherds."[4] But Eck's objection came far too late, for by 1530 the edict had long since turned the reform of the church over to the territorial lords or the mayors and councils of the Free Imperial Cities, with Reformers like Bucer arguing that the edict formed the *legal* basis upon which their reforms had been based. Depending upon the political authorities, however, the edict could create problems, as it did even for Luther who had initially welcomed its promulgation.[5] For in the end Frederick himself used the edict to coerce Luther into tolerating the full panoply of Catholic ritual and ceremonies in the Wittenberg *Stiftskirche* right under Luther's nose. And since a general church council did not meet until 1545 in Trent — and then was not recognized by the Protestants — the Edict of Nuremberg in effect permanently turned religious affairs over to the political authorities.

With the exception of the Reformation mandate issued by the Zurich city council after the First Zurich Disputation in late January of 1523, all subsequent Reformation initiatives in the empire resulted from the implementation of the Nuremberg edict. Even the Basel and Bernese Reformation decrees were modeled on the Nuremberg edict.[6] Consequently, whereas the Gospel — whether or not "in accordance with the interpretation of the Scriptures approved by the holy Christian church" — was now being preached in reform-friendly cities and territories, no immediate changes in the church's ritual or ceremonies were allowed since these might lead to "disobedience, dissention and revolt." Only when the policy itself — because of growing awareness of the ever-increasing disparity between what was being preached and the Catholic ritual and ceremonies — resulted in severe tensions in the populace, tensions that threatened the very things the edict had been designed to obviate, did city councils like that of Strasbourg begin to seek to bring ritual and ceremony into line with the new preaching of the "holy Gospel." But since no political authority, whether urban or territorial, would have tolerated the separation of church and state — the edict itself being the best evidence for this contention — the apostolic church with its believer's baptism and consequent separation of church and state was anathema. Had Frederick not been able to implement his policy in Saxony or have it realized in the Nuremberg edict for the entire empire, very different church structures might well have emerged. Indeed, some scholars have spoken of the "congregational" church structures that were beginning to emerge in Saxony before Frederick's policy was enforced.[7] This might also have happened in Zurich had not the mayor and city council taken matters into their own hands and promulgated a Reformation mandate after the First Zurich Disputation in January of 1523.

Most Reformers accommodated themselves to the new political reality after the implementation of the Nuremberg edict. Some of their followers did not. Luther objected vehemently to Frederick's policies after late 1523, and did not give in without a struggle. But he did eventually capitulate to Frederick's policy. Those who came to be known as radicals, however, by and large refused to capitulate or to compromise their principles. If the earth was indeed the Lord's and he had commanded his disciples to "go out into all the earth" in order to reclaim it for God, then surely the church was even more his and had to be restored to its apostolic reality.

The Great Commission and the Imperial Edict of Nuremberg: it was here that Christ's commands came into conflict with the ruling political wisdom and reality. The Anabaptist response to that law was very much that of John Eck: the political powers had no authority to promulgate such a law. And once it was passed, they had no right to attempt to coerce people to live in the tension created by preaching the "holy Gospel" but refusing to allow them to bring life, ritual, and ceremonies of the church, indeed its apostolic structure, into conformity with that gospel.

Epilogue

The Erasmian interpretation of Christ's Great Commission has implications for the understanding of the history of Christianity that go well beyond the search for the intellectual origins of Anabaptism. It is the purpose of this epilogue to pursue some of the more obvious of these. I do this with considerable hesitation, knowing full well the pitfalls that await the scholar who dares to venture onto terrain with which he has only a passing familiarity. Yet the implications would appear to be of such moment that I would be remiss were I to ignore them.[1]

The first of these implications touches on the missionary impulse within, and the expansion of, the primitive church. As such, it addresses one of the central themes of the history of the early church, since church historians generally,[2] and historians of missions in the apostolic church in particular,[3] either make no mention of the Great Commission in this context, or argue that it played little or no role in that church's missionary outreach. Michael Green, for example, writes in his book *Evangelism in the Early Church:*

> It is important to stress this prime motive of loving gratitude to God [in evangelism] because it is not infrequently assumed that the direct command of Christ to evangelize was the main driving force behind Christian mission. A great deal is made in some missionary writings of "The Great Commission" in Matthew 28:18-20. No doubt this was important. Obedience to the Lord was the great new commandment Jesus had left to those who loved him: "If you love

115

me, keep my commandments." But in point of fact it is quoted very little in the writings of the second century. Among the Apostolic Fathers it comes only in the spurious recension of Ignatius. Irenaeus quotes it once, in a context where he is speaking about the descent of the Spirit on the Church. This is interesting, for it shows that the command was not seen as a new legalism, the duty incumbent upon all Christians, but rather what Roland Allen called a "spiritual" as opposed to a "legal" command. No sanctions are attached to it. It is rather associated with the promised presence of Christ on mission, which "is not a reward offered to those who obey; it is rather the assurance that those who are commanded will be able to obey."[4]

Because of this, Green asserts, "it would be only a minor loss if the textual doubts surrounding these verses were proved justified, and it could be clearly demonstrated that Jesus never spoke these words."[5] Erasmus would respectfully, but also most forcefully, disagree.

From the latter's reading of the baptismal passages in Acts, from which he inferred the disciples' understanding of Matthew 28:18-20, the Great Commission is determinative. He makes this, as we have had ample occasion to note, more than a little apparent. For in every one of the baptismal passages found in Acts, Erasmus argues that what the apostles said and did took place because Christ had "commanded them [his disciples]: go forth . . . and teach all people, baptizing them, and teaching them to keep everything I have commanded you. Teach them that must be baptized, the rudiments and first beginnings of the gospel. For if a man will not believe these rudiments and principles, his baptism will avail him nothing. And teach those who have already been baptized that they must live in accordance with my teachings, proceeding always to greater perfection."[6] Now, if Erasmus was correct in his belief that the apostles had so profoundly internalized these words of Christ, then Christ's Great Commission lay not only at the very heart of what the disciples did with respect to the propagation of the gospel, but also at the very center of their theological perspective — how they went about establishing Christ's church, what they taught and in what sequence they taught it, whom they admitted into membership in the church, and what was expected of members so admitted. In other words, Erasmus's interpretation of the manner in which the apostles understood Christ's Great Commission goes well beyond any trinitarian baptismal formula or simple missionary or evangelistic imperative. Consequently, although Christ's Great Commission may not have been explicitly referred to or trumpeted abroad at every turn by the apostles as the motivation behind their proclamation of the gospel, it had been so profoundly internalized by them that it permeated every aspect of their activity. Such internalization may be difficult to pass from one generation to another, however, losing little by little the larger context within which the apostles had heard — and understood — Christ's last will and testament.

The latter appears indeed to have happened, for by the time of the Church Fathers the Great Commission had come to be applied in an entirely different context from that found in the Acts of the Apostles.[7] As Michael Green has asserted, Irenaeus cited the passage only once, and that in the context of the descent of the Holy Spirit onto the church. By Tertullian's time the context had changed even more; he was the first to speak of the "formula" of baptism with reference to the Great Commission, saying: "For the law of baptism has been imposed, and the formula prescribed: 'Go,' He says, 'teach the nations, baptizing them into the name of the Father, and of the Son, and of the Holy Spirit.'"[8]

Under Arian attack, then, this emerging emphasis on the trinitarian baptismal formula became critical, for here Christ — as a member of the Trinity — appeared co-equal with God the Father and the Holy Spirit. In this understanding, the issue driving the interpretation of Matthew 28:18-20 was the Arian heresy, not the evangelization of the world or the apostolic understanding as portrayed by Erasmus.

It was from this third/fourth-century Patristic concern for a trinitarian baptismal formula — not from the perspective of the apostles — that F. C. Conybeare addressed the apparent conflict between Matthew 28:19 and the baptismal passages in the Acts of the Apostles. He attempted to resolve this Patristic problem with a nineteenth-century solution proffered by the new higher biblical, or historical, criticism. Proceeding from the assumption that one or the other formula had to be correct, and that the trinitarian formula had become important only with the coming of the Arian heresy, Conybeare concluded that the command to baptize in the name of the Father, Son, and Holy Spirit must have been inserted into the Matthean text only after the trinitarian decisions reached in 325 at the Council of Nicea.[9] However, with his rejection of the trinitarian baptismal formula,

Conybeare also threw out the entire Great Commission — that is, Matthew 28:18-20. This doubt in the authenticity of the entire passage is still fairly widespread even today.[10] However, it is not shared by those writers who have approached the problem from different perspectives. Erasmus, as we have seen, did not even mention this conflict in his analysis; it was unimportant to him. Even Luther, who in his early Reformation years placed such a conspicuous emphasis on faith in relation to baptism, referred to the ongoing debate over the "correct" baptismal formula in the following manner: "Pointless disputes about questions of this kind are raised by those who lay no emphasis on faith; but all on works and the proper rites; whereas we lay all the stress on faith alone, and none on a mere rite; and this makes us free in spirit from all these scrupulosities and distinctions."[11] The perspective from which one viewed this "problem," therefore, was and remains the critical issue, as Luther's remarks make clear. Conybeare's doubts about the passage's authenticity — and the doubts of those who have been influenced by him — must therefore be placed in perspective. For if Erasmus was correct in his understanding, the apostles would have had no occasion to interpret the Great Commission in the manner they did were the passage spurious, or had it been inserted some three hundred years later.

The issue of the correct baptismal formula within the larger issue of the authenticity of the Great Commission — that is, Christ's apparent command to baptize in the name of the Father, Son, and Holy Spirit, and the undisputed apostolic practice of baptizing only in the name of Jesus, as the Acts passages clearly demonstrate — is a separate matter and should be treated as such, as it is in some of the more recent studies. These recent studies suggest that in its original formulation the passage was christological and that Matthew transformed it into a trinitarian form. This would better explain the fact that the apostles, from the beginning, baptized only in the name of Jesus.[12] It would also maintain the integrity of the original message of the Great Commission that Erasmus found to be implemented at every turn in the history of the apostolic church.

The second implication of Erasmus's interpretation has to do with its uniqueness. Reading the interpretations of these passages from the Church Fathers through to Karl Barth and the most recent exegetes,[13] one is forced to the conclusion that no one has interpreted the Great Commission from Erasmus's perspective or arrived at his

118

interpretation. Except for repeated references to the baptismal formula used by the apostles in Acts, no one has taken the larger Erasmian context into consideration in an analysis. All have either sought to interpret the passage in the Matthean context — that is, from below — or through their own concerns with contemporary issues. Thus the Church Fathers read it through the eyes of the Arian controversy; sixteenth-century Catholic apologists sought to exploit it to argue in favor of the church's authority over even the teachings of Christ; Luther read it in terms of his quarrel with the "papists" over the respective merits of faith and works for salvation; modern enthusiasts for missions have read it through the eyes of the great missionary movements of the last two centuries; and modern exegetes attempt to understand it from within Matthew's intellectual world or the documents upon which he may have relied. Erasmus appears to have been the only person to have sought to understand the passage from within a historical context in which the interpretation of Christ's closest followers, his earliest interpreters, was of paramount importance. Combined with his belief that both Christ and the apostles had "made it [life] correspond with confession," he was led to ask how the apostles had put their understanding into action. He discovered this apostolic implementation in the Acts of the Apostles, especially in its baptismal passages.

But why has no one — if this is indeed the case — turned to Erasmus's paraphrases in this, or any other, connection? The answer to that question would appear to lie in the reactions to the great Christian humanist in the age of the Reformation. Lauded as the prince of humanists on the eve of the conflict, Erasmus soon became the center of controversy once the Protestant rupture became apparent. Initially wooed by both sides, he soon came to be reviled by Catholics and Protestants alike, by Catholics despite his attack on Luther over the freedom of the will in 1524. Protestants called him a moral coward unable, or unwilling, to take a decisive stand on the burning issues of the day; Catholics accused him of preparing the way for the Reformers and not doing enough to denounce them once the conflict had raised its ruinous head. Eventually condemned by Catholics and rejected by the Protestants, Erasmus became more and more isolated in his later years. Belittled as a theologian by Catholics and Protestants alike already in the sixteenth century, Erasmus's reputation in this regard has not improved over the years. Why then should serious theological scholars consult this theological dilettante — this "mere grammarian," as his Scholastic critics called him — on any serious matter at all? He never founded a church, never established an Erasmus Society, and what intellectual heirs he left behind were driven, because of the increasing bitterness of the conflict, either into hiding the true meaning of their writings behind obscure language, or opting for one or the other side of the conflict. Even the present Mennonite heirs of the sixteenth-century Anabaptists, who owe him such an immense debt of gratitude with respect to their interpretation of the Great Commission, have sought to distance themselves from the great scholar as much as possible. Only in England where a translation of his paraphrases was prepared and copies placed — or at least mandated to be placed — along with Cranmer's *Book of Common Prayer,* in every "Anglican" parish church by the First Act of Uniformity of 1548, and again under Elizabeth by the Second Act of Conformity of 1559, were they publicly recognized as important.[14] However, no study exists that has attempted to assess their importance for the English Reformation.[15]

If the above is indeed the case and the Anabaptists are the only group to have adopted the Erasmian interpretation of these passages, it must follow that the Anabaptist position itself is unique, and may still be depending upon the extent to which it is held by Mennonites today. Perhaps this is why Mennonites, who still consciously stand in the Anabaptist tradition, feel both attracted to and ill at ease in North American evangelical circles; why they welcome the social emphasis on the gospel in liberal Christian circles but bemoan the lack of an emphasis on Christ, not only as the *deus incarnatus* but also as the *agnus dei* slain for the sins of humankind, an emphasis conspicuously present in Anabaptist writings. It should not surprise us, therefore, to discover that the movement known as Evangelicals for Social Action should have been founded by a person standing in the Anabaptist tradition.[16]

Third, Erasmus's interpretation also has implications for the great divide between conservative and liberal Christians in general and conservative and liberal Mennonites in particular. For not all Mennonites stand in the Anabaptist tradition. As in virtually every other denomination, many Mennonites have come under the same influences that have divided the rest of Christendom into conservative and liberal, into evangelical and rational. Mennonites, too, are therefore to be found on either side of this "Great Divide" in Christendom.

This became painfully apparent in the wake of Ludwig Keller's attempt to persuade European Mennonites to adopt the "undogmatic" Hans Denck as their ideal type in the early 1880s.[17]

Keller, a man influenced by both Pietism and Rationalism — a not uncommon phenomenon in nineteenth-century Germany — was able to integrate, or at least hold in tension, these two seemingly disparate forces in his theology. But when he imposed his synthesis upon Hans Denck in his 1882 biography[18] and sent the latter out into the Mennonite world, the book encountered a readership already divided not only along Pietist and Rationalist lines, but along Anabaptist, Pietist, and Rationalist lines. This became quickly apparent when Keller began looking for a young Mennonite scholar/theologian to write a popular account of Denck's life with which to win Mennonites for Keller's — and ostensibly also for Denck's — cause.

The first man Keller turned to was Christian Neff, newly ordained Mennonite pastor at the Weierhof in 1887. A former theology student at the universities of Erlangen, Berlin, and Tübingen, Neff had his understanding of Anabaptism shaped by his own studies and those of men like Walter Koehler. He later became a co-editor of the *Mennonitisches Lexikon* and wrote one of the first essays on Conrad Grebel in 1925. Thus, although he initially accepted Keller's invitation, within a year he gave up the work, pleading illness and the press of his pastoral duties. Not until his review of Gerhard Haake's *Hans Denck, ein Vorlaeufer der neueren Theologie* in the *Mennonitische Blaetter* some nine years later, however, did he reveal the real reasons for curtailing work on a popular Denck biography. The more he had immersed himself in the latter's writings, he said, "the more I sensed and realized the distance that existed between our religious views."[19]

But if South German Mennonites could not accept Denck's mystical theology, perhaps the more liberal North German Mennonites could. On 10 April 1897, Gerhard Haake, former student at the University of Strasbourg and now Mennonite pastor at Monsheim — but originally a North German Mennonite — contacted Keller in order to gain his consent and assistance for a dissertation on Hans Denck under the direction of Friedrich Nippold. He promised Keller that he would "work totally with your assumptions," and that he wished "to treat him [Denck] as a 'modern' theologian." For, he continued, "At every stage we encounter parallels with Lessing, Schleiermacher, Ritschl, Lipsius, [and] above all with Richard

Rothe" — a veritable "who's who" of nineteenth-century German liberal theology. Little wonder, then, that Haake could describe Denck as a "devout Pietist who earnestly heeds the voice of God in his breast," but not an uncritical one, for his "clear head [and] philosophical endowments" prevented him from getting lost in introspection. He was, said Haake, "Rationalist and Pietist in one person and as such neither of the two." Indeed, he had been a "Schleiermacher amongst the reformers."

Neff was not taken in, however. He wrote in his review: "The above-named work by Haake is, in my opinion, a partisan theological tract in the real sense of the word, from which it is impossible to expect an objective evaluation of Hans Denck. Herr Haake expressly calls himself a student of Lipsius, one of the leading exponents of theological Liberalism in the state church. He confesses himself an adherent of the 'newer,' that is modern Liberal theology. His expositions of Hans Denck's teachings are in accord with these."[20]

Keller's advocacy of Hans Denck, the "undogmatic" mystical Anabaptist, also led him quickly to disparage the "overly dogmatic" Menno Simons. His opposition to Menno reflected a more encompassing opposition to all types of orthodoxy, and especially to the resurgence of Lutheran orthodoxy in the German state churches of the post Franco-Prussian War period. Though Keller sought at first to hide his opposition to Menno, Hinrich van der Smissen, pastor of the Hamburg-Altona church and editor of the *Mennonitische Blaetter,* voiced early suspicions of Keller's motives, wondering, as early as the summer of 1883, whether Keller and his Mennonite admirers envisioned "recommending in favor of a proclamation of Denck's views as the official confession [of faith] and symbol of present-day Mennonites, and thereby indirectly rejecting the older position which appealed more or less completely to the ideas espoused by Menno Simons and the theological positions later developed in conjunction with these?"[21] Given his preference for the "undogmatic" over the "dogmatic," for the "inner Word" over the Bible or the "Written Word," it was no wonder that Keller's legacy led to an extended debate between Dutch and North German Mennonites on the one side, and South German Mennonites on the other, over the issue of biblical authority. For the Dutch and North German Mennonites had long since rejected that authority, as Bernard Brons of Emden, their spokesman, asserted. Referring to his South German "brothers," Brons wrote:

If we in the North go back a few generations in our families we
will discover similar beliefs [in the literal meaning of the Bible].
The difference is that our forefathers have followed the scholarly
research in religious matters with lively interest since the days of
Lessing and Reimarus and, as free and independent thinking people,
regarded the Bible as any other book. In this they shared the view
of Anslo, the old Mennonite preacher made famous in Rembrandt's
portrait, that the "Word of God" was, to be sure, to be found and
contained in the Bible, but that it resided and lived in the hearts of
men and would be retained there even if all the Bibles in the world
were to be destroyed. Precisely this Word of God in the hearts of
mankind is the touchstone of the content of the Bible: if a passage
of the Bible resounds in a pure human heart — in the pages of this
fine instrument — then it is a Word of God; or, to speak with Kant,
what we do we do not as slaves of some divine command, rather
we sense and believe that what we do is in conformity with God's
will if we feel ourselves bound to do it in our own heart and
conscience. For "Christ has freed us to be truly free," and the word
he so often directed against the "holy Scriptures" of his day: "but
I say unto you" also applies to us. That is the spirit that makes alive
in contrast to the letter that kills.[22]

Keller's influence reached even to North America, brought there
by a young South German Mennonite named John Horsch who, in
1885, had come increasingly under Keller's influence. Emigrating to
the United States in late 1886 or early 1887, Horsch sought at first,
through the pages of the *Herold der Wahrheit,* a Mennonite periodical
published by John F. Funk in Elkhart, Indiana, to publish the entire
corpus of what Keller had called the "Old Evangelical" literature.[23]
At the same time, he wrote articles for Mennonite periodicals in which
he promoted Keller's historical studies and sought to get American
Mennonites to adopt Denck's theology. Sometime in the early 1900s,
however, Horsch experienced an intellectual — if not spiritual —
conversion under the auspices of American fundamentalism. Gradually, as a consequence, Keller's preference for the "undogmatic"
Denck over the "dogmatic" Menno came to be reversed in Horsch's
thought. At the same time, he also began to interpret Anabaptism from
a fundamentalist perspective, referring to the "true"[24] — or dogmatic
— Anabaptists as "Anabaptist Fundamentalists."

123

Horsch's conversion to fundamentalism led, for the first time, to a clear-cut intra-Mennonite confrontation between fundamentalists and liberals over the interpretation and meaning of Anabaptism. For no sooner had Horsch returned to the Mennonite Publishing House in 1908 than an essay by his hand appeared in the *Gospel Herald* entitled "The Danger of Liberalism." Reflecting the shift from Denck to Menno, the content mirrored Horsch's move away from *Nachfolge* (discipleship) to an emphasis on the "fundamentals of the Christian religion." In the article he wrote:

> Rationalism, which is but another name for modern unbelief, makes the claim that the Bible is not what it pretends to be, that it was not given by inspiration and is not infallible. Most rationalists believe in God, but as far as man's duty toward God is concerned, they hold that reason is an adequate guide to ascertain it, and that revelation — the Word of God — is not needed. Rationalism teaches the impossibility of a miracle, and therefore denies the greatest of all wonders, namely the deity of our Lord Jesus Christ, as well as his resurrection and the atonement. The preaching of the cross of Christ and of redemption through the blood are stumbling blocks to the liberalist.[25]

By 1911 Horsch had also entered the lists in defense of Menno and the Swiss Brethren, and against the "Liberals" and "modernizers" of Anabaptist history among the Mennonites. In an essay entitled "Die geschichtliche Stellung der Mennoniten in der sog. Modernen Theologie" in the *Mennonitische Blaetter,* Horsch attacked Dr. Appeldoorn, Mennonite pastor in Emden who, in a speech at the 8-10 August *World Congress of a Free Christianity* in Berlin, had characterized the Mennonite church as "undogmatic." According to Appeldoorn, Horsch reported, "it contradicted Mennonite principles to demand belief in the authority of the Bible, the deity of Christ, indeed in the doctrine of salvation as presented in the Bible, as a condition of membership in the church. Every Mennonite was supposed to have the right, as free thinker, to believe whatever he wished, and no congregation could call him to account. This attitude is praised as the only one representative of authentic Mennonitism, as the freedom of religion and tolerance sought after by our fathers." Appeldoorn's was not an isolated opinion, said Horsch; it was broadly representative of Dutch and

North German Mennonites among whom the so-called modern theology was widely disseminated. Their spokespersons had asserted time and again that the adherents of this modern theology were the true spiritual descendants of the fathers of the Mennonite church and that those who believed in Christ did not follow in the footsteps of the old Anabaptists. This was patently false, Horsch charged, for the earliest Anabaptists, the Swiss Brethren of Zurich, had broken with Zwingli because, "according to their conviction, he did not take the practical application of the biblical teachings and requirements seriously enough." There could be no doubt, Horsch proclaimed, "that they recognized the Bible as the Word of God and the sole authority in matters of faith, and that Zwingli's disregard of the biblical commands led to the rupture between them."[26]

What had happened to Hans Denck in the meantime? He was no longer Horsch's hero as he had been in 1890. Denck, Horsch now said, was not to be confused with the Swiss Brethren, for he represented a group that had deviated in significant ways from the founders of the movement. "It cannot be denied," he proclaimed, "that Denck advocated a rationalizing view of the Scriptures; above the written Word of God he placed the 'inner Word'; his doctrine of justification, too, can hardly be described as biblical. And before he died he recanted the necessity of baptism upon confession of faith and regretted that he had helped found a church."[27]

From his attack against the "modernizing" interpreters of Anabaptism, Horsch eventually moved on to the larger issues posed by this "Great Divide" for Christendom as such. He addressed these in his book, *Modern Religious Liberalism,* published in 1921. Then, in 1924, he turned his attention to the "modernists" in the Mennonite Church in his *The Mennonite Church and Modernism.* In his later correspondence with his son-in-law, Harold S. Bender, it becomes quite apparent that Horsch, for a time, believed that even Goshen College was imperiled from the modernist wing of the church.[28]

If Horsch was right, Bender's arrival at Goshen placed him in an emerging struggle between modernists and fundamentalists for the control of the Mennonite theological soul. Horsch clearly wished his son-in-law to rally the standard of fundamentalism at Goshen and he probably assumed that Bender would, like himself, use the study of Anabaptism to do so. Somewhere along the way, however, Bender must have concluded that the polemical and ideological approach to

Anabaptist studies would be counterproductive. Not that Bender was liberal in his theological views — the exchange of letters with his father-in-law in which everything from Anabaptism to the rise of Nazism in Germany is discussed proves his essential agreement with Horsch — but he must have arrived at the conclusion that the best way to navigate the Mennonite ship between the Scylla of fundamentalism and the Charybdis of modernism/liberalism was to return, as fully as possible, to the authentic traditions of the Mennonite Church, but in as neutral a set of theological terms as the situation demanded. He therefore chose to define theology as little as possible and to concentrate, in his classic essay, "The Anabaptist Vision," on discipleship. Had he and his father-in-law been less fearful of humanism in general and of Erasmus in particular,[29] and had he not been caught between Mennonite fundamentalists and modernists, he might have come to see the importance of Erasmus's paraphrases for early Anabaptism. For in the latter, as we have seen, Erasmus sought to resolve the theological conflict of his day by focusing everyone's attention only on those Christian doctrines necessary *ad salutem*. As Hubmaier himself noted, these were contained in the Apostles' Creed. That is why Erasmus paraphrased Christ's command in Matthew 28:18 with: "Teach them that must be baptized the rudiments and first beginnings of the gospel." In the *Inquisitio de Fide,* published the very next year, he developed this approach at considerable length, making apparent in the dialogue between Aulus and Barbatius that, with respect to their belief in the doctrines contained in the Apostles' Creed, there was no difference between Catholics and Lutherans. Limiting — as had even the apostles — the doctrines necessary for salvation to those of the Apostles' Creed was therefore the solution to the conflict between Catholics and emerging Protestants in his day. At the time, however, no one appears to have paid him any heed, perhaps, because as Erasmus himself wrote on occasion: "man suffers from this *almost* congenital disease that he will not give in once a controversy has started." It should have been different in Bender's day, for he at least had a remnant of that original Anabaptist position left with which to work. Yet Bender — faced with a similar theological conflict in his own day — preferred to leave the definition of Anabaptist theology vague, arguing only that it was essentially Protestant since the Swiss Brethren had arisen in Zwingli's Zurich. In doing so, however, he was less helpful than the Erasmus whom he chose to shun.

Horsch's and Bender's struggle, as I have already suggested, was part of a larger conflict within Christendom. It in fact demonstrated that Mennonites were no longer — if they had ever been — a theological island. In this larger context, Erasmus played the "undogmatic" role assigned by Keller to Hans Denck in the Mennonite world. In this world evangelicals have by and large, in the wake of Luther's disparaging comments, rejected Erasmus, whereas more liberal Christians of the last few centuries have attempted to co-opt the great scholar, making him over in their own image, as did Preserved Smith in his 1923 biography.[30] But Erasmus, too, must be understood from within the context of his own time just as he sought to understand the Great Commission from within the context of its own time.

This rift between evangelical and liberal, conservative and modernist, might well be connected to an older division in Christianity symbolized, on the one hand, by those Christians who have taken the position *intellego ut credam* and, on the other, by those who have asserted: *credo ut intellegam.* "I understand (or seek to understand) in order (that I might) believe" is the position of the theological liberal whose faith only goes as far as his reason allows. The evangelical, however, says that one must believe in order to be able to understand. Like the Rationalists of the seventeenth and eighteenth centuries, whose writings laid the foundations for nineteenth-century liberal Christianity, the *intellego ut credam* Christian will accept only those tenets acceptable to reason — the kind of position announced by John Locke when he wrote in *The Reasonableness of Christianity* (1695):

> Thus far the dominion of faith reaches, and that without any violence or hindrance to reason; which is not injured or disturbed, but assisted and improved by new discoveries of truth, coming from the eternal fountain of all knowledge. Whatever God has revealed is certainly true; no doubt can be made of it. This is the proper object of faith: *but whether it be a divine revelation or no, reason must judge. . . . Nothing that is contrary to, or inconsistent with, the clear and self-evident dictates of reason, has a right to be urged or assented to as a matter of faith, wherein reason hath nothing to do.*[31]

Eventually, this position led to an essentially deistic Christianity — a Christianity negating even Erasmus's emphasis on the articles of faith contained in the Apostles' Creed. Instead, adherents came to stress the ethical teachings of Christ. For some of these rational Christians, Christ might still be a son of God, but he was no longer *the* Son of God.[32] Therefore his death and ostensible resurrection had to be explained in the naturalistic terms of a Schleiermacher, or rejected outright as David Friedrich Strauss did in his *Leben Jesu* of 1836.

But Anabaptists insisted that Christian ethics, Christ's injunction in Matthew 28:20 to "teach them to obey everything I have commanded you," could only be fulfilled by persons who believed the article in the Apostles' Creed regarding Christ, who responded to it in repentance and underwent a "conversion," who had died to sin and been raised to "newness of life" in Christ and had this symbolized in the waters of baptism. Without faith in the risen Christ and the transformation of life through the power of the Holy Spirit, obeying the commands of Christ was impossible. The liberal position, they would argue, was untenable, for it denied the two events necessary for the Christian life — the death and resurrection of Christ and the resultant conversion of the believer through faith in this pivotal event. Furthermore, through baptism believers were initiated into the church of Christ, into the fellowship of believers, where obedience to Christ's commands was taught and where disciples were trained. In such a church, as early Christian hermits themselves quickly recognized, the pursuit of holiness was immeasurably aided by a like-minded community.

Evangelicals, on the other hand, have placed the stress on faith in the "good news" of the gospel, saying: "I believe in order (that I might) understand." Like Luther, who struggled with the imperatives of his Nominalistic theology until his "tower experience," and like Augustine, who described his own dramatic conversion in his *Confessions* of 409, evangelicals believe that faith, being a gift from God, informs our understanding, helping us to accept the teachings about Christ our reason may find repugnant. And "justification through faith" signifies that we have been declared righteous, indeed have been granted the righteousness of Christ himself. But it is significant that the phrase says: "I believe in order to *understand*. . . ." As liberals began to reject the uniquely Christian teachings of the gospel, they moved to an ethical and moral interpretation of Christianity. Evangelicals have retained the forensic, the intellectual approach to justification and Christian teachings in general. However, as even the passage cited from Michael Green's study on missions in the early church demonstrates, evangelicals seem overly fearful of Christ's "commands" lest they should fall into a new legalism. But Christ did say: "Teach them to *obey everything* I have *commanded* you." The emphasis so central to both early monasticism and Anabaptism on the transformed, re-generated life missing in the magisterial Reformation had to be picked up by Johann Arndt in his *True Christianity* of 1609 and by Philip Jakob Spener in his *Pia Desideria,* originally written as an introduction to the 1675 edition of Arndt's book. That this emphasis is not necessarily inimical to Luther's theology is attested to by the fact that Pietists appealed to Luther's theology for justification and that Pietism has existed for centuries within the bosom of the Lutheran Church. Yet, though Pietism has emphasized the importance of "pursuing piety in community" — in the *collegiae pietatis* — as monks and Anabaptists have, only on occasion have groups separated themselves from the larger Lutheran territorial churches.

Dependent upon Erasmus, the Anabaptists sought to produce a more wholistic, perhaps apostolic, form of Christianity. As both the foregoing study and Craig R. Thompson's analysis of Erasmus's *Inquisitio de Fide* have — independently of one another — demonstrated, neither the Erasmian nor the Anabaptist position is an "undogmatic" one. On the other hand, both also stressed the ethical components of Christianity. The connection between the two, however, lay in the response to the gospel message of the individual involved, a response produced only by the Holy Spirit. The death of the "old Adam" was then symbolized by the immersion in water, and the new life by the rising out of it. Such a symbol was of any avail only if it truly reflected an inner, spiritual — not merely intellectual — transformation.

No one listened to Erasmus when he proffered his solution to the religious conflict of his day in the *Inquisitio de Fide,* nor did anyone — aside from the Anabaptists — appropriate the argument that he made in his paraphrases. Perhaps the Reformation conflict had by then in any case reached the point of no return. But then Erasmus himself, caught in the clutches of his Neoplatonic worldview, did not follow his own advice; instead, his solution remained an illusive ideal akin to other such Platonic "Ideal Forms" in the mind of God. And the Anabaptists, who sought to realize the ideal, were reviled on all sides and nearly persecuted out of existence during those early years of the Reformation. Have times changed? Could this ideal of Erasmus — implemented by the Anabaptists — be realized in the twenty-first century? Were Erasmus — and the Anabaptists — really *five*, not just four, centuries ahead of their time? The answer we give to this question, too, may depend upon our perspective.

Appendix:
The Baptism of John and of Jesus

Aside from Luther's argument that matters not explicitly forbidden in the Bible were acceptable in the church,[1] there was another way of circumventing the apparent meaning of biblical passages one might find inconvenient — and that was by creatively "reinterpreting" their meaning. The passage in Acts 19:1-7, containing the only example of rebaptism in the Bible, is a classic case in point and directly relevant to the story of Anabaptism in the sixteenth century. What makes it all the more striking is the fact that, in this instance, the Reformers were even driven to oppose the unanimous interpretation of the Church Fathers. Origen, for example, wrote: "We next remark in passing that the baptism of John was inferior to the baptism of Jesus which was given through His disciples. Those persons in Acts [xix:2] who were baptized to John's baptism and who had not heard if there was any Holy Ghost are baptized over again by the Apostle."[2] And Chrysostom wrote in his homilies on St. John: "And the proof is that He is the Son of God, and that he needed not baptism, and that the object of the descent of the Spirit was only to make him known. For it was not the Power of John to give the Spirit, as those who were baptized by him show when they say, 'We have not so much as heard whether there be any Holy Ghost.' (Acts xix:2). In truth, Christ needed not baptism, neither his nor any other: but rather baptism needed the power of Christ. For that which was wanting was the crowning blessing of all, that

131

he who baptized should be deemed worthy of the Spirit: this free gift then of the Spirit He added when He came."[3] Jerome wrote in his "Dialogue Against the Luciferians": "The baptism of John was so far imperfect that it is plain they who had been baptized by him were afterwards baptized with the baptism of Christ. For thus the history relates, (Acts xix:1-7)."[4] Even Augustine, though objecting to the fact that the Donatists rebaptized Catholics who joined their communion, wrote in his "On the Gospel of St. John": "What then are they wont to say? Behold, after John baptism was given; after heretical baptism is it not to be given? because certain who had the baptism of John were commanded by Paul to be baptized, for they had not the baptism of Christ."[5] Or, again, in his famous letter to Vincentius of 408: "I think you must already perceive that Paul administered the baptism of Christ to certain persons because they had received the baptism of John only, and not that of Christ."[6] Thieleman J. van Braght was therefore right when he wrote in his *Martyrs' Mirror:* "Notwithstanding Philips of Marnix: then, Beza; then Menso Alting; then, Abr. A. Doreslaer; and then, the latest translator of the Bible, have come to another conclusion concerning the rebaptizing of the twelve Ephesian disciples who had been baptized by John, Acts 19:1-3; there has, nevertheless, as far as we have been able to discover, before the time of P. Marnix, yea, for more than fifteen hundred years, never been a single Greek or Latin divine who doubted that those Ephesians were baptized again, because the first time they had been baptized without a knowledge of the holy Ghost."[7]

Prior to the first believer's baptism in the home of Felix Mantz's mother in Zurich on the evening of 21 January 1525, this passage was also interpreted in a straightforward manner by the Reformers, though Zwingli's 1524 *Commentary on True and False Religion* already indicates that the passage had come up for discussion between Zwingli and his increasingly disenchanted followers. Melanchthon's interpretation in his *Loci Communes* of 1521 may be taken as evidence for the first contention. There he wrote: "Those who had been washed in the baptism of John *had to be baptized again* that they might be certain that they now received the remission of sins which they had up to that time believed would come. For signs are added to make the conscience certain. Neither the baptism of John nor that of Christ justified as signs but they strengthened faith."[8] No problem here and no mention of the Church Fathers. St. Paul had rebaptized for a valid reason and all was well. But when Zwingli's radical followers began to doubt the validity of infant baptism, the Reformer also began to reinterpret the famous Acts 19 passage. That he did so because of the radicals' opposition to infant baptism — even before they proceeded to institute believer's baptism — is clear from the following passage on baptism in his 1524 *Commentary on True and False Religion:* "Those who today battle so stoutly against the baptism of infants — not seeing this distinction, namely, that baptism is sometimes used for the whole procedure of both teaching and sacrament, sometimes only for the sacrament, that is, the sign — fight blindfolded, as gladiators sometimes did."[9] Thereupon Zwingli began to clarify the issue, in the full knowledge that he was presenting a *novum,* for he remarked: "How the baptism of John and that of Christ differ is a question much mooted both in the past and today; but it is an unprofitable question, for there really is no difference at all as far as the reason and purpose are concerned, although as far as the procedure or form is concerned there is some slight difference. Yet the latter is not, properly speaking, a difference, for we can employ the same thing in various ways without detriment to faith. John's dipping effected nothing — I am speaking, here of the baptism of water, not of the inward flooding wrought through the Holy Spirit."[10]

Thereupon Zwingli, beginning with Peter's Pentecost sermon, began a discourse on the baptism of the Holy Spirit as the only and essential baptism, saying: "And this latter baptism of the Holy Spirit [the external aspect of speaking in tongues] is not necessary, but the former [the internal 'baptism by which all are flooded within who trust in Christ' — i.e., drawn to faith and converted by the Holy Spirit] is so very necessary that no one can be saved without it; for no one is saved except by faith, and faith is not born save at the instance of the Holy Spirit."[11] On this basis Zwingli contended that there could only be one baptism, be that of John or of Christ, and therefore the "apparent" differences had to be explained away. He did this by arguing that the "Evangelist [in the case of Acts 19] uses 'baptize' for 'teach,'" even though "there is here no mention at all of teaching."[12] But this explanation led him away from St. Paul's true reason for the rebaptism of the Ephesian disciples, which was that they had not even heard of the Holy Spirit. If that had indeed been the case, then there was not even the remotest chance — according to Zwingli's own emphasis on the role of the Holy Spirit in the advent of faith — that the Ephesian disciples had any faith at all! And his reinterpretation of John's baptism as "teaching" became irrelevant!

Thus, when Zwingli's radical followers proceeded — on his own earlier suggestion — to reject infant baptism and to institute adult or believer's baptism — Zwingli was not, or should not have been, caught off guard. Nevertheless, when he personally confronted some of the "rebaptized" in prison, challenging them to present biblical reasons for their actions, he does appear to have been startled. For the imprisoned did so, pointing to Acts 19:1-7. And Zwingli countered with the argument that he had already developed in his *Commentary on True and False Religion,* attempting to rationalize Paul's "rebaptism" out of existence by insisting that John's baptism had, in reality, amounted only to instruction; it had not been a true baptism. The imprisoned peasants, however, refused to be persuaded. Indeed, one Hans Hottinger, who witnessed the confrontation, reported: "Your brothers have routed Zwingli!" Intellectually — biblically — perhaps so; but Zwingli — like Augustine of old against the Donatists — had the Zurich council on his side.[13]

Heinrich Bullinger, Zwingli's successor in Zurich, carried on the fight against the Anabaptists on this point, arguing in a sermon:

> The latter testimony to maintain anabaptism, or rebaptizing, they bring out of the xix chapter of Acts; where they say that those twelve men of Ephesus were once baptized by Apollos with the baptism of water, and with that of John's likewise; but the very same afterward are rebaptized of Paul in the name of Christ. I answer, that those twelve men are not baptized again of Paul with water; they were once baptized with water, which was sufficient for them. . . . [Bullinger proceeds to argue that Paul only baptized the Ephesians with the "baptism of fire," i.e., with the Holy Spirit, and then concludes:] Therefore they [the twelve disciples] were only ignorant of that baptism of fire. As therefore Peter and John laid their hands on the Samaritans, and they therefore received the Holy Ghost; so Paul layeth hands on the men of Ephesus, and they receive the Holy Ghost. For Luke saith: "When they heard these things, they were baptized in the name of Jesus." And lest any man should understand this of the baptism of water, by and bye he addeth the manner thereof, and a plain exposition, saying: "And when Paul

134

had laid hands on them, the Holy Ghost came upon them." This, I say, he called baptizing in the name of Jesus.

And after this tortuous rationalization against the apparent meaning of the text and the unanimous opinion of the Church Father, Bullinger concluded triumphantly: "Wherefore the anabaptists have no testimony out of the scriptures for their anabaptism, or rebaptizing."[14]

John Calvin, in his commentary on the Acts of the Apostles, at least did not omit mention of the opinion of the Church Fathers; instead, he attacked their opinions, saying:

> Because the men of old had conceived an opinion that the baptism of John and of Christ were diverse, it was no inconvenient thing for them to be baptized again, who were only prepared with the baptism of John. But that that diversity was falsely and wickedly by them believed, it appeareth by this, in that it was a pledge and token of the same adoption, and of the same newness of life, which we have at this day in our baptism; and, therefore, we do not read that Christ did baptize those again who came from John to him. . . .
>
> Now the question is, whether it were lawful to repeat the same, and furious men in this our age, trusting to this testimony, went about to bring in baptizing again. Some take baptism for new institution or instruction [Zwingli], of whose mind I am not, *because, as their exposition is too much racked, so it smelleth of a starting-hole* [of evasion].
>
> Other some deny that baptism was repeated; because they were baptized amiss by some foolish enemy of John. But because their conjecture hath no colour, yea, the words of Paul do rather import that they were the true and natural disciples of John, and Luke doth honourably call them disciples of Christ; I do not subscribe to this opinion, and yet I deny that the baptism of water was repeated, because the words of Luke import no other thing, save only that they were baptized with the Spirit. First, it is no new thing for the name of baptism to be translated into the gifts of the Spirit, as we saw in the first and eleventh chapters, (Acts i,5 & xi,6) where Luke said, that when Christ promised to his apostles to send the Spirit visibly, he calleth it baptism.[15]

Even John Witgift in far-away England was forced to address the problem, arguing — in his "Of Preaching before the Administration of the Sacraments": "Moreover, it is dangerous to understand that place of the sacrament [Acts xix.5] of baptism, *lest we should seem to admit re-baptization, and to fall into the heresy of the anabaptists, who use this place for that purpose* [here one sees the real reason for the tortured and conflicting interpretations of this passage!]; or else think that there is so great difference betwixt the baptism of John and the baptism of Christ; which opinion some hold *being deceived by this place.*"[16]].

From the above Reformation passages one could think that hermeneutics is the art of rationalizing your predetermined point of view!

Notes

Notes to the Introduction

1. The term "Great Commission" was an appellation given to the command of Christ, in Matthew 28:18-20, to "go forth into every part of the world to proclaim the Gospel" by the great missionary movements of the late eighteenth and early nineteenth centuries. In earlier periods of Christian history, however, people read these verses from very different perspectives. Thus the Church Fathers, for example, caught in a controversy with the Arians over the deity of Christ, focused on the trinitarian baptismal formula as the "correct *form* of baptism." When they turned to the actual apostolic baptisms, however, they discovered that the apostles had used a christological rather than a trinitarian baptismal formula. This discovery led to endless debates as to the correct relationship between the Great Commission and the baptismal passages in the Acts of the Apostles. Even Luther referred to this debate on occasion. But he, like Erasmus — whose interpretation of these verses will form the centerpiece of this study — in their turn read them from the point of view of their own concerns. These concerns, as one might expect, had more to do with the relationship of baptism to faith than anything else because of the nature of the sixteenth-century theological quarrel. It should not be surprising therefore to find that even Menno Simons, after citing the Great Commission, could say: "Here we have the Lord's command regarding baptism." For Christians prior to the great missionary movements, therefore, the Great Commission had more to do with faith and baptism than with any missionary mandate. That is true of this study as well. But I have decided to employ the term "Great Commission" in a somewhat anachronistic sense in spite of this because it has become so widely used in contemporary literature. The reader should be aware, however, that this is not another study that deals with the missionary thrust of Anabaptism — and I am of the opinion that scholars who have sought to interpret the Anabaptist emphasis on this passage from a missionary perspective have done violence to the evidence. It is rather a study of the impact of Erasmus's reinterpretation of this passage on Anabaptist thought.

2. Preserved Smith, *Erasmus, A Study of His Life, Ideals and Place in History* (New York: Harper & Brother, 1923), p. vi. Matthew Spinka, ed., *Advocates of Reform, from Wyclif to Erasmus* (Philadelphia: Westminster Press, 1953), in his introduction also proclaimed Erasmus as the great "liberal" Christian; and John P. Dolan, ed. and trans., *The Essential Erasmus* (New York: New American Library, 1964), on the back cover declared: "Erasmus was four centuries ahead of his time."

3. *Catholic Historical Review* 79 (Jan. 1993): 107.

4. James M. Stayer, Werner O. Packull, and Klaus Deppermann, "From Monogenesis to Polygenesis: The Historical Discussion of Anabaptist Origins," *The Mennonite Quarterly Review* (henceforth *MQR*) 49 (April 1975): 83-121.

5. See my "The Radical Reformation Revisited," *Journal of Mennonite Studies* (henceforth *JMS*) 2 (1984): 124-76.

6. See Herbert Butterfield, *The Whig Interpretation of History* (London: Bell, 1950).

Notes to Chapter 1

1. It should be noted that Anabaptist/Mennonite "priests" are conspicuously absent from Collins's list! If he knew of them at all, he probably thought of them as beyond redemption.

2. See, e.g., Menno Simons's statement in his "Reply to False Accusations": "It is the manner and custom of monks to follow human statutes, commands, and institutions and not the Word of God. They have their abbots, priors, and pursers or procurators and are called Augustinians, Franciscans, Dominicans, Bernardines, and Jacobins for their founders and masters" (Menno Symons, *Opera Omnia Theologica of alle de Godgeleerde Wercken* [photographic reproduction of the 1681 edition; Amsterdam: Johannes van Ween, 1681], p. 511). Menno's remarks are reminiscent of those Erasmus made in the preface to the 1516 edition of his New Testament:

> What sort of business is this, anyhow? We keep letters written by a friend, we kiss them, we carry them about with us, we read them over and over; and yet there are thousands of Christians who, though otherwise learned enough, have never read through the evangelists and the apostolic books even once in their lifetime. The Mohamedans hold to their tenets, the Jews even today study the books of Moses from their very cradles. Why don't we in the same way devote ourselves to the study of Christ? Those who follow the discipline of Benedict accept a rule written by a mere man, and what is more an uneducated man writing for men less educated than himself; yet they study it closely and incorporate it in their lives. The Augustinian monks learn all about their founder. The Franciscans adore the little traditions of their Saint Francis; they embrace the rule passionately, surround themselves with it, and carry it with them wherever in the world they go, not thinking themselves safe unless they have the little booklet on the person. Why do they honor more a rule devised by a mere man than the entire Christian church honors its rule which

Christ granted to everyone, to which all of us alike have pledged ourselves in baptism? (Desiderius Erasmus, *The Praise of Folly and Other Writings,* trans. and ed. Robert M. Adams [New York & London: W. W. Norton, 1989], p. 125)

On occasion even Luther could assert that he wished all of his own writings would be destroyed so that people would not go back to them but rather constantly keep on returning to the Bible. But he, too, was relatively intolerant of other peoples' interpretation of the Scriptures if they disagreed with his own. See esp. Mark U. Edwards, *Luther and the False Brethren* (Stanford, Calif.: Stanford Univ. Press, 1975).

3. See esp. Brian Tierney, *Origins of Papal Infallibility, 1150-1350: A Study on the Concepts of Infallibility, Sovereignty and Tradition in the Middle Ages* (Leiden: E. J. Brill, 1972).

4. In response already to the Hussite emphasis on the primitive church and its practices, the fathers of the Council of Constance had responded:

The Primitive Church is the rite, custom, and observance of the church of the faithful, concerning the faith, at the time of the apostles and of the other, seventy-two disciples, and of their followers, up to Pope Sylvester. What is called the modern church is the custom and observance of the church, concerning the faith, from Pope Sylvester's time to the present day. Or, in a more restricted sense of the word "modern," it is what has been in existence for a couple of hundred years. And the church of the past century is called modern, at least in referring this period to the observance of the faithful concerning the faith.

And here it must be understood that in the Primitive Church everything was done in a simpler and grosser way than in the modern church. For baptism was done with ordinary water, but now with holy water. [Then by holy priests, but now with carnal priests, Erasmus would have added!] And the divine office was performed more simply, as well as many other things; while in the modern church all things are done more worthily *[digniori modo]*. So also in the Primitive Church communion among the Corinthians was performed in both kinds; in the modern church, all things having been brought to a better form, it is given in one kind. For the apostles and other followers omitted what the modern church has fulfilled. (Quoted in Howard Kaminsky, *A History of the Hussite Revolution* [Berkeley & Los Angeles: Univ. of California Press, 1967], pp. 116-17)

5. Some theologians saw it differently, but they were never in the mainstream. See both Louis Berkhof, *Reformed Dogmatics* (Grand Rapids: Eerdmans, 1937), pp. 17-27; and John Henry Cardinal Newman, *An Essay on the Development of Christian Doctrine* (New York, London, Toronto: Longmans, Green & Co., 1949), pp. 54ff. Eventually, at the Council of Trent, Aquinas's theology was enshrined as the "Catholic" interpretation.

6. Johann Walch, *Luthers Saemmtliche Schriften* (St. Louis, 1905), 15:1442, my emphasis. Note that Leo does not say that Luther's teachings are contradicted by the Bible, but "are opposed to the teachings of the Catholic church." The Edict of Worms had a somewhat different, more personal point of view. See also Johannes Eck, *Enchiridion: Handbuechlin gemainer stell unnd Artickel der jetzt schwebenden Neuwen leeren,* ed. Erwin Iserloh (Münster, 1980), p. 3.

7. See esp. Vincent of Lerins, "The Commonitory," *The Nicene and Post-Nicene Fathers,* 2nd series, vol. 11 (rpt.; Grand Rapids: Eerdmans, 1978), pp. 132-35.

8. See esp. Kaminsky, *Hussite Revolution,* and Gordon Leff, "The Making of the Myth of a True Church in the Later Middle Ages," *Journal of Medieval and Renaissance Studies* 1, no. 1 (1971): 1-15.

9. Dante Alighieri, *De Monarchia* (Oxford: Clarendon Press, 1916).

10. See esp. his *The Defender of the Peace,* trans. Alan Gewirth (New York: Harper & Row, 1967).

11. Erasmus, *Enchiridion* 24.

12. Quoted by Barbara W. Tuchman, *A Distant Mirror* (New York: Knopf, 1978), p. 29.

13. Jacques Lefevre d'Etaples, Preface to the *Commentarii initiatorii in quatuor Evangelia,* my emphasis. Eugene F. Rice, Jr., ed., *The Prefatory Epistles of Jacques Lefevre d'Etaples and Related Texts* (New York & London: Columbia Univ. Press, 1972), pp. 437-38. The translation is that of James Bruce Ross and Mary Martin McLaughlin, *The Portable Renaissance Reader* (New York: Penguin Books, 1978), pp. 85-86. Note here, as in the quotation from the Council of Constance, the emphasis on Constantine (and Pope Sylvester) as the point at which things changed; but also the diametrically opposite evaluation of the respective epochs.

14. Luther, "Wider die Verkehrer und Faelscher Kaiserlichs Mandats," *D. Martin Luthers Werke. Kritische Gesamtausgabe* (Weimar: Hermann Boehlaus Nachfolger, 1899), 15:63 (henceforth *WA*). Augustine does not use the same term, *sola scriptura,* that Luther uses, but "Scripture and right reason." And Luther cites him in this regard without criticism. What did Augustine mean to imply with the addition of "right reason"? And did Luther use "right reason" in his battle with the radicals who refused to accept such "additions" to the Bible as infant baptism?

15. John Headley, *Luther's View of Church History* (New Haven: Yale Univ. Press, 1963), p. 98.

16. *WA,* 17/1:389. But was the interpretation better? Who had the clearer understanding of what Christ had intended to say?

17. Headley, *Church History,* pp. 162-81.

18. Walch, *Luthers Schriften,* 15:1797. See also the following: "Therefore this passage [on the Parable of the Tares] should in all reason terrify the grand inquisitor and murderers of people, where they are not brazen faced, even if they have to deal with true heretics. *But at present they burn the true saints and are themselves heretics.* What is that but uprooting the wheat and pretending to exterminate the tares, like insane people" (John Nicholas Lenker, ed., *Sermons of Martin Luther,* trans. John Nicholas Lenker et al. [Grand Rapids: Baker Book House, 1983], 2:102). Or, as early as 1521: "It has not been my wish that they [the Papists] should act so foolishly and put themselves to shame; but still I gladly suffer it for the sake of the truth and because of the proverb, which comes nigh unto the Gospel: The learned are the perverted. The Gospel will come to the front and will prove that the wise are fools, and the fools are wise, *and that those who are called heretics are Christians, and those that call themselves Christians, heretics*" (*Sermons,* 1:14-15, my emphasis).

19. *WA,* 1:613, 667. Catholics such as John Eck and George Duke of Saxony had a field day with this statement of Luther's, suggesting, on occasion, that Luther should have left his gospel "under the bench."

20. For a discussion of this tradition, see my "Baptist Interpretations of Ana-

baptist History," in *Mennonites and Baptists: A Continuing Conversation,* ed. Paul Toews (Winnipeg: Kindred Press, 1993), pp. 31-46. See also the martyrologies by Adrien Haemstaed, *De Geschiedenisse ende dem doodt der vromer Martelaren, die om ghetuyghenisse des Euamgeliums Haer bloedt ghestort hebben* (Antwerp, 1559), and Ludwig Rabus, *Historien der Martyrer,* 2 vols. (Strassburg: Josias Rihel, 1572).

21. Newman, *Christian Doctrine,* p. 84. For a modern perspective on this issue, see Heiko Augustinus Obermann, *Forerunners of the Reformation* (New York: Holt, Reinhart & Winston, 1966). Erasmus even gives credence to this perspective in his preface to the third edition (1522) of his Latin New Testament, where he wrote:

> Nowadays, what quarrels and endless contentions continually distress the Christian community! The secular rulers are all engaged in bloody wars; even bishops of the church are engulfed in waves of violence. The common people are caught up in vicious mutual hatreds. While the purity of the Christian faith is corrupted in various ways, the peace of Christianity is being shattered. I don't want to pronounce here for one side or the other; wherever there is strife, there the devil is found. Who ever saw conflicts more atrocious and unrelenting among the pagans than those which for years now have raged between Christians? Without going into the causes, when was the ship of the church ever thus tossed about on the waves? Why don't we look into the causes of these events? When we have found their source, we may be able to find a remedy for them. In the gospels themselves I read that the apostolic ship was twice in danger, always at night when Jesus was not available to help, as we read in Matthew 14: "But the ship was now in the midst of the sea, tossed with waves." What wonder if tumults will arise in the church if Jesus is not present? Whenever the spirit of Christ is absent, then the waves and winds of the world toss about the ship and vex it sorely. (Erasmus, *Folly and Other Writings,* pp. 138-39)

22. Butterfield, *Whig Interpretation.* See also Gerhard Ladner, *The Idea of Reform* (New York: Harper & Row, 1967). The more one studies church history, the more Anthony Collins's observations are confirmed and the more one can apply Herbert Butterfield's conclusions, reached with respect to eighteenth- and nineteenth-century Whig history, to the field of church history. Thus Jean Michel Hornus, in his *It Is Not Lawful for Me to Fight* (Scottdale, Pa.: Herald Press, 1980), trans. from the French by Alan Kreider and Olivier Coburn, has made the case that church historians have, perhaps even willfully, distorted the primitive church's position on war and nonviolence in order to justify Christendom's participation in war. Similarly, Albert Schweitzer in his *The Quest for the Historical Jesus* (New York: Macmillan, 1957) observed: "Thus each successive epoch of theology found its own thoughts in Jesus. . . . But it was not only each epoch that found its reflection in Jesus; each individual created Him in accordance with his own character" (p. 4). And just recently Clarence Bauman arrived at similar conclusions with respect to the historical interpretations of the Sermon on the Mount. In his book *The Sermon on the Mount: The Modern Quest for Its Meaning* (Macon, Ga.: Mercer Univ. Press, 1986) Bauman writes that the various interpretations of the Sermon on the Mount "are for the most part motivated by the dubious aim of restricting the scope of its meaning, qualifying the sense of its validity, and limiting the context of its relevance" (p. 417). Perhaps, had I cast my historiographical net more widely in 1974, I might have been somewhat

more understanding of the Marxist tendency to interpret the past from their present ideological perspective. At least they did not do so under the guise of "objectivity."

23. "Ein bericht an einen guten freund von Beider gestalt des Sacraments auffs Bischoffs zu Meissen mandat" (*WA,* 26:574). Luther was not twisting the arguments of Catholic apologists like Johannes Cochlaeus and Thomas Murner in this instance! See Eck's *Enchiridion,* e.g., where Eck wrote: "Christus sagt zu den Jungern. Geet hin vnd leeret alle voelcker/tauffet sie in dem namen des vatters/vnd des sons/vnd des hayligen gaysts. *Hie hat Christus geben die form des tauffs/welliche verwandelt hat die kirch der Apostel vnd marterer/vnd haben getaufft im namen Jhesu/*wie Petrus sagt [Acts 2]/wirckend penitenz/vnd ain yetlicher werd getaufft im namen Jhesu Christi/Spricht auch Lucas. Da sie das gehoert haben/seind sie getaufft worden inn dem namen Jhesu" (p. 7).

24. See James M. Kittelson, *Luther the Reformer* (Minneapolis: Augsburg, 1986), p. 117.

25. According to an unfriendly witness, e.g., Cochlaeus is supposed to have said publicly at a breakfast in Nuremberg in 1530 that "der Papst Macht habe, Gottes Wort nach Gelegenheit der Laeufte, Zeit und Personen zu limitieren, zu maessigen oder auszulegen, eben als muesste sich Gottes Wort mit dem Papste vergleichen und nicht vielmehr wir uns in allem nach Gottes Wort richten" (quoted in Dr. Martin Spahn, *Johannes Cochlaeus: Ein Lebensbild aus der Zeit der Kirchenspaltung* [Berlin: Felix L. Dames, 1898], p. 215). It was precisely this view that Erasmus attacked in the 1516 preface to his New Testament, saying: "We drag down the teachings of heaven and force them like a Lydian rule [note: The Lydian rule was made of lead, therefore flexible, and was used to model curves and irregular surfaces.] to fit our own life-patterns, and while we make great shows of erudition by gathering together scraps of pagan literature, we — I won't say we corrupt the main point of Christian religion, but — we restrict to a very few men matters Christ wanted to be defused as widely as possible; and that nobody can deny" (Erasmus, *Folly and Other Writings,* p. 123).

26. *WA,* 26:575, my emphasis.

27. No pagination. Received from the University of Chicago Library.

28. As early as the Baden disputation of 1526, John Eck raised precisely this issue in opposition to Oecolampadius, who "propounded the principle that what was not expressly commanded by the Word of God need not be accepted. Whereupon Eck responded most adroitly: then the Anabaptists would be right, since infant baptism was not expressly commanded in the Bible" (Leonhard von Muralt, *Die Badener Disputation 1526* [Leipzig: M. Hensius Nachfolger, 1926], p. 115).

29. Newman, *Christian Doctrine,* p. 54.

30. Catholic polemicists of the sixteenth century were quick to point out that the Anabaptists had out-principled the Reformers on the matter of *sola scriptura.* John Eck, arguing in his *Enchiridion* that when the Anabaptists appeared on the scene the Reformers "could not refute them/[so] they had to depart from their fundamental principle and concede that many things were to be believed and observed which had not been written [in Scripture]/as Zwingli has pointed out with regard to the baptism of Mary/and with regard to infant baptism" (p. 23).

31. See, e.g., Joerg Voegeli in his *Die Reformationsgeschichte von Konstanz 1519-1538,* ed. Alfred Voegeli (Basel: Basileia-Verlag, 1972), 1:403, where the contemporary

Voegeli observed: "Der mererthail [of the Anabaptists] warend frumm, grecht, gotts-foerchtig und an usserlichen leben in allweg unstrafbar." See also Wolfgang Capito's letters in defense of Michael Sattler in John H. Yoder, trans. and ed., *The Legacy of Michael Sattler* (Scottdale, Pa.: Herald Press, 1973), pp. 86-107.

32. See esp. Friesen, "Die aeltere und die marxistische Muentzerdeutung," in Abraham Friesen and Hans-Juergen Goertz, eds., *Thomas Muentzer* (Darmstadt: Wissenschaftliche Buchgesellschaft, 1978), pp. 447-80; and Heinold Fast, *Bullinger und die Taeufer* (Weierhof/Pfalz: Mennonitischer Geschichtsverein, 1959).

33. An English translation in the appendix of Samuel Macauley Jackson, *Ulrich Zwingli, the Reformer of German Switzerland, 1484-1531* (New York & London: G. P. Putnam's Sons, 1901), p. 470. See Eck's rejoinder in his *Repulsio Articulorum Zwinglii* of 17 July 1530, where he wrote: "I laugh at the empty boasting of Zwingli that he was the first to teach and write against the Anabaptists, since I am aware that it was Zwingli who by his counsel and advice really founded this lost sect, and was goaded more by jealousy than love of the truth in his pursuit of Balthasar the Catabaptist, as all his neighbors testify. Wherefore let no good man believe Zwingli even under oath when he says that he has not accepted nor taught any of the doctrines of this seditious party, for his published books convict him of lying" (in Samuel Macauley Jackson and William John Hinke, eds., *Zwingli on Providence and other Essays* [rpt.; Durham, N.C.: Labyrinth Press, 1983], p. 83).

34. See esp. Fast, *Bullinger und die Taeufer.* Even Thomas Murner from Lucern, who knew Swiss conditions well, wrote: "Der Zwingly ist im anfang ein widertauffer gewesen jetz aber ist er dar von gefallen" (*Radtschlag halten der disputation zu Bern,* p. Fij; original in the University of Chicago Library).

35. A. J. F. Zieglschmid, ed., *Die aelteste Chronik der Hutterischen Brueder* (New York: Cayuga Press, 1943), pp. 41-87. The *Hutterite Chronicle* clearly traces the origins of the movement to Zurich and the Swiss Brethren, but then also strongly rejects the Münsterites. See esp. p. 144.

36. See esp. Friesen, "Menno and Muenster: The Man and the Movement," in Gerald R. Brunk, ed., *Menno Simons, A Reappraisal* (Harrisonburg, Va.: Eastern Mennonite College, 1992), pp. 144-46. Menno answered the charges especially in his 1552 "Reply to False Accusations."

37. Had van Braght been at all interested in establishing a real baptismal descent from the Waldenses to the sixteenth-century Anabaptists, he should also have made the case that the 1529 Speyer edict against "rebaptism" — as the term "Anabaptism" itself — was a fraud. Yet he did not do so. And the earliest Swiss Anabaptists justified their 21 January 1525 actions by citing St. Paul's "rebaptism" of the twelve disciples of John the Baptist as given in Acts 19. See Thieleman J. van Braght, *The Bloody Theater or Martyrs' Mirror,* trans. J. F. Sohm (Scottdale, Pa.: Herald Press, 1951).

38. John Lawrence Mosheim, *An Ecclesiastical History,* trans. Archibald Maclain (Charlestown, Mass.: Samuel Etheridge, 1810), 4:427-28, my emphasis. One of the interesting aspects of Reformation polemics is that medieval heretics — as earlier opponents of the papacy — have been much more favorably treated by church historians than have the Anabaptists, even though they may have shared ideas in common with the latter.

39. Sebastian Franck, *Chronica, Zeitbuch unnd Geschichtsbibell von anbegyn bis in diss gegenwertig 1536, iar verlengt* (Strassburg, 1536; rpt. Darmstadt: Wissenschaftliche Buchgesellschaft, 1969).

40. Gottfried Arnold, *Unparteyische Kirchen- und Ketzer-Historie, vom Anfang des Neuen Testaments biss auf das Jahr Christi 1688* (Schaffhausen, 1748).

41. Ludwig Keller, *Die Reformation und die aelteren Reformparteien* (Leipzig: S. Hirzel, 1885).

42. Sebastian Franck's mystical proclivities are well known. On Arnold, see Peter C. Erb, *Pietists, Protestants, and Mysticism: The Use of Late Medieval Spiritual Texts in the Work of Gottfried Arnold* (Metuchen, N.J.: Scarecrow Press, 1989); and on Keller see my *History and Renewal in the Anabaptist/Mennonite Tradition* (North Newton, Kans.: Bethel College, 1994), esp. chaps. 3-5.

43. See esp. Friedhelm Groth, *Die "Wiederbringung aller Dinge" im wuerttembergischen Pietismus* (Göttingen: Vandenhoeck & Ruprecht, 1984).

44. See esp. Friedrich Fabri, *Der Sensus Communis, das Organ der Offenbarung Gottes in Allen Menschen* (Barmen: W. Langenwiesche's Verlagshandlung, 1861).

45. Gustav Kawerau to Ludwig Keller, 18 August 1883. *Keller Correspondence,* Mennonite Library and Archives, North Newton, Kansas. Cited in my *History and Renewal,* p. 60.

46. Even Clarence Bauman, so perceptive in his analysis of the theological biases in regard to the interpretations of the Sermon on the Mount, when he deals with Hans Denck and seeks to legitimate his own mystical position, writes: "Hans Denck (1500-1527) represents the contemplative genius of the Anabaptist Movement at its highest and best. No undersanding of the Anabaptist Vision is complete without coming to terms with the uniqueness of Denck's intellectual spirituality: its inner dynamic, its medieval context, its mystic content, and its Jewish roots" (Clarence Bauman, trans., *The Spiritual Legacy of Hans Denck: Interpretation and Translation of Key Texts* [Leiden: E. J. Brill, 1991], p. 1). Even in far-away Winnipeg, Canada, Keller's *Hans Denck* found adherents! See T. D. Regehr, *Mennonites in Canada 1939-1970: A People Transformed* (Toronto: Univ. of Toronto Press, 1996), pp. 178-79.

47. See the review by Karl Mueller, *Theologische Studien und Kritiken* (1886), 2:337-66, and the discussion in my *History and Renewal,* pp. 103-12. In an earlier, anonymous review Mueller had written: "Ich sage es klar heraus: die waldensische und taeuferische Bewegung muesse bei Keller nach einem festen Plan in die Freimaurer auslaufen" (quoted by Keller himself in his "Zur Aufklaerung ueber die Entstehung von Dr. Keller's Schriften," *Gemeindeblatt* 11 [Nov. 1888]: 89).

48. On Friedrich Fabri see my *History and Renewal,* pp. 49-54.

49. See esp. chap. 3 of my *History and Renewal,* pp. 54-77.

50. Paul Burckhardt, *Die Basler Taeufer* (Basel, 1898), pp. 1-12.

51. Keller's interpretation even played into the Russian Mennonite problems of World War I. In 1915 these Mennonites submitted a lengthy document to the St. Petersburg government — written by Peter Braun of the "Braun Archive" fame — in which Keller's theory is given again in grand fashion. The document is entitled "Who are The Mennonites?" and sets out to prove the Dutch ancestry of the Russian Mennonites in order to save them from the government's anti-German legislation. Later on, when many of these same people, Peter Braun included, had settled in

Germany, the document became somewhat of an embarrassment that Benjamin H. Unruh sought to remove with his book on Mennonite names, entitled *Die nieder-laendischen-niederdeutschen Hintergruende der mennonitischen Ostwanderungen im 16., 18. und 19. Jahrhundert* (Karlsruhe: Heinrich Schneider, 1955).

52. John Horsch, *Modern Religious Liberalism* (rpt.; New York: Garland, 1988). See also his *The Mennonite Church and Modernism* (Scottdale, Pa.: Mennonite Publishing House, 1924).

53. In Bender's more neutral terminology "true" became "normative." See his "The Anabaptist Vision," in Guy F. Hershberger, ed., *The Recovery of the Anabaptist Vision* (Scottdale, Pa.: Herald Press, 1957), pp. 29-54.

54. On Horsch, see chap. 5 of my *History and Renewal,* pp. 113-46.

55. Stephen Dintaman, "The Spiritual Poverty of the Anabaptist Vision," *Conrad Grebel Review* 10 (1992): 205-8.

56. R. R. Palmer, *The Age of the Democratic Revolution,* 2 vols. (Princeton: Princeton Univ. Press, 1959-64).

57. See Abraham Friesen, *Reformation and Utopia: The Marxist Interpretation of the Reformation and its Antecedents* (Wiesbaden: Franz Steiner Verlag, 1974), pp. 76-113; and also "Wilhelm Zimmermann and the Nemesis of History," *German Studies Review* (May 1981): 195-236.

58. See esp. Marx and Engels, *Communist Manifesto,* ed. Samuel H. Beer (Arlington Heights, Ill.: Harlan Davidson, 1955).

59. See Claus-Peter Clasen's introduction to his *Anabaptism: A Social History* (Ithaca, N.Y.: Cornell Univ. Press, 1972). Social historians are, however, very interested in religion as a social phenomenon.

60. See esp. *Marx & Engels on Religion,* introduction by Reinhold Niebuhr (New York: Schocken Books, 1964).

61. See the recent observations by perhaps the United States' most well-known Marxist scholar, Eugene D. Genovese, "The Question," *Dissent* (Summer 1994): 371-76. A number of scholars responded to his charges, to which Genovese answered in a "Riposte," pp. 376-88.

62. On Richard Heath and his interpretation of Anabaptism, see Friesen, "Baptist Interpretations of Anabaptist History," in *Mennonites and Baptists,* pp.63-69.

63. Friesen, "Baptist Interpretations."

64. Karl Kautsky, *Die Vorlaeufer des neueren Sozialismus* (Stuttgart, 1894).

65. It has always struck me as a little odd that Marxist and some social historians believe that ideas are derivative and dependent upon one's economic and social station in life. If that were universally true, we should not have to take the "ideas" of such scholars seriously either, for they, too, would be derivative and therefore of only relative consequence. For that reason Marxist historians have argued that their studies were indeed *parteilich* — partisan. They did so, however, on the assumption that they had discovered the direction in which history was moving. But it is now definitively clear that they were mistaken.

66. See Friesen, "The Impulse toward Restitutionist Thought in Christian Humanism," *Journal of the American Academy of Religion* 44 (March 1976): 29-45.

67. See also Francis Oakley, *The Western Church in the Later Middle Ages* (Ithaca,

N.Y: Cornell Univ. Press, 1979), p. 20, for a discussion of the problems in the writing of church history.

68. See, e.g., the following statement by Menno Simons in his very first theological tract, *The Spiritual Resurrection* (1536): "I hope by the grace of God that you will find nothing in it but the infallible truth of Jesus Christ, for we have not directed you to men, nor to the doctrine nor commandments of men, *but to Jesus Christ alone and to his holy Word* which he taught and left on earth and sealed with his blood and death, *and afterwards had it preached throughout the world by his faithful witnesses and holy apostles*" (Menno Symons, *Opera Omnia Theologica,* p. 184, my emphasis).

Notes to Chapter 2

1. This chapter was first presented as a lecture at the University of Winnipeg under the auspices of the Chair in Mennonite Studies, November 1987. It was published in the *Festschrift* for Lewis W. Spitz, *The Harvest of Humanism in Central Europe,* ed. Manfred P. Fleischer (St. Louis: Concordia, 1992), pp. 232-61, and is here reprinted in a slightly revised and expanded form. Copyright 1992 Concordia Publishing House. Used with permission. Of general interest for the topic under discussion, the following Erasmus studies have been important: Lewis W. Spitz, *The Religious Renaissance of the German Humanists* (Cambridge, Mass.: Harvard Univ. Press, 1964); John B. Payne, *Erasmus: His Theology of the Sacraments* (Richmond, Va.: John Knox Press, 1970); Ernst-Wilhelm Kohls, *Die Theologie des Erasmus,* 2 vols. (Basel: Friedrich Reinhardt, 1966); Manfred Hoffmann, *Erkenntnis und Verwirklichung der wahren Theologie nach Erasmus* (Tübingen: J. C. B. Mohr, 1972); Friedhelm Krueger, *Humanistische Evangelienauslegung* (Tübingen: J. C. B. Mohr, 1986); Roland Bainton, *Erasmus of Christendom* (New York: Charles B. Scribner's Sons, 1969); Gerhard B. Winkler, *Erasmus von Rotterdam und die Einleitungsschriften zum neuen Testament* (Münster: Aschendorffsche Verlagshandlung, 1974); Edward K. Burger, *Erasmus and the Anabaptists* (Ph.D. diss., University of California at Santa Barbara, 1977); Heinz Holeczek, *Erasmus Deutsch,* vol. 1 (Stuttgart: Friedrich Frommann, 1983); and Erika Rummel, *Erasmus' Annotations on the New Testament* (Toronto: Univ. of Toronto Press, 1986).

2. Thomas S. Kuhn, *The Copernican Revolution: Planetary Astronomy in the Development of Western Thought* (Cambridge, Mass.: Harvard Univ. Press, 1957). See also his *The Structure of Scientific Revolutions* (Chicago: Univ. of Chicago Press, 1962).

3. Thomas More, *Utopia,* trans. and ed. H. V. S. Ogden (New York: Appleton, Century Crofts, 1949), p. 24, my emphasis. In the above passage, More also speaks of the "leaden rule" — the "Lydian rule" Erasmus had referred to in his introduction to his 1516 New Testament — in the same manner as did Erasmus. See Erasmus, *The Praise of Folly and Other Writings* (New York: W. W. Norton, 1989), p. 123.

4. Erasmus, *Enchiridion,* p. 75. See also the parallel statement in the preface to the 1516 edition of his New Testament. Erasmus, *Folly and Other Writings,* p. 123.

5. Philip S. Watson, *Let God be God! An Interpretation of the Theology of Martin Luther* (Philadelphia: Muhlenberg Press, 1974), p. 5. But Caspar Schwenckfeld makes

the same accusation against Luther that More and Erasmus had made against the Catholic Church. See his "An Answer to Luther's Malediction," in George H. Williams and Angel M. Mergal, eds., *Spiritual and Anabaptist Writers* (Philadelphia: Westminster Press, 1957), pp. 163-81. Blaise Pascal brought the same accusation against the Jesuits in *The Provincial Letters* (New York: Modern Library, 1941), pp. 390-95, esp. p. 393.

6. P. S. Allen, ed., *Opus Epistolarum Des. Erasmi. Roterdami* (Oxford: Clarendon Press, 1906-58), 10:388.

7. See esp. Thieleman van Braght, *The Bloody Theater or Martyrs' Mirror*, trans. Joseph F. Sohm (Scottdale, Pa.: Herald Press, 1951), pp. 15, 26.

8. Ludwig Keller, *Die Reformation und die aelteren Reformparteien* (Leipzig: S. Hirzel, 1885), pp. 330ff.

9. As quoted in Robert Kreider, "Anabaptism and Humanism: An Inquiry into the Relationship of Humanism to the Evangelical Anabaptists," *MQR* 26 (1952): 123.

10. Leonhard von Muralt, ed., *Quellen zur Geschichte der Taeufer in der Schweiz* (Zurich: S. Hirzel Verlag, 1952).

11. Leonhard von Muralt, *Glaube und Lehre der Schweizerischen Wiedertaeufer in der Reformationszeit* (Zurich: Kommissionsverlag Beer & Co., 1938), pp. 6-7.

12. Kreider, "Anabaptism and Humanism," pp. 123-41.

13. Thor Hall, "Possibilities of Erasmian Influence on Denck and Hubmaier in their Views on the Freedom of the Will," *MQR* 35 (1961): 149-70.

14. Heinold Fast, "The Dependence of the First Anabaptists on Luther, Erasmus, and Zwingli," *MQR* 30 (1956): 110.

15. Kenneth R. Davis, "Erasmus as Progenitor of Anabaptist Theology and Piety," *MQR* 47 (1973): 163-78, and *Anabaptism and Asceticism: A Study in Intellectual Origins* (Scottdale, Pa.: Herald Press, 1974), esp. chap. 5, pp. 266-92.

16. John P. Dolan, "Review of I. B. Horst, *Erasmus, the Anabaptists and the Problem of Religious Unity*," *MQR* 43 (1969): 343. This last argument would point more to the similarities between mysticism and humanism — similarities that have never been properly investigated — than to any direct influences of Erasmus on Hans Denck.

17. H. S. Bender, *Conrad Grebel c. 1498-1526, The Founder of the Swiss Brethren sometimes called Anabaptists* (Scottdale, Pa.: Herald Press, 1950). See also his "The Pacifism of Sixteenth-Century Anabaptists," *Church History* 24 (June 1955): 119-51; and my *History and Renewal in the Anabaptist/Mennonite Tradition* (North Newton, Kans.: Bethel College, 1994), pp. 139-40.

18. Dolan, "Review of I. B. Horst," p. 343.

19. Burger, *Erasmus and the Anabaptists*, pp. 43-204.

20. Paul O. Kristeller, *Renaissance Thought*, 2 vols. (New York: Harper & Row, 1955, 1965).

21. Francesco Petrarca, "On His Own Ignorance and that of Many Others," trans. Hans Nachod in *The Renaissance Philosophy of Man*, ed. Ernst Cassirer, P. O. Kristeller, and John H. Randall (Chicago: Univ. of Chicago Press, 1948), p. 103.

22. Coluccio Salutati, "A Letter in Defense of Liberal Studies," in *The Italian Renaissance*, ed. Werner L. Gundersheimer (Englewood Cliffs, N.J.: Prentice-Hall, 1965), p. 22.

23. See esp. Hanna Gray, "Renaissance Humanism: The Pursuit of Eloquence,"

in *Renaissance Essays,* ed. P. O. Kristeller and Philip Wiener (New York: Harper & Row, 1968), pp. 202-3.

24. Peter Paul Vergerio, "Letter to Ubertinus of Carrara," in *Italian Renaissance,* p. 36.

25. Vergerio, "Letter to Ubertinus of Carrara."

26. See esp. Charles Trinkaus, *In Our Image and Likeness: Humanity and Divinity in Italian Humanist Thought,* 2 vols. (Chicago: Univ. of Chicago Press, 1970).

27. See esp. Eugene F. Rice, *The Renaissance Idea of Wisdom* (Cambridge, Mass.: Harvard Univ. Press, 1958).

28. See also Kohls, *Theologie des Erasmus,* p. 24.

29. Petrarch, *Renaissance Philosophy of Man,* p. 111.

30. See also Eveleyne Luciani, *Les Confessions de Saint Augustin dans les Lettres de Petrarque* (Paris: Études Augustiniennes, 1982).

31. *Great Books of the Western World,* vol. 18, *Augustine* (Chicago: Encyclopedia Britannica, 1952), p. 47.

32. Peter Brown, *Augustine of Hippo* (Berkeley & Los Angeles: Univ. of California Press, 1967), pp. 213-14. It becomes clear from this description that Augustine's understanding of the pure church as a spiritual phenomenon derives from his Platonic thinking. How Christian is it? Perhaps Theodor Kolde was right when he observed, "Das Dogma von der unsichtbaren Kirche ist und bleibt einmal eine unfructbare Abstraktion, ein haltloser Notbehelf, um die vermeintliche Einigkeit der Kirche zu wahren" (*Luthers Stellung zu Concil und Kirche bis zum Wormser Reichstag, 1521* [Guetersloh: C. Bertelsmann, 1876], p. iv).

33. Even a Faber Stapulensis could bring a purified Aristotle into this Neoplatonic context. See Eugene F. Rice, "The Humanist Idea of Christian Antiquity: Lefevre d'Etaples and His Circle," *Studies in the Renaissance* 9 (1962): 126-60.

34. *Italian Renaissance,* p. 96.

35. See also the argument in Krueger, *Humanistische Evangelienauslegung,* p. 6.

36. Erasmus, *Enchiridion,* p. 71.

37. Erasmus, *In Novum Testamentum Praefationes,* ed. Werner Welzig and trans. Gerhard B. Winkler, vol. 3, *Ausgewaehlte Werke* (Darmstadt: Wissenschaftliche Buchgesellschaft, 1967), pp. 10-12. These words of Erasmus are echoed in the introduction to the 1536 Froschauer German Bible written by the publisher himself and widely used by the Swiss and South German Anabaptists. There one reads: "Warumb gedenckend wir nit also? Es musz ein neuwe/hohe/und wunderbare leer sein/die Gott durch seinen sun der welt hat woellen fuertragen/und damit ers thaete/hat sich Gott herab gelassen und menschliche bloedigkeit angenommen: der untoedlich unser toedtlichkeit/der hoechst unser niedere und schwachheyt/der schoepffer sein creatur. Grosz iszt und wunderbar musz die leer sein/die ein solicher hoher/nach so vil geleerter und weyser leerern/nach so vil heyliger propheten/kommen ist zeleeren" (1975 reproduction of the 1536 ed.). It would appear that Froschauer's translation was made from Erasmus's edition, to the extent of echoing the latter's preface. On the making of the Froschauer translation and its relationship to Luther's translation, see esp. Johann Jakob Mezger, *Geschichte der deutschen Bibeluebersetzungen* (Basel: Bahnmeier, 1876), pp. 33-84. The 1536 preface was probably the same one Froschauer wrote for the 1527 edition (see p. 73) and clearly shows Erasmian rather than Lutheran

influence. See Luther's preface to the New Testament where the contrast between "Law and Gospel" is emphasized: *D. Martin Luther, Die gantze Heilige Schrifft Deutsch,* ed. Hans Volz et al. (Munich: Ragner & Bernhard, 1972), 2:1962-5.

38. Kohls, *Theologie des Erasmus,* pp. 19-34.

39. See Friesen, "Anabaptism and Monasticism: A Study in the Development of Parallel Historical Patterns," *JMS* 6 (1988): 174-97.

40. Allen, *Opus Epistolarum,* 10:47. On Erasmus's view of the Anabaptists, see also Leon-E. Halkin, "Erasme et l'Anabaptisme," in *Les Dissidents du XVIIe siècle entre l'Humanisme et le Catholicisme,* ed. Marc Lienhard (Baden-Baden: Valentin Koemer, 1983), pp. 61-77. Pelargus clearly took a "Catholic" perspective on the issue, which applied Christ's "councils of perfection" only to the monastic and conventual orders.

41. Catholics like Pelargus did so as well. The difference was, however, that the Catholic Church had freed the mass of the faithful from these more onerous standards, placing them under the Mosaic or Natural Law. Erasmus quite apparently rejected this concession to the weakness of the common Christian.

42. Erasmus, *Enchiridion,* pp. 74-75.

43. This emphasis on fourteen hundred years would appear to confirm our later contention that Erasmus had earlier argued that the apostles had baptized only believers. In this piece, however, written well after the emergence of Anabaptism, he suggests that they "probably extended [it] to children." He may have done so to deflect criticism for his earlier statements.

44. Quoted in P. S. Allen, *Erasmus: Lectures and Wayfaring Sketches* (Oxford: Clarendon Press, 1934), p. 95.

45. Erasmus, *Enchiridion,* p. 71.

46. Erasmus, *The Education of a Christian Prince,* ed. Lester K. Born (New York: Columbia Univ. Press, 1968), p. 148.

47. I shall have to modify this assertion in the next chapter when Erasmus's context changes.

48. Allen, *Opus Epistolarum,* 9:318-19.

49. Erasmus, *The Praise of Folly,* in John P. Dolan, ed. and trans., *The Essential Erasmus* (New York: New American Library, 1964), p. 170.

50. Allen, *Opus Epistolarum,* 3:239.

51. Allen, *Opus Epistolarum,* 1:566.

52. Allen, *Opus Epistolarum,* 1:374.

53. Friesen, "Anabaptism and Monasticism," pp. 191-93.

54. Erasmus, *Enchiridion,* p. 83.

55. *Library of Christian Classics,* vol. 15, *Luther and Erasmus: Free Will and Salvation,* ed. E. Gordon Rupp and Philip S. Watson (Philadephia: Westminster Press, 1969), p. 44.

56. Allen, *Opus Epistolarum,* 3:482.

57. Erasmus, *Praise of Folly,* in *Essential Erasmus,* p. 158.

58. Erasmus, *Enchiridion,* p. 66.

59. Erasmus, *Education of a Christian Prince,* p. 153.

60. Erasmus, *Enchiridion,* p. 68.

61. Erasmus, *Enchiridion,* p. 68.

62. Erasmus, *Enchiridion,* p. 68.

63. Allen, *Opus Epistolarum,* 6:351-52.

64. Erasmus, *Complaint of Peace,* in *Essential Erasmus,* p. 182.

65. Erasmus, *Complaint,* p. 186.

66. Erasmus, *Complaint,* p. 187.

67. Erasmus, *Complaint,* p. 187.

68. Erasmus, *Complaint,* p. 187.

69. Erasmus, *Enchiridion,* p. 55.

70. Erasmus, *Enchiridion,* p. 55.

71. Desiderius Erasmus, *Ratio seu Methodus Compendio Perveniendi ad veram Theologiam,* vol. 3, *Ausgewaehlte Werke,* p. 375. See also Friesen, "Anabaptism and Monasticism."

72. "Monks know how to make a favorable presentation of their vows before the public by ceremonies of this sort; they perform the drama so vividly that they wring tears from the onlookers" (Erasmus, *Folly and Other Writings,* p. 136). See also Malone, "Martyrdom and Monastic Profession as a Second Baptism," and my "Anabaptism and Monasticism." In the *Confessio Augustana* this monastic view is condemned by Luther and Melanchthon.

73. Erasmus, *Folly and Other Writings,* p. 137. The kind of impact this passage — and perhaps the entire 1522 preface — had upon Zwingli and his followers at the time can be seen from the fact that Leo Jud, in the introduction to his 1535 German translation of Erasmus's paraphrases, used these very words without acknowledging their Erasmian origin, saying: "Yetz aber findt man funffzig jaerige leut/die nit wussend was der tauff bedeutet/warzu er dient/vnd wareyn sy sich im tauff gepflichtet habend/was die artickel des glaubens syend/was dz Pater noster/was die sacrament der kirchen" (*Paraphrasis Oder Erklaerung des gantzen Neuwen Testaments* [Zurich: Christoph Froschauer, 1542], p. 3).

74. In another passage Erasmus wrote: "Now that fact that we have many Christians so ignorant that they possess less knowledge of the faith than even its worst enemies, I attribute mostly to the priests" (Erasmus, *Folly and Other Writings,* p. 135).

75. Perhaps as he was himself to do in his 1524 *Inquisitio de Fide.*

76. Erasmus, *Folly and Other Writings,* p. 135. Here, clearly, Erasmus begins to move into the realm of theology, of dogma.

77. Erasmus, *Folly and Other Writings,* pp. 135-36.

78. Erasmus, *Enchiridion,* p. 52.

79. Zwingli quite apparently drew such a conclusion, as we shall see in chap. 4.

80. Erasmus, *Folly and Other Writings,* p. 136.

81. Erasmus, *Folly and Other Writings,* p. 27.

82. See esp. Brian Gerrish, *Grace and Reason: A Study in the Theology of Luther* (New York: Oxford Univ. Press, 1962).

83. Augustine, "Letters," *Works,* in *Nicene and Post-Nicene Fathers,* ed. Philip Schaff, 2nd ser., vols. 1-7 (rpt; Grand Rapids: Eerdmans, 1979), 1:239.

84. *WABr,* 2:157.

85. Holeczek, *Erasmus Deutsch,* pp. 109-18.

86. Holeczek, *Erasmus Deutsch,* pp. 16-63.

87. Robert Friedmann, "The Doctrine of the Two Worlds," in *The Recovery of*

the Anabaptist Vision, ed. Guy F. Hershberger (Scottdale, Pa.: Herald Press, 1957), pp. 105-18.

88. See also Friedhelm Krueger, "Die Bergpredigt nach Erasmus," in *Bucer und seine Zeit,* ed. Friedhelm Krueger et al. (Wiesbaden: Franz Steiner, 1976), p. 1.

89. Krueger, "Bergpredigt nach Erasmus," p. 1.

90. Leland Harder, ed., *The Sources of Swiss Anabaptism* (Scottdale, Pa.: Herald Press, 1985), p. 358.

91. H. Wayne Pipkin and John H. Yoder, trans., *Balthasar Hubmaier, Theologian of Anabaptism* (Scottdale, Pa.: Herald Press, 1989), p. 255.

92. Menno Symons, *Opera Omnia Theologica of alle de Godgeleerde Wercken* (Amsterdam: Johannes van Ween, 1618), pp. 422, 472.

93. Since Luther's translation only appeared in 1522, gradually supplementing Erasmus's New Testament editions with a vernacular translation, it may be assumed that in the formative years of the Reformation nearly everyone was using the latter's edition.

94. Harder, *Sources,* p. 358.

95. Harder, *Sources,* p. 358. Perhaps also the latest, 1522, edition with its preface "recommending" rebaptism.

96. Paul Kalkoff, "Die Vermittlungspolitik des Erasmus und sein Anteil an den Flugschriften der ersten Reformationszeit," *Zeitschrift fuer Kirchengeschichte* 1 (1903/04): 34. Smith, *Erasmus,* pp. 158-256, to the contrary.

97. Keller, *Reformation,* pp. 330ff.

98. Rummel, *Annotations,* pp. 89-121.

99. Rummel, *Annotations,* pp. 123-80. See also Leonhard von Muralt, *Glaube und Lehre der Wiedertaeufer,* p. 7.

100. In the *Martyrs Mirror* we read of a Catholic inquisitor who argued: "I could very well show you this [the legitimacy of sponsors] from the ancient fathers, but you Anabaptists will rely most firmly on the holy Scriptures alone, so that you will not hearken to the ancient fathers or teachers of the holy church." And John Eck wrote in his *Enchiridion:* "Wiewol in obgemelten vnd nachvolgenden stucken/die newchristen [Protestants] doch darauff gefuszt haben/das sie nichts wollen anne-men/dann was mit heller biblischer geschrifft muege bewert werden/noch dann so die Wiedertaeuffer auffgestanden/kunden sie inen nichts abbrechen/mussen von irem grund fallen vnd zugeben daz vil ding zu halten vnd zu glauben seindt die nit geschriben seien, wie Zwingli sagt von dem tauff Marie/also auch mit dem tauff der kinder" (Johannes Eck, *Enchiridion: Handbuechlin gemainer stell unnd Artickel der jetzt schwebenden Neuwen leeren,* ed. Erwin Iserloh [Münster, 1980], p. 23). And Stanislaus Hosius, president of the Council of Trent, wrote in his treatise on heresy:

> If you have an eye to the outwarde appearaunce of godlynes, bothe the Lutherans and the Zwinglians muste nedes graunte, that they [the Anabaptists] farr pass them. Yf you wyll be moved with the boasting of the worde of God, these be no lesse bold then Calvin to preache, and theire doctrin must stand aloft above all glory of the worlde, must stand invincible above all poure, because it is not theyre worde, but the worde of the lyving God. Nether do they creye with lesse loudeness then Luther, that with theire doctryn which is the worde of God, they shall judge the Aungelles. *And surely howe many so ever have wrytten agaynst this heresie, whether they*

were Catholykes or heretykes, they were able to overthrowe it not so muche by the testimony of the scriptures, as by the authoritie of the Church. (The Begynning of Heresyes, trans. Richard Shacklock [Antwerp: Aeg Diest, 1565], p. 49, my emphasis)

101. Quoted in Heinold Fast, "Hans Kruesis Buechlein über Glauben und Taufe," in *A Legacy of Faith: A Sixtieth Anniversary Tribute to Cornelius Krahn,* ed. C. J. Dyck (Newton, Kans.: Faith and Life Press, 1962), p. 224.

102. Walter Koehler, "Die Zuercher Taeufer," in *Gedenkschrift zum 400 jaehrigen Jubilaeum der Mennoniten oder Taufgesinnten,* ed. D. Christian Neff (Ludwigshafen: Konferenz der Sueddeutschen Mennoniten, 1925), p. 53.

103. See note 101 above.

104. Fast, "Hans Kruesis Buechlein," p. 225.

105. Fast, "Hans Kruesis Buechlein," p. 228.

106. Fast, "Hans Kruesis Buechlein," p. 229.

107. Rummel, *Annotations,* pp. 156-58.

108. Rummel, *Annotations,* p. 159. See also Holeczek, *Erasmus Deutsch,* pp. 182-84.

109. Rummel, *Annotations,* p. 160.

110. Rummel, *Annotations,* p. 160.

111. Rummel, *Annotations,* p. 161.

112. Menno Symons, *Opera Omnia Theologica,* p. 472. See also Cornelis Augustijn, "Der Epilog von Menno Simons' *Meditation,* 1539 (Leringhen op den 25. Psalm), Zur Erasmusrezeption Menno Simons," in *Anabaptistes et dissidents au XVIe siecle,* ed. Jean-Georges Rott and Simon L. Verheus (Baden-Baden & Bouxwiller: Valentin Koemer, 1987), pp. 175-88.

113. John H. Yoder, trans. and ed., *The Legacy of Michael Sattler* (Scottdale, Pa.: Herald Press, 1973), p. 82, n. 23.

114. Rummel, *Annotations,* p. 164.

115. Rummel, *Annotations,* p. 164.

116. Rummel, *Annotations,* p. 164.

117. Rummel, *Annotations,* p. 172.

118. Robert Stupperich, ed., *Die Schriften B. Rothmanns* (Münster: Aschendorffsche Verlagsbuchhandlung, 1970), p. 184 has "Adnotationibus." Marpeck, as given in the translation of William Klassen and Walter Klaassen, *The Writings of Pilgram Marpeck* (Scottdale, Pa.: Herald Press, 1978), p. 280, has "Advocationibus." The editors do not note the change.

119. Stupperich, *Schriften B. Rothmanns,* pp. 184-85.

120. Robert Friedmann, "Eine dogmatische Hauptschrift der hutterischen Taeufergemeinschaften in Maehren," *Archiv fuer Reformationsgeschichte* 28 (1933): 234-35.

121. Certainly, he never read Erasmus's paraphrases.

Notes to Chapter 3

1. Erasmus could just as well have substituted "ceremonies of the Catholic Church" in its place. Indeed, it is probable that Erasmus had these in mind when he spoke of the "Mosaic law."

2. "Quicquid igitur ego praecepi vobis, id illis servandum tradite. Non autem praescripsi vobis Mosaicae Legis ceremonias, quas jam velut umbras ad lucem Evangelicae veritate evanescere oportet, non Pharisaicas constitutiunculas, sed ea quae sola praestant veram innocentiam ac pietatem, quaeque sola vos Deo caros reddant, vereque felices" (*Desiderii Erasmi Roterodami Opera Omnia,* vol. 7, *Paraphrasis in N. Testamentum* [Leiden, 1706], p. 146. Photographic reproduction [Hildesheim: Georg Olms Verlagsbuchhandlung, 1962], my emphasis).

3. Walter Koehler, *Huldrych Zwingli* (Leipzig: Koehler & Amelang, 1954), pp. 30ff. For a discussion of the literature on the subject, see Gottfried W. Locher, "Zwingli and Erasmus," in *Zwingli's Thought: New Perspectives* (Leiden: E. J. Brill, 1981), pp. 233-55.

4. Koehler, *Zwingli,* p. 41.

5. Heinz Holeczeck, *Erasmus Deutsch,* vol. 1 (Stuttgart: Friedrich Frommann, 1983), p. 47.

6. Holeczeck, *Erasmus Deutsch,* p. 47, n. 2.

7. W. Schwarz, *Principles and Problems of Biblical Translation: Some Reformation Controversies and their Background* (Cambridge: The University Press, 1955), p. 142.

8. Schwarz, *Principles and Problems,* p. 146.

9. 1522 is about the time that the questioning of infant baptism began in Zurich.

10. See chap. 2, n. 81. As I shall note later, Oecolampadius was to use the identical argument against the Anabaptists in 1527.

11. Quoted in Johann Jakob Mezger, *Geschichte der deutschen Bibelueberzetzungen* (Basel: Bahnmeier, 1876), p. 34. See also Locher, "In Spirit and in Truth," in *Zwingli's Thought,* pp. 27-28.

12. Mezger, *Bibelueberzetzungen,* p. 38.

13. If not for Zwingli, this sequence appears in many ways to have been determinative for his radical followers: the teachings of Christ and the practice — or implementation — by his disciples. The biblical point of departure appears here to have been very different from that of a Luther who took his point of departure from Paul's Epistle to the Romans. On the different points of departure for Luther and Zwingli, see Locher, "Huldrych Zwingli's Message," in *Zwingli's Thought,* pp. 31-36.

14. Ernst Haenchen, *The Acts of the Apostles. A Commentary,* trans. from the 14th German ed. (Philadelphia: Westminster Press, 1971), p. 97, writes: "Now if the earthly life of Jesus, brought to a close by his Ascension, represents an epoch in chronologically regarded history, one is drawn to the highly important inference that it had a chronological sequel. With bold logic Luke considers this sequel also a historical event, and presents it as a continuation of his gospel! This was a daring enterprise which none of his predecessors had thought to execute, and in which he found no successors."

15. Haenchen, *Acts,* p. 99, n. 1.

16. Haenchen, *Acts,* pp. 136-37.

17. Luke writes, "He told them, 'This is what is written: The Christ will suffer and rise from the dead on the third day, and repentance and forgiveness of sins will be preached in his name to all nations, beginning in Jerusalem. You are witnesses of these things. I am going to send you what my Father has promised; but stay in the city until you have been clothed with power from on high'" (24:46-49; NIV).

18. See esp. the Epilogue.

19. *The Ante-Nicene Fathers,* vol. 3, *Tertullian* (rpt.; Grand Rapids: Eerdmans, 1978), p. 676. It is the emphasis on this "trinitarian formula," contained only in Matthew's version of the Great Commission, that brought about the association with the baptismal passages in Acts during the Arian controversy. Mark's version makes no mention of the Trinity in this connection, and Luke — as already noted — makes only a vague reference to the commission. Nor did Mark or Luke make the distinction, which was to become so important for Erasmus and the Anabaptists, between the first, initial preaching of the gospel and the "teaching them to obey everything I have commanded you" after repentance, conversion, and baptism had taken place. It is therefore, as we shall see, of considerable significance that it was Matthew's version of the Great Commission that came to be associated with the baptismal passages in Acts.

20. *The Nicene and Post-Nicene Fathers,* vol. 14, *The Seven Ecumenical Councils,* ed. Henry R. Percival (rpt.; Grand Rapids: Eerdmans, 1979), p. 40.

21. See Appendix.

22. This entire question has been investigated, from the earliest pronouncements to the controversy regarding the possible later interpolation of the Matthew 28 passage debated by scholars at the turn of the last century, by Bernard Henry Cuneo, *The Lord's Command to Baptise. An Historical Critical Investigation with Special Reference to the Works of Eusebius of Caesarea* (Washington, D.C: The Catholic University of America, 1923).

23. Cuneo, *Lord's Command,* pp. 29-33.

24. *The Anti-Nicene Fathers,* vol. 3, *Tertullian,* pp. 669-79.

25. Tertullian's dates are generally given as 145-220.

26. For a discussion of the Renaissance approach to the past, see Peter Burke, *The Renaissance Sense of the Past* (New York: St. Martin's Press, 1970); and for Erasmus's understanding, see Peter Bietenholz, *History and Biography in the Work of Erasmus of Rotterdam* (Geneva: Eugene Droz, 1966).

27. Vincent of Lerins, *The Commonitory,* vol. 11 of *The Nicene and Post-Nicene Fathers,* pp. 131-56. Vincent, the first person to articulate this position, wrote at the outset of the second chapter,

> I have often then inquired earnestly and attentively of very many men eminent for sanctity and learning, how and by what sure and so to speak universal rule I may be able to distinguish the truth of Catholic faith from the falsehood of heretical pravity; and I have always, and in almost every instance, received an answer to this effect: That whether I or any one else should wish to detect the frauds and avoid the snares of heretics as they rise, and to continue sound and complete in the Catholic faith, we must, the Lord helping, fortify our own belief in two ways; first,

154

by the authority of the Divine Law, and then, by the tradition of the Catholic Church. (P. 132)

28. *Commonitory,* p. 132.

29. See Leo X's bull of August 1519 threatening Luther with excommunication, where it is written: "we have discovered that Luther's errors, as expected, were not Catholic articles but were opposed to the teachings of the Catholic church and in *opposition to the correct interpretation of the holy Scriptures accepted by the church*" (Johann Walch, *Luthers Saemmtliche Schriften* [St. Louis, 1905], p. 1442, my emphasis).

30. Pierre Fraenkel, *Testimonia patrum; the Function of the Patristic Argument in the Theology of Philip Melanchthon* (Geneva: Eugene Droz, 1961). In so doing, they implied that the Catholic Church had not been guided by the Holy Spirit. But nowhere do they appear to have said so explicitly.

31. We have already seen him argue, in his 1516 and 1519 *Paraclesis,* that a true Christian theology could only be achieved on the basis of the New Testament documents.

32. Modern interpreters of the Gospels are not so much interested in what Christ said here as they are in Matthew, the author of the Gospel. See, e.g., the following: Daniel Patte, *The Gospel According to Matthew: A Structural Commentary on Matthew's Faith* (Philadelphia: Fortress Press, 1987); A. W. Argyle, *The Gospel According to Matthew: A Commentary* (Cambridge: The University Press, 1963); and David B. Howell, *Matthew's Inclusive Story: A Study in the Narrative Rhetoric of the First Gospel* (Sheffield: JSOT Press, 1990). Older commentaries were interested in discovering the historical sources that the writers used.

33. It has nearly always been argued that Erasmus, good Christian humanist that he was, emphasized only Christ's teachings and not the teachings about Christ. He is often contrasted with Luther in this regard. Such an argument, however, does Erasmus an injustice.

34. The term "repent" became a bone of contention between Catholics and Protestants because the Vulgate had "do penance" in its place. The matter came up for discussion, e.g., between Gregory Martin, a Catholic biblical scholar but former English Protestant, and William Fulke, Master of Pembroke Hall, Cambridge, with specific reference to Erasmus's paraphrase. Martin accused Theodore Beza of having mistranslated the passage in order to prove their heresy. To this charge Fulke responded:

> Of purpose against the heresy of satisfaction, Beza will not translate the Greek word, as the vulgar Latin translator doth, but yet as the Greek word ought to be translated. Erasmus, finding the Latin insufficient, hath added *vitae prioris,* that is, "repent ye of your former life." Neither doth Beza find fault with the English word "repent," but with the Latin *agite poenitentiam,* when you translate it, "do penance," meaning thereby pain or satisfaction for sins passed, to be a necessary part of true repentance, which is not contained in the Greek word . . . , which signifieth changing of the mind; that is, not only sorrow for the sin past, but also a purpose of amendment, which is best expressed by the Latin word *resipiscere.* (William Fulke, *A Defence of Translations of the Holy Scriptures,* The Parker Society Publications [Cambridge: The University Press, 1853], p. 155)

See the Douai translation, which renders the passage (Acts 2:38): "But Peter said to them: Do penance, and be baptized every one of you in the name of Jesus Christ, for the remission of your sins." The Vulgate reads: "Petrus vero ad illos: Poenitentiam (inquit) agite, et baptizetur unusquisque vestrum in nomine Jesu Christi in remissionem peccatorum vestrorum: et accipietis donum Spiritus sancti."

Leo Jud's later (1535) German translation of Erasmus's paraphrases gives the following weakened rendering: "So jr disz ercleert habend/glaubend sy euch denn unnd nemmends an/habend sy am vorigen laeben ein reuewen/sind sy bereit die Evangelische leer anzenemmen/so tawffend sy mit wasser in den namen des vatters/des suns/und des heyligen geists" (*Paraphrasis,* p. 69).

35. "Haec ubi illos docueritis, si crediderint quae docuistis, si poenituerit vitae prioris, si parati fuerint amplecte doctrinam Evangelicam, tum tingite illos aqua, in nomine Patris, & Filii, & Spiritus Sancti, ut hoc sacro symbolo confidant sese liberatos ab omnium peccatorum suorum sordibus gratuito beneficio mortis mea, jamque cooptatos in numerum filiorum Dei" (*Erasmi Opera Omnia,* 7:146).

36. "Sic enim mandarat illis Dominus: *Ite docete omnes gentes, baptizantes eos, docentes eos fervare quaecumque praecepi vobis.* Docete baptizandos Euangelicae Philosophiae rudimenta, quibus nisi quis crediderit, frustra tingitur aqua. Docete baptizatos, ut juxta doctrinam meam viventes, semper ad perfectiora proficiant" (*Erasmi Opera Omnia,* 7:674).

37. "Subita mutatio" (*Erasmi Opera Omnia,* 7:674). The concept of conversion in the writings of Erasmus — as in the Reformation generally — is extremely problematic. For Luther, see Marilyn J. Harran, *Luther on Conversion* (Ithaca: Cornell Univ. Press, 1983); for Calvin, see Wm. J. Bouwsma, *John Calvin: A Sixteenth-Century Portrait* (New York: Oxford Univ. Press, 1988); for Capito, see James M. Kittelson, *Wolfgang Capito: From Humanist to Reformer* (Leiden: E. J. Brill, 1975); for Thomas Müntzer and mystics in general, see Friesen and Hans-Jürgen Goertz, eds., *Thomas Muentzer* (Darmstadt: Wissenschaftliche Buchgesellschaft, 1978). The great examples of conversion for the period were those of St. Paul and Augustine; for mystics, John Tauler; for monks, St. Anthony. A fundamental problem, seldom discussed, however, is the fact that the conversions of both Paul and Augustine took place before their baptisms; not those of pseudo-Tauler and St. Anthony. Did baptism have the same import for both sets of persons? If one is "converted" after baptism, what does the latter mean? Especially if one speaks of "baptismal regeneration," as did many Church Fathers, sixteenth-century Catholics, and even some Reformers? To a certain extent, at least, the subject was broached — though apparently never fully investigated — during the Patristic controversy over the rebaptism of heretics. If one is "regenerated" in baptism, does "conversion" become meaningless? But the monks revived the concept and argued that anyone who wished to enter a monastery had to be converted (see the Rule of St. Benedict). Such an argument virtually necessitated a "second baptism"; and this is indeed what they called their initiation rites. Furthermore, what actual effect did baptism have if — as Erasmus wrote — "Who ever saw conflict more atrocious and unrelenting among the pagans than those which for years have raged between Christians?" One could speak — as Erasmus himself did — "of pledging ourselves to Christ in baptism," but to do so apparently meant little or nothing at all because "Christians" were worse than pagans. The whole Renaissance attempt to use

the "moral pagan" to flail the "immoral Christian" — More's entire *Utopia* is such an argument — implied that baptismal grace, regeneration, was a theological figment. It was for this reason that Erasmus himself, in 1522, called for a "second baptism" in all but name. The larger theological and ecclesiological context within which one discusses the term is therefore of critical importance.

38. "Mirabantur quid homini accidisset, quod subito factus esset alius" (*Erasmi Opera Omnia,* 7:704).

In his colloquy *Inquisitio de Fide,* Erasmus presents the following dialogue:

Aulus: So far I hear nothing heretical; but he died to recall to life us who were dead in sin. Yet why did he come to life again?

Barbatius: For three reasons, mainly.

Aulus: What?

Barbatius: First, to provide us with a sure hope of resurrection. Next, that we might know that he to whom we entrusted the safeguarding of our salvation is immortal and will never die. *Finally, that we, dead to sins through repentance, buried along with him through baptism, might be recalled by his grace to newness of life* [my emphasis].

39. "Priusquam autem adscenderet in coelum, praecepit nobis, ad hoc munus selectus, ut palam omnibus praedicaremus, testificantes, quod ipse sit onus, quem Deus evexit in summam potestatem, ut in fine mundi fit judex omnium, vivorum ac mortuorum" (*Erasmi Opera Omnia,* 7:711-14).

40. "Tradidit hoc sius Apostolis Dominus Jesus, ut qui credidissent Euangelico sermoni, eos baptizarent in nomine Patris & Filii & Spiritus Sancti. Hunc in modum doceri merebantur, qui simpliciter errabant" (*Erasmi Opera Omnia,* 7:741-44). Erasmus seems not to have been concerned about the conflict between Christ's ostensible command to baptize in the names of the Trinity and the apostolic practice of baptizing only in the name of Jesus. Not once does it enter his discussion. Indeed, immediately after he has spoken of Christ's command to baptize in the name of the Father, Son, and Holy Spirit, he proceeds to say: "Atque illi moniti, promte obtemperaverunt monitori, moxque baptizati sunt in nomine Domini Jesu" (7:742-45). Furthermore, unlike the other authors cited in Appendix 1, Erasmus appears to have had no problems with St. Paul's "rebaptism" of the twelve Ephesian disciples of John the Baptist. His preface to the 1522 edition of his Bible would seem to confirm this.

41. Hubmaier read Erasmus correctly when he emphasized "the articles of faith as they are contained in the *Symbolo Apostolorum,*" for this was precisely the point Erasmus was to make in his colloquy *Inquisitio de Fide,* published shortly after his paraphrases of the Acts of the Apostles in March of 1524. There Aulus, the Catholic, examines Barbatius, a Lutheran, on the various articles of faith contained in the Apostles' Creed. As Craig R. Thompson writes in the introduction to his English translation: "Barbatius passes the examination. Aulus the Catholic satisfies himself, to his surprise, that the Lutheran is sufficiently orthodox on the Apostles' Creed — the Creed which it is necessary to believe *ad salutem.* A reader's inference must be that, putting aside all the vexed questions of custom, discipline, ceremonies, indulgences, and other such matters not necessary to salvation" (Craig R. Thompson, trans., *The Colloquies of Erasmus* [Chicago: Univ. of Chicago Press, 1965], p. 177). In

his essay on the colloquy, Thompson proceeds to explain this dialogue in the context of Erasmus's gradual estrangement from Luther and the Protestant Reformation. His overriding attention is directed to Erasmus's *De Libero Arbitrium,* but he never once mentions the humanist's paraphrases of the Gospels and the Acts of the Apostles. Judging from what we have delineated above, and Hubmaier's response to Erasmus's analysis, it would appear that the *Inquisitio de Fide* must rather be placed into the context of these paraphrases. We shall return to Thompson's analysis of this colloquy at various other points in this study because his conclusions overlap virtually completely with my own, even though my study has an altogether different point of departure. Professor Ken Gouwens of the University of South Carolina drew my attention to this colloquy and Thompson's analysis of it when I had already virtually completed this study. I wish to express my thanks to him here.

42. H. Wayne Pipkin and John H. Yoder, trans., *Balthasar Hubmaier, Theologian of Anabaptism* (Scottdale, Pa.: Herald Press, 1989), p. 255. In this connection it is interesting, and perhaps not coincidental, that Hubmaier is the author of the oldest Anabaptist catechism. It is entitled *Ein Christennliche Leertafel, die ein yedlicher mensch, ee vnd er im Wasser getauft wirdt, vor wissen solle* (Nikolsburg, 1526), written in the very year Hubmaier wrote the words quoted above about Erasmus's paraphrases. For an English translation see Denis Janz, *Three Reformation Catechisms: Catholic, Anabaptist, Lutheran* (New York & Toronto: Edwin Mellen Press, 1982), pp. 141-78. In his article on "Catechism" in the *Mennonite Encyclopedia,* Harold Bender argues that "It is not probable that Hubmaier's catechism was actually used as such" (1:529). But he cites no evidence that it was not. Perhaps Bender's statement can be ascribed to his "non-creedal" predilections.

43. Pipkin and Yoder, *Hubmaier,* pp. 255-56.

44. Peter Walpot, "Das Grosze Artikelbuch oder Ein schoen lustig Buechlein etlicher Hauptartikel unseres christlichen Glaubens, etc.," in Robert Friedmann, ed., *Glaubenszeugnisse oberdeutscher Taufgesinnter,* vol. 12 of *Quellen zur Geschichte der Taeufer* (Gütersloh: Gerd Mohn, 1967), pp.117-18.

45. Pipkin and Yoder, *Hubmaier,* pp. 104, 114-15, 129, 179, 191, 198, 207, 211, 222, 228, 249-50, 253, 255, 263, 267, 270, 302, 370.

46. Here one sees the importance, once again, of the Matthean version of the Great Commission with its unique trinitarian emphasis and its emphasis upon the "two kinds" of teaching — preaching the good news of the gospel and, after acceptance, repentance, conversion, and baptism, teaching the baptized "to obey everything I have commanded you."

47. Quoted in Abraham Friesen, "Acts 10: The Baptism of Cornelius as Interpreted by Thomas Muentzer and Felix Mantz," *MQR* 64 (Jan. 1990): 7, my emphasis. One is led to wonder, under these circumstances, what Zwingli's influence was in all of this. The above passage would appear to suggest that Mantz and the Anabaptists, using the Erasmian argument, were responding here to Zwingli's argument about the sacrament of baptism being an external sign of an interior, spiritual reality. Zwingli, as we shall have occasion to note, argued that the external sign, in the Catholic ritual, had not produced the interior spiritual regeneration. Therefore there could be no connection between the two. But Mantz does assert that they belong together; however, the external baptism is a mere sign that the work of the Holy Spirit has been accomplished within.

These two paraphrases of Erasmus were not immediately translated into the German by Leo Jud; he only did so later, having the entire set published in 1535, after Zwingli's death. In the introduction to his 1542 edition (virtually unchanged from the 1535 edition), Jud wrote that he had at first not wished to translate the Gospels and Acts, "vermeinende die lautere leer des Herren Jesu Christi in den vier Euangelisten/seye ein soelicher leer/die nit mit menschlichen glosen vermengt soelle werden: denn es moechte hierinn im verstand Goettlicher warheit bald ein grosser vnd gefarlicher faeler geschaehen" (p. 1). Was this because of the use the radicals made of these paraphrases? Would this factor have contributed to Zwingli's alienation from Erasmus?

48. This emphasis on the role of the Holy Spirit in conversion may well derive from Zwingli himself. See esp. Locher, "In Spirit and in Truth," in *Zwingli's Thought,* pp. 12-15. The entire movement appears to have grown out of a revival movement begun by Zwingli's own preaching. Locher states: "Until recently the origins of the Anabaptist movement lay in darkness. But the subtle researches of Fritz Blanke have shown that the first Anabaptist communities constituted a revival movement called into being by the preaching of Zwingli" (Locher, "The Image of Zwingli in Recent Research," in *Zwingli's Thought,* p. 70).

49. The *Hutterite Chronicle,* indeed, placed even the first baptisms of 21 January 1525 into the context of the Great Commission, saying:

> Es begab sich das Vlrich Zwingel/vnd Conrad Grebel/einer vom Adel/vnd Felix Mantz/alldrey vast erfarne vnd geleerte Maenner/Inn Teutscher/Latteinischer/Griechischer vnnd auch Hebreischer sprach/zusammen kamen/Anfiengen sich miteinander zu ersprachen Inn glaubens sachen/Vnd haben erkenndt/das der Kindstauf vnnoetig sey/Auch den selben fuer kein tauff erkenndt.
>
> Die zwen aber/Conrad vnd Felix haben Im herren erkenndt vnd glaubt/das man muesz vnd solle nach Christlicher ordnung vnd einsatzung des Herren recht getaufft werden/dieweil Christus selbs sagt/wer glaubt vnnd getaufft wirt/der wirt selig. Da hat Vlrich Zwingel (welchem vor Christi Creutz schmach vnd vuolgung grauset) nit gewoelt/vnd fuergeben/Es wuerde ein auffruer auszgeben. Die andern zwen aber/Conrad vnd Felix sprachen/Man kuende vmb deszwillen gottes lautern beuelch vnd angeben nit vnderwegen lassen. (*Die aelteste Chronik,* pp. 45-46)

It is interesting to note here, with respect to what will follow, that the writer includes Zwingli in this triumvirate that recognized, on the basis of Christ's Great Commission, that infant baptism was wrong.

This emphasis on the Great Commission is even to be found in the Anabaptist hymns. See, e.g., Liepolt Schneider's *In gnad thu mein gedencken,* where one reads:

> 4. Gar klaerlich sein geschriebn
> Marci am letzten staht,
> Darwider nichts kan treiben,
> es ist sein wunderthat,
>   Dasz, wer da glaubt und wirt getaufft,
> derselb sol sehlig werden:
> wer es liszt, der merck drauff!
>
> 5. Was laszt ihr euch betrueben,
> dasz man hell Christi brauch?

In Gottes wort euch ueben,
so werd ihr sehen auch
    Was Jesus Christus, Gottes Sohn,
uns allen hat befohlen,
was wir dan sollen thun.

50. Leland Harder, ed., *The Sources of Swiss Anabaptism* (Scottdale, Pa.: Herald Press, 1985), p. 299.

51. Hans Denck, *Schriften,* vol. 2, ed. Walter Fellmann (Gütersloh: Gerd Mohn, 1960), p. 83. I shall note the differences in Denck's reading of this passage from that of the Swiss Brethren at a later point in this study.

52. Quoted in Walter Koehler, "Die Zuericher Taeufer," in *Gedenkschrift zum 400 jaehrigen Jubilaeum der Mennoniten oder Taufgesinnten,* ed. D. Christian Neff (Ludwigshafen: Konferenz der Sueddeutschen Mennoniten, 1925), p. 55.

53. Emil Egli, *Die Zuericher Wiedertaeufer zur Reformationszeit nach den Quellen des Staatsarchivs dargestellt* (Zurich: Friedrich Schultess, 1878), p. 27.

54. The Zurich Anabaptist's use of Romans 6:4 may have been a direct response to Zwingli's attempt to separate the baptism of the Holy Spirit from water baptism.

55. Egli, *Zuericher Wiedertaeufer,* pp. 66-67.

56. Emil Egli, *Die St. Galler Taeufer. Geschichte im Rahmen der staedtischen Reformationsgeschichte* (Zurich: Friedrich Schulthess, 1887), pp. 30-31.

57. Harder, *Sources,* p. 366.

58. Robert Stupperich, ed., *Die Schriften B. Rothmanns* (Münster: Aschendorffsche Verlagsbuchhandlung, 1970), p. 161.

59. Donald J. Ziegler, ed., *Great Debates of the Reformation* (New York: Random House, 1969), p. 129.

60. On this matter see Frank J. Wray, "The 'Vermahnung' of 1542 and Rothmann's 'Bekenntnisse,'" *Archiv für Reformationsgeschichte* 47 (1956): 243-51.

61. See the parallel passages in William Klassen and Walter Klaassen, *The Writings of Pilgram Marpeck* (Scottdale, Pa.: Herald Press, 1978), pp. 211-12.

62. Robert Friedmann, "Eine dogmatische Hauptschrift der hutterischen Taeufergemeinschaften in Maehren," *Archiv für Reformationsgeschichte* 28 (1933): 222.

63. The emphasis on Matthew 28:18-20 first appears in the writings of Hessian Anabaptists in 1531 where, in a document dated 11 November, it is recorded that Melchior Rinck used the argument from Matthew 28:19, though without any reference to the Acts passages. Günther Franz et al., eds., *Wiedertaeuferakten,* vol. 4 of *Urkundliche Quellen zur Hessischen Reformationsgeschichte* (Marburg: N. G. Ewert'sche Verlagsbuchhandlung, 1951), pp. 43-44. In an earlier interrogation by Hessian authorities on 17 and 18 August 1528, however, even with reference to the specific issue of infant baptism, Rinck makes no mention of the text (*Wiedertaeuferakten,* pp. 3-9). Rinck must surely have done so had Thomas Müntzer or Hans Hut justified their initial opposition to infant baptism on the interpretation given in the Erasmian paraphrases. Only three years later does the argument crop up with reference to Rinck. This can mean only that Rinck picked up the argument later, after it had filtered into Hessian territories, probably brought in by South German missionaries.

64. Franz, *Wiedertaeuferakten,* pp. 8, 40, 44, 91, 148, 155, 184, 186, 197, 202, 226, 236.

65. Franz, *Wiedertaeuferakten,* p. 184. As shall become evident, this simplistic view of the Anabaptist interpretation of the Great Commission fails, by far, to do them justice.

66. Menno Symons, *Opera Omnia Theologica of alle de Godgeleerde Wercken* (Amsterdam: Johannes van Ween, 1618), p. 12.

67. See Rothmann, *Schriften,* p. 147.

68. See first Friesen, "The Radical Reformation Revisited," *JMS* 2 (1984): 166; then also Friesen, "Menno and Muenster: The Man and the Movement," in *Menno Simons, A Reappraisal,* ed. Gerald R. Brunk (Harrisonburg, Va.: Eastern Mennonite College, 1992), pp. 150-51.

69. See Friesen, "Menno and Muenster," p. 151.

70. When I wrote the essay in which this argument was first made, I was not yet aware of Menno's — and Rothmann's — dependence on Erasmus with respect to their common interpretation of the Great Commission.

71. Rothmann, *Schriften,* 282.

72. For a discussion of the problem and the literature, see Friesen, "Radical Reformation Revisited," pp. 148-54.

73. For the more comprehensive argument, see my forthcoming essay, "Present at the Inception: Menno Simons and the Beginnings of Dutch Anabaptism."

74. In George H. Williams and Angel M. Mergal, eds., *Spiritual and Anabaptist Writers* (Philadelphia: Westminster Press, 1957), pp. 204-25.

75. I address this problem much more fully in my "Present at the Inception."

76. Symons, *Opera Omnia Theologica,* p. 525, my emphasis.

77. "It must however be acknowledged, that Menno does not seem to have been unchangeably wedded to this opinion. For in several places he expresses himself ambiguously on this head, and even sometimes falls into inconsistencies" (John Lawrence Mosheim, *An Ecclesiastical History,* trans. Archibald Maclain [Charlestown, Mass.: Samuel Etheridge, 1810], 4:456).

78. See Cornelius Krahn, *Dutch Anabaptism: Origin, Spread, Life and Thought (1450-1600)* (The Hague: Martinus Nijhoff, 1968), p. 173.

79. One should note that Huizinga speaks of "Menno," not Obbe or Dirk Philips. Indeed, I have come to the conclusion that the entire relationship between Menno and the peaceful Melchiorites must be rethought. For Menno does not — with the exception of the doctrine of the incarnation foisted upon him — accept their theology; rather, he continues to develop his own theology based on Erasmus's interpretation of the Great Commission, as is clearly evident in his 1539 *Fundament-boek.* Further, Dirk Philips has his Melchiorite views modified by Menno. This will become evident when Dirk later begins to expound Erasmus's interpretation of the Great Commission.

80. J. H. Huizinga, *Dutch Civilization in the Seventeenth Century and other Essays,* trans. Arnold J. Pomerans (New York: Frederick Ungar, 1968), pp. 50-51.

81. Thieleman van Braght, *The Bloody Theater or Martyrs' Mirror,* trans. Joseph F. Sohm (Scottdale, Pa.: Herald Press, 1951), pp. 367-68.

82. J. Ten Doornkaat Koolman, *Dirk Philips 1504-1568* (Haarlem: H. D. Tjeenk Willink & Zoon N. V., 1964), p. 63. Koolman rejects a 1544 first and a 1562

second edition, declaring: "Weliswaar lezen we op het titelblad van het bekende Enchiridion van 1564 'nv nieus gecorrigeert ende vermeerdert,' maar dit doelt niet op de mysterieuze uitgaven van 1544 en 1562, maar op een erste druk van het Enchiridion in 1564, waarvan twee eendere exemplaren door mij gevonden werden, nl. Te Amsterdam (Universiteits-Bibliotheek) en te Zurich (Zentralbibliothek)."

83. See, e.g., *Martyrs' Mirror,* pp. 476-77, 494, 522, 544, and many more examples.

84. See esp. Friesen, "Menno and Muenster," pp. 140-42.

85. *Martyrs' Mirror,* p. 1050.

86. *Martyrs' Mirror,* p. 996. Never once in the entire book (over one thousand pages) does the author refer to Dirk or Obbe Philips in this manner.

87. Gustav Bossert, ed., *Quellen zur Geschichte der Wiedertaeufer I. Band Herzogtum Wuerttemberg* (Leipzig: M. Hensius Nachfolger, 1930), p. 542.

88. See Bossert, *Quellen,* pp. 560, 584, 683, 725, 727, 800, 802, 911, 1128.

89. Bossert, *Quellen,* p. 911.

90. Manfred Krebs, ed., *Baden und Pfalz,* vol. 4 of *Quellen zur Geschichte der Taeufer* (Gütersloh: C. Bertelsmann, 1951), p. 208. Cf. the 1835 reproduction of the 1575 *Ein Fundament und Klare Anweisung von der seligmachenden Lehre unsers Herrn Jesu Christi* (Lancaster, Pa.: Johann Baer, 1835), p. 38.

91. George Warren Richards's introduction to the English translation cites a letter of 7 October 1524 to Zwingli from Anton Papilio, which speaks of Zwingli's *De vera et falsa religione commentarius* (Ulrich Zwingli, *Commentary on True and False Religion,* ed. Samuel Macauley Jackson [Durham, N.C.: Labyrinth Press, 1981], p. 1). About one month earlier Grebel et al. wrote their famous letter to Müntzer, along with others to Carlstadt and Luther.

92. See Zwingli, *Commentary,* pp. 192-97, where he attacks the position, especially the Acts 19 passage.

93. Edward K. Burger, *Erasmus and the Anabaptists* (Ph.D. diss., University of California at Santa Barbara, 1977), p. 26.

94. Emil Duerr and Paul Roth, *Aktensammlung zur Geschichte der Basler Reformation in den Jahren 1519 bis Anfang 1534,* vol. 2 (Basel: Universitaetsbibliothek Basel, 1933), p. 557.

95. Günther Franz, ed., *Thomas Muentzer, Schriften und Briefe* (Gütersloh: Gerd Mohn, 1968), pp. 354-55.

96. Franz, *Muentzer Schriften,* p. 539. On a comparison of water baptism and the Holy Spirit in the thought of Thomas Müntzer, see Friesen, "Acts 10," pp. 5-22.

97. Franz, *Muentzer Schriften,* p. 503.

98. See Hermann Barge, *Andreas Bodenstein von Karlstadt,* 2 vols. (Leipzig: Friedrich Brandstetter, 1905), 1:170, 177-78, 195, 239, 395; 2:39, 217, 220, 253, 465, 512, 542; Ronald J. Sider, *Andreas Bodenstein von Karlstadt* (Leiden: E. J. Brill, 1974), pp. 85, 149, 240; Friedel Kriechbaum, *Grundzuege der Theologie Karlstadts* (Hamburg: Evangelischer Verlag, 1967), p. 11; James S. Preus, *Karlstadt's Ordinaciones and Luther's Liberty: A Study of the Wittenberg Movement* (Cambridge: Harvard Univ. Press, 1974); and Gordon Rupp, *Patterns of Reformation* (Philadelphia: Fortress Press, 1969), p. 63. Even Calvin Augustine Pater, *Karlstadt as Father of the Baptist Movements: The Emergence of Lay Protestantism* (Toronto: Univ. of Toronto Press, 1984), pp. 10, 23, 37, 54, 123,

127-28, 138, 143, 178, 292, never mentions Erasmus in connection with the para-phrases, nor even with Carlstadt's reference to Matthew 28:18-20.

99. See esp. Kriechbaum, *Grundzuege.*

100. Quoted in Pater, *Karlstadt,* p. 105, my emphasis.

101. Williams and Mergal, *Spiritual and Anabaptist Writers,* p. 184.

102. Williams and Mergal, *Spiritual and Anabaptist Writers,* pp. 187-88.

103. Williams and Mergal, *Spiritual and Anabaptist Writers,* p. 193, my emphasis.

104. See also Peter Kawerau, *Melchior Hoffmann als Religioeser Denker* (Haarlem: De Erven F. Bohn N.V., 1954), pp. 118-20, and Klaus Deppermann, *Melchior Hoffmann, Social Unrest and Apocalyptic Visions in the Age of the Reformation,* trans. Malcolm Wren, ed. Benjamin Drewry (Edinburgh: T. & T. Clark, 1987).

105. See esp. Grete Mecenseffy, ed., *Oesterreich I. Teil,* vol. 11 in *Quellen zur Geschichte der Taeufer* (Gütersloh: Gerd Mohn, 1964), pp. 42-45, 81-82, and 158-59.

106. Rupp, *Patterns,* pp. 379-99.

107. Rupp, *Patterns* p. 383. This passage is reminiscent of the following passage in Müntzer's *Prague Manifesto:* "Frey unde frisz sage ich, das ich keinen eselfortzigen doctor im allergeringesten mytlein adder spitzleyn von der ordennuenge (in Gott vnnd alle creaturn gesatzth) habe horen wispele, schweige den lauth reden" (Franz, *Muentzer Schriften,* p. 496).

108. Rupp, *Patterns,* p. 390. This would appear to be a reference to the mystical concept of the baptism of the Holy Spirit.

109. Franz, *Wiedertaeuferakten,* p. 4. Müntzer made the very same argument in his letter to Melanchthon of 22 March 1522. See Friesen and Goertz, *Muentzer,* pp. 124-27.

110. "Auch leren sie, das der mensch durch die verzeihung, verleucknunge und absagung seiner werk der creatur und seiner selbst (das ist nicht anders dan durch seine naturliche craft, so ime von got geben in der schepfung) muge zum glauben und geist gottes sich bereiten und kommen" (Franz, *Wiedertaeuferakten,* p. 5).

111. Franz, *Wiedertaeuferakten,* p. 8.

112. Franz, *Wiedertaeuferakten,* pp. 42-45.

113. See Friesen and Goertz, *Muentzer,* pp. 23-24.

114. Clarence Bauman, trans., *The Spiritual Legacy of Hans Denck: Interpretation and Translation of Key Texts* (Leiden: E. J. Brill, 1991), pp. 1-3.

115. See his recantation in Bauman, *Hans Denck,* pp. 248-59.

116. Johannes Bader, *Bruederliche Warnung fuer dem newen Abgoettischen orden der Widertaeuffer* (Landau, 1527).

117. Bader, *Bruederliche Warnung,* p. 14.

118. Bader, *Bruederliche Warnung,* p. 10.

119. John P. Dolan, *John Calvin & Jacopo Sadoleto: A Reformation Debate* (New York: Harper Torchbooks, 1966), pp. 59-61.

120. Hubmaier wrote of this exchange in his "Final Accounting": "Here let everyone who has ears hear that we, in light of the above Scriptures, are quite willingly to be subject to, and obey, the governmental authorities; we are also willingly to turn away from and avoid all disputes, revolts and dissension. It is on this account that I am so ill-pleased with Hans Hut and his followers, for they secretly and in out of the way places entice the people, misleading them to conspiracy and [outright]

revolution under the semblance of baptism and the Lord's Supper, as though one had to attack with the sword and the like."

121. *Geschichtsbuch,* pp. 102-3, n. 1.

122. Leonhard von Muralt, ed., *Quellen zur Geschichte der Taeufer in der Schweiz* (Zurich: S. Hirzel Verlag, 1952), 4:297, 341.

123. John H. Yoder, trans. and ed., *The Legacy of Michael Sattler* (Scottdale, Pa.: Herald Press, 1973), pp. 35-36.

124. Klassen and Klaassen, *Pilgram Marpeck,* pp. 44-45.

125. The baptismal part of Bader's tract is contained in Denck, *Schriften,* 3:100.

126. Denck, *Schriften,* 3:101.

127. Denck, *Schriften,* 3:117. That Denck makes no distinction between the first and second command to teach seems to be confirmed by his own following words: "Dann der tauff solle ye on vorgende predig nichts, und mag nyemants mit Gott sagen, das es on geferdt geschehen sey, das die lere vor und nach dem tauff befolhen ist, wie dann die schrifft vermag" (p. 116).

128. See Friesen and Goertz, *Muentzer,* pp. 10-32.

129. None of the persons discussed above appear to have encountered it from the Erasmian source. But then if they truly believed in the enlightenment within from the Inner Word, why should they study the work of a "scribe" like Erasmus?

Notes to Chapter 4

1. Ulrich Zwingli, *Selected Works,* ed. Samuel Macauley Jackson (Philadelphia: Univ. of Pennsylvania Press, 1901), p. 28. Perhaps Zwingli was more indebted to Luther in the above citation of Mark 16:16 than to Erasmus, for this was the passage that Luther cited in his *Babylonian Captivity*.

2. Zwingli, *Saemtliche Werke,* ed. Emil Egli and Georg Finsler (1908), 2:123. This passage was cited by Menno Simons (*Opera Omnia Theologica of alle de Godgeleerde Wercken* [Amsterdam: Johannes van Ween, 1618], p. 272) as proof of Zwingli's earliest position and by John Eck, who, in his response to Zwingli's boast in his *Fidei Ratio ad Carolum Imperatorem* of 1530, "I have been the first to teach and write against them [the Anabaptists]," wrote:

> I laugh at the empty boasting of Zwingli that he was the first to teach and write against the Anabaptists, since I am aware that it was Zwingli who by his counsel and advice really founded this lost sect, and who was goaded more by jealousy than love of truth in his pursuit of Balthasar the Catabaptist, as all his neighbors testify. Wherefore let no good man believe Zwingli even under oath when he says he has not accepted or taught any of the doctrines of this seditious party, for his published books convict him of lying. [Eck quotes from Art. 18 of Zwingli's *Auslegung und Gruende der Schluszreden* (1523), and *De vera et falsa Religione* (1524).] Balthasar the Catabaptist also, in a pamphlet published at Nikolsburg in Moravia had words of Zwingli printed which advised against the baptism of infants, and said in a note that he had a writing to that effect.

Clearly, Eck took the word of Hubmaier over that of Zwingli, while Usteri, a Zwinglian partisan, wrote: "Es waere an und für sich wenig glaubwuerdig, was der fluechtige Balthasar Hubmaier in einem 1526 zu Nikolsburg herausgegebenen Gespraech Zwingli nachredet, derselbe habe, als sie im Jahre 1523 zweimal in Zuerich in einer Privatunterredung die Schriftstellen von der Taufe verglichen, ihm darin recht gegeben, dasz man die Kinder, ehe sie unterrichtet seien, nicht taufen solle, er habe auch versprochen, in seinem Artikelbuch davon Meldung zu thun, und dies sei wirklich im 18. Artikel von der Firmung (sowie in dem Buechlein 'von den aufruehrischen Geistern') geschehen" (Usteri, "Darstellung der Tauflehre Zwinglis," *Theologische Studien und Kritiken* 2 [1882]: 211). On the next page, however, Usteri referred to Zwingli's "strange" confession that he had himself been deceived some years earlier to believe "it would be better not to baptize children until they came of age." Perhaps, Usteri grudgingly conceded, Hubmaier's statement was not totally unbelievable after all (p. 212).

3. See the argument in Friesen, "The Radical Reformation Revisited," *JMS* 2 (1984): 124-76.

4. Leland Harder, ed., *The Sources of Swiss Anabaptism* (Scottdale, Pa.: Herald Press, 1985), p. 366.

5. A careful reading of Mantz's *Protestation* reveals that he employs both the Erasmian argument as well as the one we will argue Zwingli uses. Perhaps Zwingli used his argument to attack the Erasmian argument while Mantz used the Erasmian argument to attack Zwingli's.

6. See, e.g., the following from Eck's *Enchiridion:* "In tauff werden wir wider geboren zu dem leben/nach dem tauff werden wir gefirmt vnd bestet zu dem streyt/im tauff werden wir abgeweschen nach dem tauff werden wir gesterckt" (Johannes Eck, *Enchiridion: Handbuechlin gemainer stell unnd Artickel der jetzt schwebenden Neuwen leeren,* ed. Erwin Iserloh [Münster, 1980], p. 27). Or again: "sonder red von der ernewerung der widergeburt des Taufs" (p. 81).

7. This is an argument that smacks of precisely that passage in Erasmus's 1522 preface to his New Testament that Leo Jud was to lift for the introduction of his 1535 translation of the paraphrases. See chap. 2 n. 73 above.

8. Zwingli, *Commentary on True and False Religion,* ed. Samuel Macauley Jackson (Durham, N.C.: Labyrinth Press, 1981), pp. 182-83, my emphasis.

9. It is very clear that Zwingli uses the term very differently from the Mystics. See Friesen and Hans-Jürgen Goertz, eds., *Thomas Muentzer* (Darmstadt: Wissenschaftliche Buchgesellschaft, 1978), pp. 10-32.

10. Zwingli, *Commentary,* p. 187, my emphasis.

11. Zwingli, *Commentary,* p. 183.

12. Zwingli, *Commentary,* p. 183. Zwingli's separation of water and Spirit baptism has usually been attributed to his Neoplatonism. See esp. John H. Yoder, *Läufertum und Reformation im Gespräch* (Zurich: EVZ-Verlag, 1968), pp. 13-32. With regard to baptism, however, it derives clearly from his conviction that the Catholic sacrament of baptism does not regenerate the baptized. The water alone accomplishes nothing; it was the baptism of the Holy Spirit that transformed a person.

13. Zwingli, *Commentary,* p. 189.

14. Matthew 21:25 reads: "Jesus replied, 'I will ask you one question. If you

answer me, I will tell you by what authority I am doing these things. John's baptism —
where did it come from? Was it from heaven, or from men?'" No wonder Calvin was
to say later: "Some take baptism for new institution or instruction [Zwingli], of whose
mind I am not, *because, as their exposition is too much racked, so it smelleth of a starting-hole* [of
evasion]" ("Commentary upon the Acts of the Apostles," in *Calvin's Commentaries* [rpt.;
Grand Rapids: Baker Book House, 1981], 19:209-10). Zwingli himself recognized how
formidable a difficulty he faced, for in his *Of Baptism* he wrote: "And when John came
he baptized, as we may see quite plainly in all the evangelists. But if he came to initiate
and prepare the way of the Lord, and in fulfilling that mission he baptized, then assuredly
he initiated the baptism of the Lord. But here the Anabaptists say: The baptism of John
and that of Christ are not the same. And they are not alone when they say that, for all
the theologians that I have ever read or can call to mind say exactly the same. Therefore
it is not easy for me to assert the contrary, for if the Anabaptists and the papists are in
league against me, I am inevitably confronted by more formidable adversaries than any
theologian of our age has ever previously encountered" (G. W. Bromiley, *Zwingli &
Bullinger* [Philadelphia: Westminster, 1969], p. 161).

15. Harder, *Sources,* p. 305.

16. Harder, *Sources,* p. 306.

17. Harder, *Sources,* p. 308.

18. Harder, *Sources,* p. 309, my emphasis.

19. Bromiley, *Zwingli & Bullinger,* p. 141.

20. That Zwingli was arguing against the Erasmian interpretation may also be
indirectly inferred from Mantz's *Protestation.* For there Mantz clearly employs the
Erasmian context together with Zwingli's argument concerning the internal reality
and external sign of a sacrament, saying: "After the receiving of this teaching and the
descent of the Holy Spirit, . . . water was then poured over them. This meant that,
just as they were cleansed within by the coming of the Holy Spirit, so they were also
poured over with water externally to signify the inner cleansing and dying to sin."
See p. 54 above.

21. Bromiley, *Zwingli & Bullinger,* p. 142.

22. Quoted in John Horsch, *Infant Baptism: Its Origin Among Protestants and the
Arguments Advanced for and against It* (Scottdale, Pa.: Mennonite Publishing House,
1917), p. 23, my emphasis.

23. Quoted in Horsch, *Infant Baptism,* p. 25, my emphasis.

24. See Horsch, *Infant Baptism,* pp. 23-28.

25. Emil Duerr and Paul Roth, *Aktensammlung zur Geschichte der Basler Reformation in den Jahren 1519 bis Anfang 1534* (Basel: Universitaetsbibliothek Basel, 1933),
2:31-32.

26. Nikolaus Mueller, "Die Wittenberger Bewegung 1521 und 1522," *Archiv
für Reformationsgeschichte* 6 (1908-1909): 396.

27. See Luther's letter of 13 January 1522 to Philip Melanchthon, where Luther
tells him that he disapproves of "your timidity" (*Luther's Works,* ed. Gottfried G.
Krodel and Helmut T. Lehmann [Philadelphia: Fortress Press, 1955], 48:365).

28. It was the threat of social unrest that probably motivated Frederick the most
to cut off further discussion with regard to infant baptism, especially since Carlstadt's

Protestant eucharistic service only a few days before, on Christmas day 1522, had already caused such unrest.

29. Melanchthon may be indebted to Erasmus for this judgment, for Menno Simons cites Erasmus as having made this observation about the Church Fathers in general (*Opera Omnia Theologica*, pp. 272, 409).

30. Mueller, "Die Wittenberger Bewegung," pp. 394-95, my emphasis. Hermann Pfister explains Melanchthon's indecision with respect to infant baptism at this point by asserting that "Melanchthon befindet sich also in der Sakramentslehre auf dem Weg zu einer *Ueberbetonung* des Glaubens im sakramentalen Akt" (*Die Entwicklung der Theologie Melanchthons unter dem Einflusz der Auseinandersetzung mit Schwarmgeistern und Wiedertaeufern* [Ph.D. diss.: Univ. of Freiburg, 1968], p. 38, my emphasis). So much for the doctrine of *sola fide*. And Wilhelm Maurer, in *Der junge Melanchthon* (Göttingen: Vandenhoeck & Ruprecht, 1967), 2:207, places the blame on Melanchthon's Christian humanistic background. But the "blame," as we shall see, is to be placed at Luther's own door, and his initial "Ueberbetonung des Glaubens"!

31. Perhaps upon reading Erasmus's observation on the matter.

32. *WA*, 2:736.

33. Bertram Lee Woolf, trans. and ed., *Reformation Writings of Martin Luther* (New York: Philosophical Library, 1953), 1:255.

34. Woolf, *Reformation Writings*, 1:261.

35. Woolf, *Reformation Writings*, 1:263.

36. Woolf, *Reformation Writings*, 1:265. Walter Koehler also points to this emphasis on faith in Luther's early writings, saying: "der wahre Luther war den Schweizern verhuellt geblieben, *sie sahen ihn durch die eigene Brille, empfanden die Betonung des Glaubens, die Luther wie fuer jedes Sakrament auch fuer das Abendmahl* [and baptism] *forderte und in seinen Fruehschriften ganz in den Vordergrund gerueckt hatte*" (*Huldrych Zwingli*, 2nd ed. [Leipzig: Koehler & Amelang, 1954], p. 179, my emphasis).

37. Woolf, *Reformation Writings*, p. 271.

38. Woolf, *Reformation Writings*, pp. 271-72.

39. Had there been dissent on this issue among the Wittenberg Reformers?

40. If the above is correct — that is, that the Zwickau Prophets based their doubts about *baptismi parvulorum* and *fides aliena* on Luther's writings (esp. his *Captivity*), an assertion Melanchthon made no effort to refute and indeed tacitly appears to have accepted — then Luther is, at least to an extent, responsible for their convictions. Add to this Luther's publication of the fragmentary *German Theology* in 1516 and the complete document in 1518 with their laudatory prefaces regarding John Tauler, whom Luther at first assumed to have written the document, and one can begin to see the critical influence of Luther on the radical mystical movement that was to emerge in his own backyard. This further implies that these radicals never absorbed Erasmus's argument as propounded in his paraphrases. Indeed, the Prophets appeared in Wittenberg with their views before the publication of Erasmus's paraphrases. Because of this they never shared the basic assumptions upon which the Swiss Anabaptists and the Dutch Anabaptists after Münster based their views.

41. Woolf, *Reformation Writings*, pp. 260-61, my emphasis.

42. Mueller, "Wittenberger Bewegung," p. 304, presents a document dated 14 December 1521 and signed by a group of Wittenberg personalities headed by Lorenz

Schlamau, dean of the *Stiftskirche* and Luther's staunchest Catholic opponent. The document is a response to the Elector's memorandum on the subject of church reform in Wittenberg dated 25 October 1521, and contains the following passage: "In the same way the church at the time of the apostles soon changed the *form* of baptism. Those who baptized in the holy name of Jesus in chapters 2, 8, 9 and 19 of Acts did so according to the *form* of baptism they had received from Christ in Matthew 28: go ye into all the world, teach the people and baptize them in the name of the Father, Son and Holy Ghost."

In my *History and Renewal,* I argued that this reflected an Erasmian influence in the Wittenberg discussion concerning infant baptism. I no longer believe that, having traced the issue back to the Church Fathers through the Medieval Scholastics and, as the first chapter of this book demonstrates, having seen how the Catholic apologists of the Reformation era sought to exploit the problem in favor of the authority of the church over the Bible. But the fact that we should refer to this interpretive tradition on both the Lutheran side as well as the Catholic side in Wittenberg is a strong indication that the issues that Luther addressed in his *Captivity* had probably been pretty thoroughly discussed within the Wittenberg university community.

43. "Grund und Ursach aller Artivkel D. Martin Luthers, so durch roemische Bulle unrechtlich verdammt sind," *WA,* 7:321.

44. That even Zwingli found this passage as interpreted by Erasmus persuasive is indicated by the following passage taken from his letter to Franz Lambert and the "Brethren in Strasbourg" of 16 December 1524: "Their third objection is this: 'He who believes and is baptized shall be saved; but he who believes not shall be damned' [Mark 16:16]. Faith must therefore be present first, or one might just as well baptize a raven. I answer: This verse cannot be applied to children, for just before these words, he said, 'Preach the gospel to every creature' [Mark 16:15], and then 'he who believes' — that is, when he has heard the gospel. But since it can neither be preached to infants nor heard by them, it clearly follows that they were not meant in this admittedly very important passage, but only those who hear the preaching and then either believe it or evade it" (Harder, *Sources,* p. 309).

45. John Nicholas Lenker, ed., *Sermons of Martin Luther,* trans. John Nicholas Lenker et al. (Grand Rapids: Baker Book House, 1983), 2:197-98.

46. Lenker, ed., *Sermons,* 2:201.

47. Lenker, ed., *Sermons,* 2:203.

48. Lenker, ed., *Sermons,* 2:188-89.

49. Lenker, ed., *Sermons,* 2:225.

50. Lenker, ed., *Sermons,* 2:226.

51. Lenker, ed., *Sermons,* 2:226, my emphasis.

52. Lenker, ed., *Sermons,* 2:226-27, my emphasis. Luther accentuated this sequence even more a little later on when he wrote:

When one understands and believes this text, then the teaching of the other text should follow, namely, that we should also do good works. Yet good works must accompany faith, which always clings to Christ and pleads before God that he will graciously and for Christ's sake accept and be pleased with the supplicant's life and works, and not impute to him that which might be imperfect and sinful in him. Hereupon follows properly the text, Mt 28,20: "Teaching them to observe all things whatsoever I commanded you." Fail not to observe the first and essential condition; for if faith is absent, all our good works and upright life count for naught before God. Indeed, it is not possible to do truly good works without faith. Christ says in John 15,5: "For apart from me ye can do nothing" etc. (Lenker, ed., *Sermons*, 2:230)

This emphasis on "Jewish law and ceremonies" is reminiscent of Erasmus's paraphrase of the Great Commission in the Gospel of Matthew. The fact that Luther now also turned to Matthew in this fashion may well derive from his reading of the Erasmian paraphrase.

53. Lenker, ed., *Sermons*, 2:237.

54. Lenker, ed., *Sermons*, 2:237.

55. Lenker, ed., *Sermons*, 2:228.

56. The Anabaptist sect was just as troublesome for Melanchthon. As late as 1536 he was still reacting to the Anabaptist justification of believer's baptism, but now within the Erasmian context of that argument. In his *Adversus Anabaptistas* of 1536 he wrote: "Dagegen sollen alle Christen wohl unterrichtet seyn, dasz die Kindertaufe recht und noethig sey. Denn das Gebot: tauffet alle Voelker, begreift auch die Kinder" (*Corpus Reformatorum* [Halis Saxonum: C. A. Schwetschke et filium, 1836], 3:33).

57. Duerr and Roth, *Basler Reformation*, 2:557, 559.

58. Duerr and Roth, *Basler Reformation*, 2:556-57.

59. Duerr and Roth, *Basler Reformation*, 2:552.

60. "Dan dieweil die armen, einfeltigen, von ynen verfierte widerteuffer von allen christlichen breuchen, ordnungen und satzungen allein uff den heitern, dirren buchstaben sind gezogen worden, haben sie denselben fleissiger betrachtet, dan yren meistern wil gefallen. Dann wie dirr und beschnitten er ist, so ist er dannocht ynen, ja yren meistern ze hert und ze streng, ihres fleischlichen sauff- und bauchlebens halben. Dan hausz und hoff, garten und matten, sylbern und guldne kleinod kauffen, wil sein dirre nit tragen. Darumb die fleischmeyster, sich hand understanden, das arm voelcklin, die teuffer, also von ynen vertüefft, versenckt und verblendt, wellen auszleschen nit des widertauffs (welchen sie uns nu fuer ein schein fuerwenden, *dan er geet von ynen ausz, wie du weist*), sondern des sauffslebens halben, das ynen wolt dorch solch yr juenger abgestrikt werden. *Haben aber solchs in keinerley weg muegen durch alleyn heytere [a 3:], blosze und (wie sie reden) dirre schrifft kuenden thuen. Darumb sie geurschet sind worden, ausz yr eygene ban uff unseren platz ze tretten und sich der christenlichen kirchen waffen und mit der schrifft geist ze fechten underfangenn.* Welches yr christenlichen seulen, so yrs habent gemerckt, wie namlich Eck in seinem Enchiridion ausz Hueszscheinischen [Oecolampadius] biechern eylff argumenta anzeiget, ausz dem schatz kirchliches (!) geists genommen, habent yr gesagt, wie do selbest Eck redet: Schaw zue, so ein ketzer wil den andern bestreiten, kan ers nit thuen on die waffen der christenlichen kirchen. Disz habent die heicklen geist nit muegen erleiden. Darumb sie wider zu der schrifft sind gelauffen und *haben alle oerter, so die notte anzeigenn, das man sol getaufft werden mit dem wassertauff, well man anderst selig werden, uberzogen mit tropen, unnd getaufft werden, wie auch das nachtmal ze nuessen (wie sie sagen), in die frey wilkoerung gesetzt, wie dann yre buecher anzeigen, so in den nechsten tzweien vergangenen jaren sind auszgangen. Darinn alle schrifften, so je und je das sie von den sacramenten*

redent, nit allein von der christenlichen kirchen und den gotlichen lerern, sondern auch von yrem meister Luthero und nu yrenn juengern, den widerteuffern, sind worden anzogen, dermassen von ynen sind vertropet und ausz natuerlichem verstand in frembde figurliche sinn by dem har gezogenn, das ynen gar nach an den schematen, tropen und figuren, von allen poeten unnd oratoren gebraucht, thuet zerinnen, dem armen, einfeltigen man die augen zerblendend, als ob niemant fuer ynen nie Hebraisch oder Kriechisch buchstaben hab gesehen, Latin oder Tuetsch geredt, dieweil doch nichts minders rechtgeschaffens kinden, dan die frembden, kuenstlichen sprachen. Und steet nu ir gantzes fundament auff einem einygen syllogismo" (Duerr and Roth, *Basler Reformationsakten,* 2:582-83). And that one syllogism had as its major premise the doctrine of predestination!

61. Duerr and Roth, *Basler Reformationsakten,* 2:594-95.

62. Eck, *Enchiridion,* p. 161. This is a photographic reproduction of the 1532 edition. Acts 10 was the passage Felix Mantz also had used for his purposes.

63. On the problem of Dionysius during the age of the Renaissance and the Reformation, see Jean Leclercq, "Influence and Noninfluence of Dionysius in the Western Middle Ages," in *Pseudo-Dionysius: The Complete Works* (New York: Paulist Press, 1985).

64. Eck, *Enchiridion,* p. 157.

65. *The Decades of Henry Bullinger,* trans. H. I. and ed. Rev. Thomas Harding, The Parker Society (Cambridge: Cambridge Univ. Press, Johnson rpt., 1968), 5:337-38.

66. John Calvin, "Brieve instruction pour armer tous bons fideles contre les erreurs de la secte commune des Anabaptistes," *Ioannis Calvini Opera quae supersunt omnia,* ed. Guilielmus Baum, Eduardus Cunitz, and Eduardus Reuss (Brunsvigae: C. A. Schwetschkte et filium, 1863-1900), 7.49-142. Calvin refers to the Great Commission and its use by the Anabaptists in his discussion of baptism, the very first article.

67. John Calvin, *Commentary on a Harmony of the Evangelists, Matthew, Mark, and Luke* (Edinburgh: Calvin Translation Society; rpt., Grand Rapids: Baker Book House, 1981), 3:386, my emphasis.

68. John Calvin, *Commentary upon the Acts of the Apostles* (Edinburgh: Calvin Translation Society; rpt., Grand Rapids: Baker Book House, 1981), 1:333, 452-54; 2:208-10.

69. John Calvin, *Institutes of the Christian Religion,* vol. 21 of the *Library of Christian Classics* (Philadelphia: Westminster Press, 1960), p. 1346.

70. I will attempt to establish this argument even more fully in the epilogue to this study.

71. The "polygenesis" argument is in fact based on an improper use of historiography. The latter can at best be used to trace the development of an interpretive tradition; it cannot, however, in and of itself confirm an interpretation. The latter must always be done on the basis of the historical evidence. Therefore, all that the Stayer, Deppermann, and Packull study proves is that there were in fact these three major interpretive traditions. Most scholars already knew this.

But what is more disturbing about that study is that all three historiographical traditions end in one or the other of the three authors' own studies! This is a development worthy of the great Hegel himself. The individual studies, therefore, serve to determine both the point of departure as well as the culmination of each tradition. Should such authors be so critical of the "Bender school"?

Notes to Chapter 5

1. Franklin H. Littell, *The Origins of Sectarian Protestantism* (New York: Macmillan, 1963), p. 109.

2. See Littell, *Origins,* p. 109.

3. See chap. 3 n. 50 above.

4. See esp.: Franklin H. Littell, "The Anabaptist Theology of Missions," *MQR* 21, no.1 (1947): 5-17; Wilhelm Wiswedel, "Die alten Taeufergemeinden und ihr missionarisches Wirken," *ARG* 40 (1943): 183-200, *ARG* 45 (1948): 115-32; Roland H. Bainton, "The Great Commission," *Mennonite Life* 7, no. 4 (1953): 183-89; Wolfgang Schaeufele, *Das missionarische Bewusstsein und Wirken der Taeufer* (Neukirchen: Neukirchener Verlag des Erziehungsvereins, 1966); and Hans Kasdorf, "The Great Commission and the Reformation," *Direction* (April 1975): 303-318, as well as "Teaching the Great Commission," in *Called to Teach,* ed. David Ewert (Fresno: Center for Mennonite Brethren Studies, 1980), pp. 115-42.

5. Menno Symons, *Opera Omnia Theologica of alle de Godgeleerde Wercken* (Amsterdam: Johannes van Ween, 1618), p. 168.

6. This argument would appear to be confirmed by Erasmus's colloquy, *Inquisitio de Fide,* first published in March 1524 — that is, very shortly after his completion of the paraphrases of the Gospels and the Acts of the Apostles. In the introduction to his English translation of this colloquy, Craig R. Thompson writes: "Barbatius passes the examination. Aulus the Catholic satisfies himself, to his surprise, that the Lutheran is sufficiently orthodox on the Apostles' Creed — the Creed which it is necessary to believe *ad salutem.* A reader's inference must be that, putting aside all the vexed questions of custom, discipline, ceremonies, indulgences, and other such matters *not* necessary to salvation, Catholics and Lutherans could agree on the articles of the Creed" (Craig R. Thompson, trans., *The Colloquies of Erasmus* [Chicago: Univ. of Chicago Press, 1965], p. 177).

7. In opposition to Preserved Smith, who saw in Erasmus the great exemplar of liberal, "undogmatic" Christianity. See Preserved Smith, *Erasmus: A Study of His Life, Ideals and Place in History* (New York: Harper & Brother, 1923), p. xi.

8. Robert Friedmann, *The Theology of Anabaptism* (Scottdale, Pa.: Herald Press, 1973), pp. 27-35.

9. Craig R. Thompson makes the same argument with respect to Erasmus's position, upon which the Anabaptists appear to have been dependent, saying:

> It might be convenient to conclude, as one writer has done, that *Inquisitio de Fide* is a tract on the superiority of religion to theology, and that it shows us that "Ce qui le [Luther] separe de la communion romaine ce n'est pas la religion; c'est la theologie." [J. B. Pineau, *Erasme: sa pensee religieuse* (1924), p. 257.] This oversimplifies matters. We should do better, in my opinion, to say that *Inquisitio de Fide* [we should also add, his paraphrases] argues the supremacy of *fundamental* theological doctrines and the sufficiency of those doctrines (about which, it is discovered, Luther and the Roman Church agree) for establishing and preserving concord among Christians. For Erasmus did insist on the necessity of accepting the primary dogmas, those of the Apostles' Creed. The articles of that Creed are certainly

dogmatic theology, and Erasmus' elucidation of them is certainly theological in character. As for theological questions not treated in the Apostles' Creed, they should be differently regarded: they are important, to be sure, but agreement about them is not necessary *ad salutem,* nor basic to Christian unity. The Church should tolerate local or individual disagreements about such questions as far as it possibly can; which meant, for Erasmus, sacrificing conformity to unity. We must not make Erasmus more modern than he was. He did not believe in the wisdom or even the right of secession. He did believe that authority should require conformity only in essentials. Beyond that it was to exhort, to persuade, but to refrain from compulsion and tyranny. (Thompson, trans., *Colloquies,* pp. 43-44)

Whereas liberal theologians and those, like Keller, influenced by medieval mysticism speak of an "undogmatic" Christianity — whatever they may mean by that — some Mennonite historians and theologians speak of the "non-creedal" nature of Anabaptist thought. Thus, in his article on "Confessions of Faith" in the *Mennonite Encyclopedia* (1:679), Harold S. Bender wrote: "The Anabaptists never attached the weight to creeds or confessions given to them by the remainder of Christendom; they were Biblicists who produced a large number of confessions, not as instruments to which the laity or ministry subscribed *ex anima,* but as instructional tools for the indoctrination of their young people and as witnesses to their faith for distribution in society or as a means of better understanding between differing groups." Or, a little later on: "For the most part these ministers' meetings deal with life rather than doctrine; the concern is with Christian conduct and church regulations, not dogmatics. The outcome is typically precepts, not creeds" (p. 680). And in his article on "Catechism" Bender wrote: "This and the obvious *nonuse* of the catechetical method and nonpublication of a catechism by Anabaptist-Mennonites in any country for the first century and a quarter of their history . . ." (1:531). In the introduction to Howard John Loewen's *One Lord, One Church, One Hope, and One God: Mennonite Confessions of Faith in North America* (Elkhart, Ind.: Institute of Mennonite Studies, 1985), C. J. "Dyck suggested that Anabaptists and Mennonites were non-creedal because of a combination of factors, including a rejection of the established churches' habit of stressing doctrine at the expense of ethics, a desire to be biblical, a feeling that an emphasis on creeds did not fit with the idea of the priesthood of all believers, and a fear that spontaneity in worship could be eliminated by a need for confessional recital" (Russel Snyder-Penner, "The Ten Commandments, The Lord's Prayer, and the Apostles' Creed as Early Anabaptist Texts," *MQR* 68 [July 1994]: 319-20, n. 4). Snyder-Penner himself conludes: "With respect to the place of the Apostles' Creed in these presuppostions, one is led at the very least to conclude that some of the assumptions about the non-creedal character of early Anabaptism call for careful reconsideration" (p. 335). In both Bender's and Dyck's pronouncements there appears to be a curious non-Anabaptist polarity at work: Anabaptists were non-creedal because of magisterial Protestantism's overemphasis on creeds; and they emphasized ethics because the latter did not. This is to misinterpret Anabaptism's central emphasis on the integration of precepts — of statements of belief — with action. Like both Erasmus and Thomas More, Anabaptists argued for a congruence between beliefs and actions. The demand for such a congruence lies at the heart of the movement.

10. More, *Utopia,* trans. and ed. H. V. S. Ogden (New York: Appleton, Century

Crofts, 1949), p. 24. In his *Inquisitio de Fide* Erasmus has Barbatius respond to Aulus' statement: "Since you agree with us in so many and so difficult questions, what hinders you from being wholly on our side?" with: "I want to hear about that from you, for I think I'm orthodox. Even if I wouldn't vouch for my life, *still I try diligently to make it correspond to my confession*" (Thompson, trans., *Colloquies,* p. 188). Erasmus also made this argument clearly in the preface to the 1522 edition of his New Testament, which all of the Swiss Anabaptist leaders must have used.

11. *Hutterite Chronicle,* p. 45.

12. Symons, *Opera Omnia Theologica,* p. 15.

13. The "Zofinger Gespraech," in Leonhard von Muralt, ed., *Quellen zur Geschichte der Taeufer in der Schweiz* (Zurich: S. Hirzel Verlag, 1952), 4:100.

14. Menno's views on the incarnation were adopted from the pacific Melchiorites under difficult circumstances. As the later debates made clear, there were differences on predestination and free will as well as on a number of other issues.

15. Augustine's use of this phrase, and what he intended to imply with it, needs to be investigated, as does Luther's use of the same phrase.

16. It may be Peter's use of the Old Testament passages that influenced the Anabaptist view of the relationship between Old and New Testaments. For, as Walter Klaassen has described this view,

> The Anabaptists seem to have been the only Protestants in the 16th century who took a historical view of the Bible [due to Erasmian influence?]. They viewed the drama of God's redemption as a process, initiated by God in particular with Abraham, and moving forward to a climax in Jesus Christ, in whom God would conclude human history. The Old Testament with its Abrahamic, Mosaic and Davidic covenants they viewed as preparatory, as paving the way, for the final and complete revelation of God in Christ Jesus. The Old Testament institutions and the understanding of God and his ways and will are seen as lacking finality; they are unfinished. Men there move in the world of shadow in comparison with the brightness of the world in which Christ is revealed. ("The Bern Debate of 1538: Christ the Center of Scripture," *MQR* 40 [April 1966]: 148-49)

17. Symons, *Opera Omnia Theologica,* p. 128, my emphasis.

18. See Friesen, "Anabaptism and Monasticism: A Study in the Development of Parallel Historical Patterns," *JMS* 6 (1988): 174-97.

19. Leland Harder, ed., *The Sources of Swiss Anabaptism* (Scottdale, Pa.: Herald Press, 1985), p. 313.

20. John H. Yoder, trans. and ed., *The Legacy of Michael Sattler* (Scottdale, Pa.: Herald Press, 1973), p. 36.

21. See the argument following this quotation in Martin Haas, ed., *Quellen Schweiz* (Zurich: Theologischer Verlag, 1974), 4:104-5.

22. Harder, ed., *Sources,* p. 290.

23. For a fuller treatment of this subject, see Friesen, "Menno and Muenster: The Man and the Movement," in *Menno Simons, A Reappraisal,* ed. Gerald R. Brunk (Harrisonburg, Va.: Eastern Mennonite College, 1992), pp. 131-62.

24. Yoder, *Legacy,* pp. 37-38.

25. John Nicholas Lenker, ed., *Sermons of Martin Luther,* trans. John Nicholas Lenker et al. (Grand Rapids: Baker Book House, 1983), 3:226-27.

26. Lenker, ed., *Sermons,* 3:237.

27. *Desiderii Erasmi Roterodami Opera Omnia,* vol. 7, *Paraphrasis in N. Testamentum* (Leiden, 1706), p. 674 (photographic reproduction; Hildesheim: Georg Olms Verlagsbuchhandlung, 1962).

28. Nowhere, however, is it to be found in Thomas Müntzer's writings. And in the writings of those Anabaptists influenced by mystical (spiritualistic) tendencies, it often plays a secondary role and is quite frequently employed for different purposes, as noted in chap. 3.

29. For example:

Diewyll durch die predicannten angezogenn, der touff sye ein anheblich zeichenn der christennlichen kilchen, so hetten Christus billichen sinen aposteln bevolchenn unnd Johannes gelertt: Lannd uech zum ersten touffen und darnach thund busz. Dwyll sy aber disers vor gelertt unnd es Christus sinen aposteln bevolchenn: thund busz, werdennt von nuewem geboren unnd den erst toufft, so vollgett, das der toyff nitt ein anheblich zeichenn, *sunder busz, gloubenn, widergeburt* musz vorgan. Unnd das ist das anheblich zeichen der christenlichen kilchen; Wellicher gloubt, wirtt wider geborenn durch die gaben gottes, sich der sundenn bekhennt, ruew unnd leid treitt [traegt], dem ist der touff zugelassenn, das er verfasset werde in ein christenliche versamlung. (Haas, ed., *Quellen Schweiz,* 4:385)

See also p. 350, where the emphasis on the gospel — "das man zum ersten leren den glaubenn inn Christum" — is even clearer; and p. 110 where a greater emphasis is placed on discipleship after baptism. Note also the central emphasis on conversion in the above and also even in the Rothmann quotation above.

30. Rothmann, *Schriften,* p. 147. Rothmann's tract may well have influenced Menno, but it most certainly influenced the Swiss and South German Anabaptists through Marpeck's *Vermahnung* of 1542, which was taken nearly verbatim from Rothmann's tract, and reads:

This is the first instruction, namely, that the gospel is openly proclaimed to all creatures and salvation is freely offered to everyone. This proclamation is included in the words the Lord speaks: 'Teach all nations.' Wherever, then, the Holy Spirit touches the heart, so that man can truly believe the gospel, a child of God is born and his birth is witnessed in baptism, openly revealed and carried as we shall note later.

After baptism, a different kind of teaching follows, a teaching which is directed to the regenerate and baptized children of God; they are taught to observe all that Christ has commanded, as is fitting for obedient children, and at all times to seek to do the will of their Father. (William Klassen and Walter Klaassen, *The Writings of Pilgram Marpeck* [Scottdale, Pa.: Herald Press, 1978], p. 199)

31. Dirk Philips, *Enchiridion, oder Handbüchleia von der Christlichen Lehre und Religion* (rpt.; Aylmer, Ohio, and LeGrange, Ind.: Pathway, 1986), pp. 19-20.

32. Speaking with reference to Matthew 28:19-20, van Imbroeck observed: "Hence, the words of Christ declare, that teaching must take place before and after baptism, in order that the person baptized may use diligence to observe, after baptism,

the Gospel (which was presented to him before baptism), and all things commanded him; for he is no more lord over himself; but, as a bride surrenders herself to her bridegroom, so he, after receiving baptism, surrenders himself to Christ" (Thieleman van Braght, *The Bloody Theater of Martyrs' Mirror,* trans. Joseph F. Sohm [Scottdale, Pa.: Herald Press, 1951], p. 367. See also p. 396).

33. Günther Franz et al., eds., *Wiedertaeuferakten,* vol. 4 of *Urkundliche Quellen zur Hessischen Reformationsgeschichte* (Marburg: N. G. Ewert'sche Verlagsbuchhandlung, 1951), p. 184.

34. Lenker, ed., *Sermons,* 3:237.

35. See *The Decades of Henry Bullinger,* trans. H. I. and ed. Rev. Thomas Harding, The Parker Society (Cambridge: Cambridge Univ. Press, Johnson rpt., 1968), 10:386-87. But he too argued that "Yea, he teacheth them also the way and means how to gather disciples unto him out of all nations, or all nations, by baptizing and teaching them. By baptizing and preaching ye shall gather me together a church. And he setteth out both of them severally one after another, sweetly and shortly, saying: 'Baptizing them in the name of the Father and of the Son and of the Holy Ghost; teaching them to observe all things which I have commanded you.' Now therefore baptism goeth before teaching" (p. 286). Bullinger and Luther were the only ones to speak of the "Trine" baptismal formula. See also Calvin, "Commentary on a Harmony of the Evangelists," in *Commentaries* (rpt.; Grand Rapids: Baker Book House, 1981), 17:386-87.

36. This sequence was even expressed in their hymns. E.g., in a hymn entitled *Gott fuehrt ein recht Gericht,* we read:

> Sein Wort laeszt er hie zeugen an,
> der Mensch soll sich bekehren.
> Glauben dem wort und tauffen lahn,
> und folgen seiner lehren.

37. Erasmus, *Enchiridion,* p. 75.

38. Ulrich Zwingli, *Selected Works,* ed. Samuel Macauley Jackson (Philadelphia: Univ. of Pennsylvania Press, 1901), p. 28.

39. More, *Utopia,* p. 24.

40. Harder, *Sources,* p. 286.

41. Symons, *Opera Omnia Theologica,* p. 168.

42. Symons, *Opera Omnia Theologica,* p. 168, my emphasis.

43. Zwingli, *Works,* p. 132, my emphasis.

44. Zwingli, *Works,* p. 133.

45. See Emilien Lamirande, "Augustine and the Discussion on the Sinners in the Church at the Conference of Carthage (411)," *Augustinian Studies* 3 (1972): 97-112.

Notes to Chapter 6

1. On 9 December 1993 I delivered a paper at the Institut für europaeische Geschichte in Mainz, Germany, entitled "Reichsgesetz und Evangelium: Martin

Luther und das Reichsmandat vom 6. Maerz 1523." I have begun work on the larger project, to be entitled *Imperial Law and Holy Gospel: The Political Limits of Protestant Reform in the Early Years of the German Reformation.* What follows here is based on my research for that study.

2. A copy of the original edict was graciously made for me by the archivist at the Stadtarchiv in the city of Constance.

3. Robert Stupperich, ed., *Martin Bucer's Deutsche Schriften* (Gütersloh & Paris, 1960), 3:43.

4. Stupperich, *Bucer's Deutsche Schriften,* 3:209-10.

5. See Luther's "Wider die Verkehrer und Faelscher Kaiserlichs Mandats," *WA,* 15:60-64.

6. In contrast to the argument made by the editors of Zwingli's *Saemtliche Werke,* 1:442-50.

7. Esp. Hermann Barge, *Andreas Bodenstein von Karlstadt,* 2 vols. (Leipzig: Friedrich Brandstetter, 1905), and a number of other writings.

Notes to the Epilogue

1. This epilogue is in reality a response to the challenge posed to me by my friend and colleague, Professor Victor G. Doerksen of the University of Manitoba, after he had read a penultimate (I think there have already been four) version of the manuscript. Therefore, if blame is to be assessed, please blame him!

2. E.g., W. H. C. Frend, *The Rise of Christianity* (Philadelphia: Fortress Press, 1984); John Lawrence von Mosheim, *An Ecclesiastical History,* vol. 1, trans. Archibald Maclaine (Charlestown: Samuel Etheridge, 1810); Philip Schaff, *History of the Christian Church,* vol. 1 (Grand Rapids: Eerdmans, 1910); Joseph Cullen Ayer, *A Source Book for Ancient Church History,* vol. 1 (New York: Scribners, 1939); Albert Henry Newman, *A Manual of Church History,* vol. 1 (Philadelphia: American Baptist Publ. Society, 1933); Gunnar Westin, *The Free Church through the Ages,* trans. Virgil A. Olson (Nashville: Broadman Press, 1958); E. H. Broadbent, *The Pilgrim Church* (London: Fleming H. Revell, 1955); Kenneth Scott Latourette, *A History of the Expansion of Christianity* (New York: Harper & Row, 1937-1945).

3. See Jean-Marie Sevrin, et al., eds., *The New Testament in Early Christianity* (Peeters: The Univ. of Louvain Press, 1989); Gerald H. Anderson, ed., *The Theology of the Christian Mission* (New York: McGraw-Hill, 1961); Johannes Blauwe, *The Missionary Nature of the Church* (New York: McGraw-Hill, 1962); Adolf von Harnack, *The Mission and Expansion of Christianity: The First Three Centuries,* trans. James Moffatt (New York: Harper Torchbooks, 1961); Michael Green, *Evangelism in the Early Church* (Grand Rapids: Eerdmans, 1970); Stephen Neill, *A History of Christian Missions* (New York: Penguin Books, 1964); E. Glenn Hinson, *The Evangelization of the Roman Empire* (Macon, Ga.: Mercer Univ. Press, 1981).

4. Green, *Evangelism,* pp. 239-40.

5. Green, *Evangelism,* pp. 239-40.

6. *Erasmi Opera Omnia,* 7:674.

7. I have gone through the entire corpus of the Ante-Nicene and Post-Nicene Fathers, and have found no interpretations of the Great Commission even remotely similar to that of Erasmus.

8. *The Ante-Nicene Fathers,* vol. 3, *Tertullian* (rpt.; Grand Rapids: Eerdmans, 1978), p. 676.

9. See F. C. Conybeare, "The Authorship of the Contra Marcellum," *Zeitschrift für neutestamentliche Wissenschaft* 6 (1905): 250-70.

10. See the above observations by Michael Green as well as those by Adolf von Harnack in his *Mission and Expansion*.

11. Bertram Lee Woolf, trans. and ed., *Reformation Writings of Martin Luther* (New York: Philosophical Library, 1953), 1:260-61.

12. These arguments have been made by Robert H. Gundry, *Matthew: A Commentary on His Literary and Theological Art* (Grand Rapids: Eerdmans, 1982), p. 596, and Otto Michel, "Der Abschluss des Matthaeusevangelium," *Evangelische Theologie* 10 (1950): 16-26. Both argue that the trinitarian emphasis is Matthean in origin, and that the original emphasis was christological, Michel asking — in dependence upon Bultmann: "oder ist nicht diese Komposition *von anfang an christologisch?* Dabei wuerde die These, das Matth. 28:18-20 christologisch zu verstehen sein, durch die Vermutung R. Bultmanns, dasz im Missionsbefehl urspruenglich nicht ein triadisches . . . , sondern ein christologisches (. . .) gestanden haben, nur verstaerkt" (p. 22).

13. Karl Barth, "An Exegetical Study of Matthew 28:16-20," in *The Theology of the Christian Mission,* ed. Gerald H. Anderson (New York: McGraw-Hill, 1961), pp. 55-71.

14. As we have seen, a German translation of the complete paraphrases was prepared by Leo Jud in Zurich, published in 1535, but how influential it may have been, or how widely used, is not apparent.

15. In spite of the fact that virtually everyone of any theological consequence in the early sixteenth century appears to have attacked the way the Anabaptists used these passages and the interpretation given them by Erasmus, no one seems to have mentioned Erasmus, or his paraphrases, by name. The same thing appears to have happened to his colloquy, the *Inquisitio de Fide.* Of that colloquy Thompson writes, in a footnote:

> The more surprising, then, that it has seldom been seriously examined. I have found no mention of it in Luther's writings, or in whatever has been published to date of the correspondence of Zwingli, Pellican, Aleander, Beatus Rhenanus, Boniface Amerbach, Oecolampadius, Ambrose and Thomas Blaurer, Bugenhagen, Camerarius, G. Helt, Hutten, Jonas, Mutianus, Peutinger, Reuchlin, Pirckheimer, and Sadoleto. Kaspar Schatzgeyer's *Scrutinium,* 1522, and Hutten's *Expostulatio cum Erasmo,* 1523, contain no references to any work of this character. I have failed to find any contemporary allusion to it beyond those in Erasmus' later correspondence, though we do know that two important readers thought highly enough of it to translate it (see below, pp. 49-51). There is no modern edition, nor has it received attention in the abundant biographies and studies of Erasmus and Luther except for some remarks in J. B. Pineau's *Erasme: sa pensee religieuse,* 1924, pp. 256-62; Preserved Smith's *A Key to the Colloquies of Erasmus,* 1927, pp. 24-25; P. S. Allen's

Erasmus, 1934, pp. 88-89; A Renaudet's *Etudes Erasmiennes* (1521-1529), 1939, passim; and M. Betaillon's edition of J. De Valdes *Dialogo de Doctrina Cristiana (1529),* 1925, and his *Erasme et l'Espagne,* 1937. On Valdes' *Dialogo* see below, pp. 50-51. Some of Pineau's comments are good, but there are many aspects of *Inquisitio de Fide* that he does not touch upon. (Thompson, *Inquisitio de Fide,* p. 3, n. 3.)

16. I.e., Ronald J. Sider.

17. What liberal Christians like Preserved Smith and others have done with Erasmus, liberal Pietists like Ludwig Keller have done with Anabaptist mystics like Hans Denck. For the full account of the above case, see Friesen, *History and Renewal in the Anabaptist/Mennonite Tradition* (North Newton, Kans.: Bethel College, 1994), pp. 41-77. Keller's influence went well beyond European Mennonite circles, however. Under the influence of the latter's biography of Hans Denck, Frederick Lewis Weiss, *Life, Teaching and Works of Johannes Denck* (Strasbourg, 1924), wrote, quoting H. E. Dosker: "It seems evident that there must be a very close connection between the Anabaptist and Socinian movements and that many late liberal views in the Protestant world were anticipated by, if they did not originate in, the Anabaptist communion" (p. 5). And Alfred Coutts wrote: "no one . . . seems more deserving of remembrance than . . . Hans Denck." He spoke further of his generation as being "more or less sympathetic with views that in various ways resemble his [Denck's]." These were views that "had no definite creed, for its primary doctrine of the Inner Word, and its belief in a continuous and progressive Revelation, left no room for the rigid theological systems with which the sixteenth century Church of the Reformation seemed resolved to replace the scholastic theology of the Medieval Church" (Alfred Coutts, *Hans Denck, 1495-1527, Humanist and Heretic* [Edinburgh: Macniven & Wallace, 1927], p. 10).

18. Gustav Kawerau, in a letter to Keller of 18 August 1883, referred to Denck's ideas — as Keller had portrayed them — as "this mixture of Medieval Mysticism and modern Rationalism." See Friesen, *History and Renewal,* p. 60.

19. Quoted in Friesen, *History and Renewal,* p. 66.

20. Friesen, *History and Renewal,* p. 66.

21. Friesen, *History and Renewal,* p. 57.

22. Quoted in Friesen, *History and Renewal,* pp. 74-75.

23. This included virtually the entire corpus of medieval mystical literature, culminating in the anonymous fifteenth-century *German Theology* and the writings of Hans Denck.

24. These he held to be the Swiss Brethren, the Hutterites, and Menno Simons and his followers.

25. John Horsch, "The Danger of Liberalism," *Gospel Herald* 1, no. 12 (20 June 1908): 178-79.

26. John Horsch, "Die geschichtliche Stellung der Mennoniten in der sog. Modernen Theologie," *Mennonitische Blaetter,* no. 1 (Jan. 1911): 4-5.

27. Horsch, "Die geschichtliche Stellung der Mennoniten in der sog. Modernen Theologie," pp. 4-5.

28. See his letter to Bender of 18 May 1524, *Mennonite Archives,* Hist. Mss. 1-278.

29. Perhaps Bender and Horsch saw Erasmus only through the eyes of "modernizers" like Preserved Smith.

30. Smith, *Colloquys of Erasmus,* p. vi.

31. John Locke, *The Reasonableness of Christianity, as Delivered in the Scriptures* (London, 1695), my emphasis.

32. See, e.g., Henry P. Van Dusen, *The Vindication of Liberal Theology* (New York: Charles Scribner's Sons, 1963), esp. pp. 93-148.

Notes to the Appendix

1. See also Glanmor Williams, *Reformation Views of Church History* (Richmond, Va.: John Knox Press, 1970), pp. 16-17.

2. Origen, "Commentary on the Gospel of John," in *The Ante-Nicene Fathers* (rpt.; Grand Rapids: Eerdmans, 1978), 10:367.

3. Chrysostom, "Homilies on St. John," in *The Nicene and Post-Nicene Fathers* (rpt.; Grand Rapids: Eerdmans, 1978), 14:60.

4. Jerome, "Dialogue Against the Luciferians," in *Nicene and Post-Nicene Fathers,* 6:323.

5. Augustine, "On the Gospel of St. John," in *The Nicene and Post-Nicene Fathers,* 7:37.

6. Augustine, in *The Nicene and Post-Nicene Fathers,* 1:399.

7. Thieleman J. van Braght, *The Bloody Theater of Martyrs Mirror of the Defenseless Christians,* trans. J. F. Sohm (Scottdale, Pa.: Mennonite Publishing House, 1950), p. 16, note.

8. Wilhelm Pauck, ed., *Melanchthon and Bucer* (Philadelphia: Westminster Press, 1969), p. 139, my emphasis.

9. Ulrich Zwingli, *Commentary on True and False Religion,* ed. Samuel Macauley Jackson (Durham, N.C.: Labyrinth Press, 1981), p. 186.

10. Zwingli, *Commentary,* p. 189.

11. Zwingli, *Commentary,* p. 187.

12. Zwingli, *Commentary,* p. 195.

13. See also Martin Hass's introduction to Leonhard von Muralt, ed., *Quellen zur Geschichte der Taeufer in der Schweiz* (Zurich: S. Hirzel Verlag, 1952), vol. 4.

14. Heinrich Bullinger, *The Decades of Henry Bullinger* (Cambridge: The University Press, 1852), 10:395-96.

15. John Calvin, "Commentary on the Acts of the Apostles," *Calvin's Commentaries* (rpt.; Grand Rapids: Baker Book House, 1981), 19:209-10, my emphasis.

16. John Witgift, "Of Preaching before the Administration of the Sacraments," in *The Works of John Witgift,* The Parker Society (Cambridge: Cambridge Univ. Press, 1853), 3:17, my emphasis.

Bibliography

Primary Sources

Alighieri, Dante. *De Monarchia.* Oxford, 1916.

Arnold, Gottfried. *Unparteyische Kirchen- und Ketzer-Historie, von Anfang des Neuen Testaments biss auf das Jahr Christi 1688.* Schaffhausen, 1748.

Ayer, Joseph Cullen. *A Source Book for Ancient Church History.* Vol. I. New York, 1939.

Bader, Johannes. *Bruderliche Warnung fuer dem newen Abgoettischen orden der Widertaeuffer.* Landau, 1527.

Bauman, Clarence, trans. *The Spiritual Legacy of Hans Denck: Interpretation and Translation.* Leiden, 1991.

Braght, Thieleman J. Van. *The Bloody Theater or Martyrs' Mirror of the Defenseless Christians.* Trans. J. F. Sohm. Scottdale, Pa, 1950.

Bossert, Gustav, ed. *Quellen zur Geschichte der Taeufer I. Band Herzogtum Wuerttemberg.* Leipzig, 1930.

Bromiley, G. W., ed. *Zwingli and Bullinger.* Philadelphia, 1969.

Calvin, John. *Calvin's Commentaries.* 22 vols. Rpt. Grand Rapids, 1981.

———. *Institutes of the Christian Religion.* 2 vols. Philadelphia, 1960.

———. *Ioannis Calvini Opera quae supersunt omnia.* Eds. Guilelmus Baum et al. Brunsvigae, 1863-1900.

Cassirer, Ernst, P. O. Kristeller, and John Herman Randall, eds. *The Renaissance Philosophy of Man.* Chicago, 1948.

Cochlaeus, Johannes. *Vortedigung Bischofflichs Mandats zu Meissen/wider Martin Luthers scheltwordte.* 1529.

Dolan, John P. *John Calvin and Jacopo Sadoleto: A Reformation Debate.* New York, 1966.

Eck, Johannes. *Enchiridion: Handbuechlin gemainer stell unnd Artickel der jetzt schwebenden Neuwen leeren.* Ed. Erwin Iserloh. Muenster, 1980.

Egli, Emil, and Georg Finsler, eds. *Zwingli, Saemmtliche Werke.* Vols. I-III. Zurich, 1905-14.

Erasmus, Desiderius. *Ausgewaehlte Werke.* 8 vols. Ed. Werner Welzig. Trans. Gerhard B. Winkler. Darmstadt, 1967.

————. *The Colloquies of Erasmus.* Trans. and ed. Craig R. Thompson. Chicago, 1965.

————. *Desiderii Erasmi Roterodami Opera Omnia.* Leiden, 1706. Rpt. Hildesheim, 1962.

————. *Desiderius Erasmus: The Praise of Folly and Other Writings.* Ed. Robert M. Adams. New York and London, 1989.

————. *The Education of a Christian Prince.* Ed. Lester K. Born. New York, 1968.

————. *The Essential Erasmus.* Ed. John P. Dolan. New York, 1964.

————. *Luther and Erasmus: Free Will and Salvation.* Eds. Gordon Rupp and Philip S. Watson. Philadelphia, 1969.

————. *Opus Epistolarum Des. Erasmi. Roterodami.* Ed. P. S. Allen. Oxford, 1906-58.

Franck, Sebastian. *Chronica, Zeitbuch unnd Geschichtsbibell von anbegyn bis in diss gegenwertig 1536, iar verlengt.* Rpt. Darmstadt, 1969.

Franz, Guenther. *Thomas Muentzer, Schriften und Briefe.* Guetersloh, 1968.

———— et al., eds. *Wiedertaeuferakten.* Vol. 4 of *Urkundliche Quellen zur Hessischen Reformationsgeschichte.* Marburg, 1951.

Friedmann, Robert, ed. *Glaubenszeugnisse oberdeutscher Taufgesinnter.* Vol. 12 of *Quellen zur Geschichte der Taeufer.* Guetersloh, 1967.

Fulk, William. *A Defence of Translations of the Holy Scriptures.* Cambridge, 1853.

Gundersheimer, Werner L., ed. *The Italian Renaissance.* New Jersey, 1965.

Haemstaed, Adrien. *De Geschiedenisse ende dem doodt der vromer Martelaren, die om ghetuyghenisse des Euangeliums Haer bloedt ghestort hebben.* Antwerp, 1559.

Harder, Leland, ed. *The Sources of Swiss Anabaptism.* Scottdale, PA, 1985.

Harding, Rev. Thomas, ed. *The Decades of Heinrich Bullinger.* 10 vols. Rpt. New York, 1968.

Hosius, Stanislaus. *The Begynning of Heresyes.* Trans. Richard Schacklock. Antwerp, 1565.

Janz, Denis, ed. *Three Reformation Catechisms: Catholic, Anabaptist, Lutheran.* New York and Toronto, 1982.

Jud, Leo. *Paraphrasis Oder Erklaerung des gantzen Neuwen Testaments.* Zurich, 1542.

181

Klassen, William, and Walter Klaassen, trans. *The Writings of Pilgram Marpeck.* Scottdale, PA, 1978.

Krebs, Manfred, ed. *Quellen zur Geschichte der Taeufer.* Vols. VII and VIII, *Elsass I. und II. Teil.* Guetersloh, 1959, 1960.

Luther, Martin. *D. Martin Luther, Die gantze Heilige Schrift Deutsch.* Eds. Hans Volz et al. Munich, 1972.

————. *D. Martin Luthers Werke. Kritische Gesammtausgabe.* Weimar, 1833–1948.

————. *Luthers Saemmtlich Schriften.* Ed. Johann Walch. St. Louis, 1905.

————. *Luther's Works.* Eds. Gottfried G. Krodel and Helmut T. Lehmann. Philadelphia, 1955.

————. *Sermons of Martin Luther.* Trans. and ed. John Nicholas Lenker. Grand Rapids, 1983.

Loewen, Howard John. *One Lord, One Church, One Hope, and One God: Mennonite Confessions of Faith in North America.* Elkhart, IN, 1985.

Marsiglio of Padua. *The Defender of the Peace.* Trans. Alan Gewirth. New York, 1967.

Marx, Karl, and Friedrich Engels. *Communist Manifesto.* Ed. Samuel H. Beer. Arlington Heights, IL, 1955.

Mecenseffy, Grete, ed. *Quellen zur Geschichte der Taeufer,* vol. II, *Oesterreich I. Teil.* Guetersloh, 1964.

More, Thomas. *Utopia.* Trans. and ed. H. V. S. Ogden. New York, 1949.

Muralt, Leonhard von, ed. *Quellen zur Geschichte der Taeufer in der Schweiz.* Vol. I. Zurich, 1952.

Murner, Thomas. *Radtschlag halten der disputation zu Bern.* 1529.

Newman, Albert Henry. *A Manual of Church History.* Vol. I. Philadelphia, 1933.

Niebuhr, Reinhold, ed. *Marx and Engels on Religion.* New York, 1955.

Pauck, Wilhelm, ed. *Melanchthon and Bucer.* Philadelphia, 1969.

Pipkin, H. Wayne, and John H. Yoder, trans. *Balthasar Hubmaier: Theologian of Anabaptism.* Scottdale, PA, 1989.

Rabus, Ludwig. *Historien der Martyrer.* Strassburg, 1572.

Rice, Eugene F., Jr., ed. *The Prefatory Epistles of Jacques Lefevre d'Etaples and Related Texts.* New York and London, 1972.

Ross, James Bruce, and Mary Martin McLaughlin, eds. *The Portable Renaissance Reader.* New York, 1978.

Roth, Paul, and Emil Duerr, eds. *Aktensammlung zur Geschichte der Basler Reformation in den Jahren 1519 bis Anfang 1534.* 4 vols. Basel, 1933.

Spinka, Matthew, ed. *Advocates of Reform, from Wyclif to Erasmus.* Philadelphia, 1953.

Stupperich, Robert, ed. *Martin Bucer's Deutsche Schriften.* Vol. I. Guetersloh and Paris, 1960.

————. *Die Schriften B. Rothmanns.* Muenster, 1970.

Symons, Menno. *Ein Fundament und Klare Anweisung von der seligmachenden Lehre unsers Herrn Jesu Christi.* Lancaster, PA, 1835.

————. *Opera Omnia Theologica of alle de Godgeleerde Wercken.* Rpt. Amsterdam, 1983.

Voegeli, Joerg. *Die Reformationsgeschichte von Konstanz 1519-1538.* 2 vols. Ed. Alfred Voegeli. Basel, 1972.

Williams, George H., and Angel M. Mergal, eds. *Spiritual and Anabaptist Writers.* Philadelphia, 1957.

Woolf, Bertram Lee, trans. and ed. *Reformation Writings of Martin Luther.* 2 vols. New York, 1953.

Yoder, John Howard, ed. *The Legacy of Michael Sattler.* Scottdale, PA, 1973.

Ziegelschmidt, A. J. F., ed. *Die aelteste Chronik der Hutterischen Brueder.* New York, 1943.

Ziegler, Donald J., ed. *Great Debates of the Reformation.* New York, 1969.

Zwingli, Ulrich. *Commentary on True and False Religion.* Ed. Samuel Macauley Jackson. Durham, NC, 1981.

————. *Zwingli on Providence and other Essays.* Eds. Samuel Macauley Jackson and Wm. John Hinke. Durham, NC, 1983.

Secondary Sources

Allen, P. S. *Erasmus: Lectures and Wayfaring Sketches.* Oxford, 1934.

Anderson, Gerald H., ed. *The Theology of the Christian Mission.* New York, 1961.

Argyle, A. W. *The Gospel according to Matthew: A Commentary.* Cambridge, 1963.

Bainton, Roland. *Erasmus of Christendom.* New York, 1969.

————. "The Great Commission." *Mennonite Life* 7 (1953): 183-89.

Barge, Hermann. *Andreas Bodenstein von Karlstadt.* 2 vols. Leipzig, 1905.

Barth, Karl. "An Exegetical Study of Matthew 28:16-20." *The Theology of Christian Mission.* Ed. Gerald H. Anderson. New York, 1961.

Bauman, Clarence. *The Sermon on the Mount: The Modern Quest for Its Meaning.* Macon, GA, 1986.

Bender, Harold S. *Conrad Grebel c. 1498-1526, The Founder of the Swiss Brethren sometimes called Anabaptists.* Scottdale, PA, 1950.

————. "The Pacifism of Sixteenth-Century Anabaptists." *Church History* 24 (1955): 119-51.

Berkhof, Louis. *Reformed Dogmatics.* Grand Rapids, 1937.

Bietenholz, Peter. *History and Biography in the Work of Erasmus of Rotterdam.* Geneva, 1966.

Blauwe, Johannes. *The Missionary Nature of the Church.* New York, 1962.

Bouwsma, William. J. *John Calvin. A Sixteenth Century Portrait.* New York and Oxford, 1988.

Broadbent, E. H. *The Pilgrim Church.* London, 1955.

Brown, Peter. *Augustine of Hippo.* Berkeley and Los Angeles, 1967.

Burckhardt, Paul. *Die Basler Taeufer.* Basel, 1898.

Burger, Edward K. *Erasmus and the Anabaptists.* Ph.D. dissertation, University of California, Santa Barbara, 1977.

Burke, Peter. *The Renaissance Sense of the Past.* New York, 1970.

Butterfield, Herbert. *The Whig Interpretation of History.* London, 1950.

Clasen, Claus-Peter. *Anabaptism: A Social History.* Ithaca, NY, 1972.

Collins, Anthony. *A Discourse on Free Thinking.* London, 1713.

Conybeare, F. C. "The Authorship of the Contra Marcellum." *Zeitschrift fuer neutestamentliche Wissenschaft* 6 (1905): 250-70.

Cornelis, Augustijn. "Der Epilog von Menno Simons' *Meditation,* 1539 (Leringhen op den 25. Psalm), Zur Erasmusrezeption Menno Simons." *Anabaptistes et dissidents au XVIe siècle.* Eds. Rott, Jean-Georges, and Verheus, Simon L. Baden-Baden and Bouxwiller, 1987.

Coutts, Alfred. *Hans Denck, 1495-1527, Humanist and Heretic.* Edinburgh, 1927.

Cuneo, Bernard Henry. *The Lord's Command to Baptise: An Historical Critical Investigation with Special Reference to the Works of Eusebius of Caesarea.* Washington, D.C., 1923.

Davis, Kenneth R. *Anabaptism and Asceticism: A Study in Intellectual Origins.* Scottdale, PA, 1974.

———. "Erasmus as Progenitor of Anabaptist Theology and Piety." *The Mennonite Quarterly Review* 47 (1973): 163-78.

Deppermann, Klaus. *Melchior Hoffmann, Social Unrest and Apocalyptic Visions in the Age of the Reformation.* Trans. Malcolm Wren and ed. Benjamin Drewry. Edinburgh, 1987.

Dintaman, Stephen. "The Spiritual Poverty of the Anabaptist Vision." *Conrad Grebel Review* 10 (1992): 205-208.

Dolan, John P. "Review" of I. B. Horst, *Erasmus, the Anabaptists and the Problem of Religious Unity. The Mennonite Quarterly Review* 43 (1969): 343.

Edwards, Mark U. *Luther and the False Brethren.* Stanford, 1975.

Egli, Emil. *Die St. Galler Taeufer. Geschichte im Rahmen der staedtischen Reformationsgeschichte.* Zurich, 1887.

———. *Die Zuercher Wiedertaeufer zur Reformationszeit nach den Quellen des Staatsarchivs dargestellt.* Zurich, 1878.

Erb, Peter C. *Pietists, Protestants, and Mysticism: The Use of Late Medieval Spiritual Texts in the Work of Gottfried Arnold.* Metuchen, NJ, 1989.

Fabri, Friedrich. *Der Sensus Communis, das Organ der Offenbarung Gottes in Allen Menschen.* Barmen, 1861.

184

Bibliography

Fast, Heinold. *Bullinger und die Taeufer.* Weierhof/Pfalz, 1959.

———. "The Dependence of the First Anabaptists on Luther, Erasmus, and Zwingli." *The Mennonite Quarterly Review* 30 (1956): 110.

———. "Hans Kruesis Buch ueber Glauben und Taufe." *A Legacy of Faith: A Sixtieth Anniversary Tribute to Cornelius Krahn.* Ed. C. J. Dyck. Newton, KS, 1962.

Fleischer, Manfred P., ed. *The Harvest of Humanism in Central Europe.* St. Louis, 1992.

Fraenkel, Peter. *Testamonia patrum: The Function of the Patristic Argument in the Theology of Philip Melanchthon.* Geneva, 1961.

Frend, W. H. C. *The Rise of Christianity.* Philadelphia, 1984.

Friedmann, Robert. "The Doctrine of the Two Worlds." *The Recovery of the Anabaptist Vision.* Ed. Guy F. Hershberger. Scottdale, PA, 1957.

———. "Eine dogmatische Hauptschrift der hutterischen Taeufergemein-schaften in Maehren." *Archiv fuer Reformationsgeschichte* 28 (1933): 234ff.

Friesen, Abraham. "Acts 10: The Baptism of Cornelius as Interpreted by Thomas Muentzer and Felix Mantz." *The Mennonite Quarterly Review* 64 (1990): 5-21.

———. "Anabaptism and Monasticism: A Study in the Development of Parallel Historical Patterns." *Journal of Mennonite Studies* 6 (1988): 174-97.

———. "Baptist Interpretations of Anabaptist History." *Mennonites and Baptists. A Continuing Conversation.* Ed. Paul Toews. Winnipeg, 1993.

———. *History and Renewal in the Anabaptist/Mennonite Tradition.* North Newton, KS, 1994.

———. "The Impulse Toward Restitutionist Thought in Christian Humanism." *Journal of the American Academy of Religion* 44 (1976): 29-45.

———. "Menno and Muenster: The Man and the Movement." *Menno Simons: A Reappraisal.* Ed. Gerald R. Brunk. Harrisonburg, VA, 1992.

———. "Present at the Inception: Menno Simons and the Beginning of Dutch Anabaptism." Forthcoming in *The Mennonite Quarterly Review.*

———. "The Radical Reformation Revisited." *Journal of Mennonite Studies* 2 (1984): 124-76.

———. *Reformation and Utopia: The Marxist Interpretation of the Reformation and Its Antecedents.* Wiesbaden, 1974.

———. *Thomas Muentzer.* Eds. Abraham Friesen and Hans-Juergen Goertz. Darmstadt, 1978.

———. *Thomas Muentzer: A Destroyer of the Godless.* Berkeley, Los Angeles, Oxford, 1990.

———. "Wilhelm Zimmermann and the Nemesis of History." *German Studies Review* 4 (1981): 195-236.

Genovese, Eugene D. "The Question." *Dissent* (1994): 371-76.

185

Gerrish, Brian. *Grace and Reason: A Study in the Theology of Luther.* New York, 1962.

Gray, Hanna. "Renaissance Humanism: The Pursuit of Eloquence." *Renaissance Essays.* Eds. P. O. Kristeller and Philip Wiener. New York, 1968.

Green, Michael. *Evangelism in the Early Church.* Grand Rapids, 1970.

Groth, Friedhelm. *Die "Wiederbringung aller Dinge" im wuerttembergischen Pietismus.* Goettingen, 1989.

Gundry, Robert H. *Matthew: A Commentary on His Literary and Theological Art.* Grand Rapids, 1982.

Haenchen, Ernst. *The Acts of the Apostles: A Commentary.* Philadelphia, 1971.

Halkin, Leon-E. "Erasme et l'Anabaptisme." *Les Dissidents du XVI siècle entre l'Humanisme et le Catholicisme.* Baden-Baden, 1983.

Hall, Thor. "Possibilities of Erasmian Influence on Denck and Hubmaier in Their Views on the Freedom of the Will." *The Mennonite Quarterly Review* 35 (1961): 149-70.

Harnack, Adolf von. *The Mission and Expansion of Christianity: The First Three Centuries.* Trans. James Moffatt. New York, 1961.

Harran, Marilyn J. *Luther on Conversion.* Ithaca, 1983.

Headley, John. *Luther's View of Church History.* New Haven, 1963.

Heath, Richard. *Anabaptism, From Its Rise at Zwickau to Its Fall at Muenster 1521-1536.* London, 1895.

Hershberger, Guy F., ed. *The Recovery of the Anabaptist Vision.* Scottdale, PA, 1957.

Hinson, E. Glenn. *The Evangelization of the Roman Empire.* Macon, GA, 1981.

Hoffmann, Manfred. *Erkenntnis und Verwirklichung der wahren Theologie nach Erasmus.* Tuebingen, 1986.

Holeczeck, Heinz. *Erasmus Deutsch.* Vol. I. Stuttgart, 1983.

Hornus, Jean Michel. *It Is Not Lawful for Me to Fight.* Trans. Alan Kreider and Olivier Coburn. Scottdale, PA, 1980.

Horsch, John. "The Danger of Liberalism." *Gospel Herald* 1 (1908): 178-79.

———. "Die Geschichtliche Stellung der Mennoniten in der sog. Modernen Theologie." *Mennonitische Blaetter* 1 (1911): 4-5.

———. *Infant Baptism: Its Origin among Protestants and the Arguments Advanced for and against It.* Scottdale, PA, 1917.

———. *The Mennonite Church and Modernism.* Scottdale, PA, 1924.

———. *Modern Religious Liberalism.* Rpt. New York, 1988.

Howell, David B. *Matthew's Inclusive Story: A Study of the Narrative Rhetoric of the First Gospel.* Sheffield, 1990.

Huizinga, J. H. *Dutch Civilization in the Seventeenth Century and other Essays.* Trans. Arnold J. Pomerans. New York, 1968.

Jackson, Samuel Macauley. *Ulrich Zwingli: The Reformer of German Switzerland, 1484-1531.* New York and London, 1901.

Kalkoff, Paul. "Die Vermitlungspolitik des Erasmus und sein Anteil an den Flugschriften der ersten Reformationszeit." *Zeitschrift fuer Kirchengeschichte* 1 (1903/4).

Kaminsky, Howard. *A History of the Hussite Revolution.* Berkeley and Los Angeles, 1976.

Kasdorf, Hans. "The Great Commission and the Reformation." *Direction* (1975): 303-18.

———. "Teaching the Great Commission." *Called to Teach.* Ed. David Ewert. Fresno, 1980.

Kautsky, Karl. *Die Vorlaeufer des neueren Sozialismus.* Stuttgart, 1894.

Kawerau, Peter. *Melchior Hoffmann als Religioeser Denker.* Haarlem, 1954.

Keller, Ludwig. "Zur Aufklaerung ueber die Entstehung von Dr. Keller's Schriften." *Gemeindeblatt* 11 (1888): 89.

———. *Die Reformation und die aeltere Reformparteien.* Leipzig, 1885.

Kittelson, James M. *Luther the Reformer.* Minneapolis, 1986.

———. *Wolfgang Capito: From Humanist to Reformer.* Leiden, 1975.

Klassen, Walter. "The Bern Debate of 1538: Christ the Center of Scripture." *The Mennonite Quarterly Review* 40 (1966): 148-56.

Koehler, Walter. *Huldrych Zwingli.* Leipzig, 1954.

———. "Die Zuercher Taeufer." *Gedenkschrift zum 400 jaehrigen Jubilaeum der Mennoniten oder Taufgesinnten.* Ed. D. Christian Neff. Ludwigshafen, 1925.

Kohls, Ernst-Wilhelm. *Die Theologie des Erasmus.* 2 vols. Basel, 1966.

Kolde, Theodor. *Luther's Stellung zu Concil und Kirche bis zum Wormser Reichstag 1521.* Guetersloh, 1876.

Koolman, J. Ten Doornkat. *Dirk Philips 1504-1568.* Haarlem, 1964.

Krahn, Cornelius. *Dutch Anabaptism: Origin, Spread, Life and Thought (1450-1600).* The Hague, 1968.

Kreider, Robert. "Anabaptism and Humanism: An Inquiry into the Relationship of Humanism to Evangelical Anabaptism." *The Mennonite Quarterly Review* 26 (1952): 123.

Kriechbaum, Friedel. *Grundzuege der Theologie Karlstadts.* Hamburg. 1967.

Kristeller, Paul Oskar. *Renaissance Thought.* 2 vols. New York, 1955, 1965.

Krueger, Friedhelm. *Humanistische Evangelienauslegung.* Tuebingen, 1986.

——— et al., eds. *Bucer und Seine Zeit.* Wiesbaden, 1976.

Kuhn, Thomas S. *The Copernican Revolution: Planetary Astronomy in the Development of Western Thought.* Cambridge, MA, 1957.

———. *The Structure of Scientific Revolutions.* Chicago, 1962.

Ladner, Gerhard. *The Idea of Reform.* New York, 1967.

Lamirande, Emilien. "Augustine and the Discussion on the Sinners in the Church at the Conference of Carthage (411)." *Augustinian Studies* 3 (1972): 97-112.

Latourette, Kenneth Scott. *A History of the Expansion of the Church.* 6 vols. New York, 1937-45.

Leff, Gordon. "The Making of the Myth of a True Church in the Later Middle Ages." *Journal of Medieval and Renaissance Studies* 1 (1971): 1-15.

Littell, Franklin H. "The Anabaptist Theology of Missions." *The Mennonite Quarterly Review* 21 (1947): 5-17.

———. *The Origins of Sectarian Protestantism.* New York, 1963.

Locher, Gottfried W. *Zwingli's Thought: New Perspectives.* Leiden, 1981.

Locke, John. *The Reasonableness of Christianity, as Delivered in the Scriptures.* London, 1695.

Luciani, Eveleyne. *Les Confessions de Saint Augustine dans les Lettres de Petrarque.* Paris, 1982.

Maurer, Wilhelm. *Der junge Melanchthon.* 2 vols. Goettingen, 1967.

Mezger, Johann Jakob. *Geschichte der deutschen Bibeluebersetzungen.* Basel, 1876.

Michel, Otto. "Der Abschluss des Matthaeusevangeliums." *Evangelische Theologie* 10 (1950): 16-26.

Mosheim, John Lawrence. *An Ecclesiastical History.* 6 vols. Trans. Archibald MacLain. Charlestown, MA, 1810.

Mueller, Nikolaus. "Die Wittenberger Bewegung 1521 und 1522." *Archiv fuer Reformationsgeschichte* 6 (1908-9).

Muralt, Leonhard von. *Die Badener Disputation 1526.* Leipzig, 1926.

———. *Glaube und Lehre der Schweizerischen Wiedertaeufer in der Reformationszeit.* Zurich, 1952.

Neill, Stephen. *A History of Christian Missions.* New York, 1964.

Newman, John Henry Cardinal. *An Essay on the Development of Christian Doctrine.* New York, London, and Toronto, 1949.

Oakley, Francis. *The Western Church in the Later Middle Ages.* Ithaca, NY, 1979.

Oberman, Heiko Augustinus. *Forerunners of the Reformation.* New York, 1966.

Palmer, R. R. *The Age of Democratic Revolution.* 2 vols. Princeton, 1959-64.

Pascal, Blaise. *The Provincial Letters.* New York, 1941.

Pater, Calvin Augustine. *Karlstadt as Father of the Baptist Movements: The Emergence of Lay Protestantism.* Toronto, 1984.

Patte, Daniel. *The Gospel according to Matthew: A Structural Commentary on Matthew's Faith.* Philadelphia, 1987.

Payne, John B. *Erasmus: His Theology of the Sacraments.* Richmond, VA, 1970.

Pfister, Hermann. *Die Entwicklung der Theologie Melanchthons unter dem Einflusz der Auseinandersetzung mit Schwarmgeistern und Wiedertaeufern.* Freiburg i.B., 1968.

Preus, James S. *Karlstadt's Ordinaciones and Luther's Liberty: A Study of the Wittenberg Movement.* Cambridge, MA, 1974.

Regehr, T. D. *Mennonites in Canada 1939-1970: A People Transformed.* Toronto, 1996.

Rice, Eugene F. "The Humanist Idea of Christian Antiquity: Lefevre d'Etaples and His Circle." *Studies in the Renaissance* 9 (1962): 126-60.

————. *The Renaissance Idea of Wisdom*. Cambridge, MA, 1958.

Rummel, Erika. *Erasmus' Annotations on the New Testament*. Toronto, 1986.

Rupp, Gordon. *Patterns of Reformation*. Philadelphia, 1969.

Schaeufele, Wolfgang. *Das missionarische Bewusstsein und Wirken der Taeufer*. Neukirchen, 1966.

Schaff, Philip. *History of the Christian Church*. Vol. I. Grand Rapids, 1910.

Schwarz, W. *Principles and Problems of Biblical Translation: Some Reformation Controversies and Their Background*. Cambridge, 1955.

Schweitzer, Albert. *The Quest for the Historical Jesus*. New York, 1957.

Sevrin, Jean-Marie, et al., eds. *The New Testament in Early Christianity*. Peeters, 1989.

Sider, Ronald J. *Andreas Bodenstein von Karlstadt*. Leiden, 1974.

Smith, Preserved. *Erasmus: A Study of His Life, Ideals and Place in History*. New York, 1923.

Snyder-Penner, Russell. "The Ten Commandments, the Lord's Prayer, and the Apostles' Creed as Early Anabaptist Texts." *The Mennonite Quarterly Review* 68 (1994): 318-35.

Spahn, Dr. Martin. *Johannes Cochlaeus: Ein Lebensbild aus der Zeit der Kirchenspaltung*. Berlin, 1898.

Spitz, Lewis W. *The Religious Renaissance of the German Humanists*. Cambridge, MA, 1964.

Stayer, James M., Werner O. Packull, and Klaus Deppermann. "From Monogenesis to Polygenesis: The Historical Discussion of Anabaptist Origins." *The Mennonite Quarterly Review* 49 (1975): 83-121.

Strauss, Gerald. Review in *Catholic Historical Review* 79 (1993): 107.

Tierney, Brian. *Origins of Papal Infallibility, 1150-1350: A Study on the Concepts of Infallibility, Sovereignity and Tradition in the Middle Ages*. Leiden, 1972.

Trinkaus, Charles. *In Our Image and Likeness: Humanity and Divinity in Italian Humanist Thought*. 2 vols. Chicago, 1970.

Unruh, Benjamin H. *Die niederlaendischen-niederdeutschen-Hintergruende der mennonitischen Ostwanderungen im 16., 18. und 19. Jahrhundert*. Karlsruhe, 1955.

Usteri, Georg. "Darstellung der Tauflehre Zwinglis." *Theologische Studien und Kritiken* 2 (1882): 205-84.

Van Dusen, Henry. *The Vindication of Liberal Theology*. New York, 1963.

Watson, Philip S. *Let God Be God! An Interpretation of the Theology of Martin Luther*. Philadelphia, 1974.

Weiss, Frederick Lewis. *Life, Teaching and Works of Johannes Denck*. Strasbourg, 1924.

Westin, Gunner. *The Free Church through the Ages.* Trans. Virgil A. Olson. Nashville, 1958.

Williams, Glaanmor. *Reformation Views of the Church.* Richmond, VA, 1970.

Winkler, Gerhard B. *Erasmus von Rotterdam und die Einleitungsschriften zum neuen Testament.* Muenster, 1974.

Wiswedel, Wilhelm. "Die alten Taeufergemeinden und ihr missionarisches Wirken." *Archiv fuer Reformationsgeschichte* 45 (1948): 115-32.

Wray, Frank J. "The 'Vermahnung' of 1542 and Rothmann's 'Bekenntnisse.'" *Archiv fuer Reformationsgeschichte* 47 (1956): 243-51.

Index